AN EMPIRE OF PLANTS

AN EMPIRE OF PLANTS

PEOPLE AND PLANTS
THAT CHANGED THE WORLD

TOBY & WILL MUSGRAVE

CASSELL&CO

First published in the United Kingdom in 2000 by Cassell & Co
Text copyright © Toby and Will Musgrave, 2000
Design and layout copyright © Cassell & Co, 2000

Distributed in the United States of America by
Sterling Publishing Co., Inc.
387 Park Avenue South
New York
NY 10016-8810
A CIP catalogue record for this book
is available from the British Library.

ISBN 0304 35443 0
Editor: Catherine Bradley
Text editor: Slaney Begley
Art editor: Briony Chappell
Designer: Nigel Soper
Proofreader: Liz Cowen
Picture researcher: Cee Weston-Baker
Additional text research: Judy Spours
Indexer: Drusilla Calvert

Typeset in Centaur
Printed in Hong Kong

Endpapers: A map of the world produced by the Imperial Federation,
showing the extent of the British empire, c.1886.
Front cover photograph: A botanist and his dog explore the Brazilian rainforest,
from the *Historia Naturalis* of Carl Friedrich Philip von Martius, early 19th century.

Cassell & Co
Wellington House
125 Strand
London WC2R 0BB

CONTENTS

INTRODUCTION
THE SEEDS OF WEALTH

'MEN HAVE TRAVELLED, as they have lived, for religion, for wealth, for knowledge, for pleasure, for power and the overthrow of rivals ... The discovery of the new Western World followed, as an incidental consequence, from the long struggle of the nations of Europe for commercial supremacy and control of the traffic with the East. In all these dreams of the politicians and merchants, sailors and geographers, who pushed back the limits of the unknown world, there is the same glitter of gold and precious stones, the same odour of far-fetched spices.'

Sir Walter Raleigh, 1509

From foodstuffs and fabrics to medicines and industrial materials, plants have dominated trade between countries for centuries. They sustained the power and influence of empires from the Mediterranean to Asia and the Far East, and were integral to the colonial expansion of Europe in the last 300 years. Raleigh's percipient words recognize the financial motives behind travel and exploration, demonstrated again and again in the economic imperative to find new overseas trade routes and markets. Profit was the engine that drove European powers beyond their own shores, and crops such as tea, cotton, sugar, rubber and tobacco changed the destinies of regions where they were grown. As territorial claims were established, plant products also became a focus for tensions between the mother country and increasingly restive settlers, challenging their traditional relationship and the tariffs and controls through which it was expressed.

At the beginning of the 16th century, as Raleigh observed, the spice trade was one of the most lucrative in existence. The immense value attached to seemingly everyday commodities such as cinnamon, cloves, nutmeg and mace, ginger and pepper — the last, amazingly, once more expensive, weight for weight, than gold — seems almost incredible today, yet the trade was critical in motivating initial

European exploration of distant lands. In conditions where food went off quickly, illness was common and the smells of day-to-day life were pervasive, the need for spices was immense, and they had enriched people's lives for hundreds of years — as medicines, culinary flavour enhancers, perfumes, emollients and aphrodisiacs. Centuries of Arab control of the trade had created a complex network of trading links from the Mediterranean to the Far East; cargoes of cinnamon from Ceylon (Sri Lanka), pepper from India and cloves and nutmeg from southeast Asia were transported by sea and overland along the Silk Routes for consumption in the West. So profitable was the trade that the Arab merchants went to great lengths to conceal the plant sources of their wares, even to the extent of telling outlandish stories. Such a practice was long established; the Ancient Greek historian Herodotus recounts that when the Arabians went out to collect cassia, they had to cover their whole bodies save their eyes in ox-hide to protect them from attack by bat-like creatures that inhabited the shallow lakes where cassia grew. Cinnamon, it was alleged, was either found in deep glens infested with poisonous snakes or came from the nests of terrifying birds of huge size (the spice was collected when the nests fell to the ground).

In early medieval times the ever-expanding Islamic empire exerted influence well beyond the Mediterranean region, extending from Spain in the west to northern India in the east. Ships returning from the Crusades in the Holy Land (which took place between 1095 and 1291) brought back rich cargoes of spices, jewels, tapestries and silks, making the West fully aware of the wealth that lay beyond the Mediterranean's shores. To their frustration, however, the Muslims rigorously controlled the trading routes to the east; only the city-states of Genoa and Venice possessed trade agreements with the Muslims and they quickly became the most powerful entrepôts in the northern Mediterranean.

Western curiosity about Asia increased even further when the Mongols expanded their empire from China to the Black Sea and it became relatively safe for missionaries and merchants to travel along the Silk Roads to the east. The most famous journey was made by Marco Polo (1254–1324), who, according to his own account, seems to have been particularly impressed by the abundance of spices in places such as India and Malaysia. He records that the Chinese city of Hangzhou imported an astonishing 5 tons of pepper a day — probably something of an exaggeration, as it would mean that annually Hangzhou imported twice as much pepper as the whole of Europe (an avid consumer at the time). Polo also noted with interest the social aspects of consumption in China, in which the upper classes ate meat preserved in several spices, while the lower orders had only garlic to flavour their dishes.

Compared to the powerful Ming dynasty of China, with its technological and cultural sophistication, Europe in 1400 was a relative backwater: parochial in outlook, ravaged by wars and the Black Death. Indeed, until the 15th century

ABOVE The lucrative spice trade in Asia was held under Muslim control for centuries, with Istanbul acting as a thriving commercial gateway between Europe and the East. This spice and flower market, illustrated in a 16th-century manuscript, shows an intriguing bustle of buying and selling.

the only Europeans to sail more than 800 miles (1,300 km) into uncharted waters were the Vikings. However, within 125 years European ships had crossed the Atlantic, Indian and Pacific oceans, and discovered the riches of the Americas, Africa and Asia in an 'Age of Discovery' fuelled primarily by the profit motive. The seismic shift in world relationships that was to characterize this period effectively began when the kingdoms of Castile, Aragon and Portugal won their freedom from the occupying Muslims. Each kingdom possessed strong nautical traditions, and their knowledge of boat building and sailing techniques was close to the point at which lengthy ocean voyages were possible, if perilous. Iberian merchants realized that obtaining spices from their source of origin would enable them to bypass the exorbitant mark-ups of not only Mediterranean dealers, but also the Arabian and Persian middlemen.

One man was to prove essential to the formidable economic ascendancy achieved by Portugal in the 16th century. A Portuguese prince, Henry the Navigator (1394–1460) – so named because he established a 'school of navigation' at Sagres near Lagos – was to set into motion the great period of European exploration that would change the world. Little is known about Henry's navigation school, for the Portuguese were always secretive about their ocean voyages, but it appears that training included map-making, the use of nautical instruments and, of course, navigation skills. This literal and metaphorical expansion of horizons was to transform Europe's position in the world over the next four centuries; the historian J.M. Roberts has observed how even by 1500 a distinctive psychological make-up was in evidence, defined above all by a 'growing confidence in the power to change things … Europe was open to the future and its possibilities in a way that other cultures were not'. Such conviction in its own supremacy was to foster many destructive aspects of the continent's colonial legacy, but it was also to transform the shape of trade and bring new and accessible materials into the domestic marketplace.

Although Henry died in 1460, the Portuguese continued with their exploration of Africa's west coast in the hope of discovering a route to the East Indies. In 1487 an expedition led by Bartolomeu Dias rounded the Cape of

SERVITUDO ESTO PERPETUA

Cotton. Tobacco. Sugar.

ABOVE Plants were to play a key role in shaping America's future, as the country evolved from early colonial settlements to independent nation. The Confederate Shield, the symbol of its Southern states, illustrated three of the most important: sugar, cotton and tobacco.

Good Hope and sailed on to Algoa Bay, where the south coast of Africa begins curving northwards. At the same time Dom Pedro de Covilham reached India and sent back compelling descriptions of the busy spice trade in Calicut and Goa. It now appeared possible to sail around Africa and then directly to India. However, the Portuguese hesitated in sending such an expedition after hearing Columbus's claims in 1492 that he had discovered a western passage to the Orient. Eventually concluding that Columbus must have been mistaken, they dispatched Vasco da Gama and four ships to India in 1497 via the southern sea route. Da Gama arrived at Calicut without mishap, although he was not received with warmth and the gifts he thought fit for a king were derided by those familiar with the luxuries of Asia. He was nevertheless able to fill his ships with nutmegs, cloves, ginger, cinnamon and peppercorns, and a letter from the Indian rulers agreeing to a trade partnership with Portugal capped his triumphant homecoming in 1499. Lisbon had now become the centre for the spice trade in Europe.

Expanding eastwards, Portugal quickly strengthened its incipient empire, building forts and trading posts, cementing foreign alliances and establishing itself in the Malaya Archipelago, the home of the celebrated Spice Islands, or Moluccas, first reached in 1513. Four years later Portugal had opened up trading links with China and were subsequently permitted by the Chinese authorities to use the island of Macao as a trading base; they also dominated trade over the Indian Ocean for the second half of the century. Yet the spices remained Portugal's most prized commodity; of particular importance in the Moluccas were cloves (*Eugenia caryophyllus*: the dried flower bud of a non-hardy tree related to the myrtle) and nutmeg and mace (*Myristica fragrans*: two parts of the fruit of the nutmeg tree native to the Banda Islands in the Moluccas).

As the Portuguese empire waned, the Dutch took control of the Spice Islands, maintaining a tight grip on their Indonesian colonies under the auspices of the Dutch United East India Company. The 17th century saw the peak of Dutch influence in the region, their authority focused on the Malacca Strait and encompassing trade with China through a station at Formosa (Taiwan). Yet it was Britain, doggedly establishing trading posts through organizations such as the Muscovy Company (founded in 1555), the Levant Company (1581) and the English East India Company (1600), who eventually achieved economic supremacy in the Indian Ocean. This slowly expanding web of international trade and naval domination allowed Britain to become a global power over the next two centuries, with much of its wealth obtained from plant products.

Each of the seven plants discussed in the following chapters played a crucial, if at times unexpected and even paradoxical, role in the shaping of overseas trade. All were interlinked with the development and extension of Britain's colonial interests abroad, and also had a significant impact upon social changes at home. Many of the ordinary domestic items that we take for granted today were once luxuries, relished by the few and enjoyed in ignorance of how they were cultivated or processed. The origins of tea, for example, were virtually unknown outside China until the intervention of plant hunter Robert Fortune, who smuggled samples from that country to create plantations in India, with unfortunate consequences for China, but great benefits for the subcontinent.

The dubious legitimacy of such economic botany was a hallmark of 19th-century imperialism. The transfer of rubber seedlings from the Amazonian basin, for example, seriously damaged Brazil's economy, but proved extremely profitable for Malaya, where plantations were established. Rubber, the last plant considered in this book, is interlinked with the industries that define late 19th- and early 20th-century technology – motor transport, aviation, specialized industrial processing and the mechanics of war. It also transformed the trading potential of the British empire, and those of other European powers. Improvements in transport enabled bulk products to be moved efficiently by rail

and steamship, opening up new tracts of land and redefining national
perceptions of their colonies. Their needs and problems both became much
nearer to home – by 1900 any part of Britain's empire could be reached in six
weeks from London.

Three centuries earlier, the first settlers on the American seaboard must have
felt completely isolated. The struggles of the colonists of Jamestown in
Chesapeake Bay, founded as a commercial enterprise by the Virginia Company in
1607, were almost overwhelming; only the successful cultivation of tobacco from
the West Indies was to sustain the colony as a viable proposition. Paradoxically,
the plant that ensured the colony's survival was to become a key feature in its
demand for independence, as Britain's mercantile perspectives on trade were
challenged by the newly successful planters.

The traditional view was that colonies existed to provide raw materials for their
mother country; they were also perceived as useful captive markets for processed
goods from Europe. The fate of India's cotton industry, long celebrated for its
fine handspun and woven muslins and calicoes, illustrates the impact of such
trading relationships in action. In the 17th century cotton provided a valuable
export for the East India Company, who were establishing themselves in the east

of the country. However, the development of Britain's industrial technology required a finer quality of thread to manufacture at home, and raw cotton was instead imported from America. Manufactured cotton goods, in turn, were exported to India and sold more cheaply than native produce, even as the free trade movement sought to liberalize trading structures in domestic markets.

The volume of cotton cultivation in America's Deep South was sustained by slavery, as the sugar industry had been in the previous century. The labour-intensive plantations on Caribbean islands were worked by slaves brought as part of the notorious triangular trade from the stations of the West African coast. The physical demands of sugar production created terrible working conditions on the plantations, in stark contrast to the elegant houses and lifestyles of sugar barons and their families. As Europe's demand for sugar soared, the valuable crop gave Caribbean planters significant influence in their country's economic affairs.

The patterns of international trade reveal the intriguing connections between different crops. The success of one plant product often impacted upon another, such as the corresponding increase in exports of both sugar and tea. One of the most iniquitous associations, however, was that of opium and tea in the 18th and 19th centuries. The illicit opium trade, in which the crop was cultivated in India and smuggled into China to fuel spiralling national addiction, was linked to the West's rising demand for Chinese tea and the inability of the East India Company to obtain enough silver to meet these requirements. As China was uninterested in other Western produce, opium was an effective, if unacknowledged, method of securing sufficient tea supplies for Europe's markets. Only when Turkish opium began to have a significant effect on European countries was an attempt made to limit, and eventually to suppress, the Indo-China smuggling nexus.

In contrast, the cultivation of cinchona trees for their bark (a source of the anti-malarial drug, quinine) was prompted by political rather than commercial expediency. As more territories were acquired by Britain in the late 19th century, high-quality supplies of quinine were required, not only for the Empire's officials and troops, but also for the workers on key plantations. Seedlings were therefore discreetly transported by plant hunters from their native Peru and established in plantations, initially in India and later in many British colonies, from Burma and Fiji to Tanganyika, Jamaica and the Cameroons. Quinine enabled the settlement of previously inhospitable parts of Africa and southeast Asia, and the presence of wives and families changed the landscape of colonial life. As competition for land and raw materials intensified, the 'Scramble for Africa' was translated in the West from a crude economic imperative into a dramatic rivalry of nations.

The role of key plants in shaping history is therefore as undisputed as it is complex. The need to cultivate, harvest, transport and process them has changed the ecology, population and economy of former colonies and their rulers alike, and left an ambivalent legacy whose consequences still influence us today.

ESTABLISHED 1760.

PETER LORILLARD,

PAUL NEFFLIN, DEL.

LITH. OF SARONY, MAJOR & KNAPP, 449 BROADWAY, N.Y.

SNUFF & TOBACCO,

16 Chambers St. New York.

TOBACCO –
'THAT TAWNY WEED'

OPPOSITE A legend of the Huron people, in which tobacco was given to them by a beautiful female spirit, provided humorous inspiration *c.*1860 for a tobacconist's advertisement.

ABOVE Huge barrels containing tobacco are loaded on to sailing ships bound for Europe in this detail from a map of 1775.

ALTHOUGH ITS ROLE IN MEDICAL OPINION has shifted from hero to villain, tobacco continues to play a major role in the world's economies. First brought to Europe by the crew of Columbus's voyage of 1492, the next century saw it both celebrated as miracle panacea and denounced as an agent of the devil. Nevertheless its fascination for addicted consumers made tobacco one of the most valuable export crops for New World colonies. Plantations were established in the Caribbean and on mainland America, where its commercial success ensured the survival of the Chesapeake Bay colony of Jamestown in Virginia. The darker aspects of this burgeoning industry – smuggling, piracy and the development of the slave trade – were obscured by the lustre of high profits, not least in the form of government tax revenues, the catalyst for the end of Britain's colonial role in America.

DISCOVERY AND EARLY USE

Exactly when tobacco was first used for ceremonial and/or recreational purposes
is not known, but certainly it was widespread amongst the pre-Columbian Native
Americans. Tobacco is indigenous to the Americas; between 50 and 70 varieties
of *Nicotiana* grow wild in North America, at least eight of which were smoked by
the native tribes. In central and eastern America, *Nicotiana rustica* was the most
frequently used, and in the Upper Missouri Valley the preferred variety was
Nicotiana quadrivalis; both were often blended with dried willow bark, leaves and
even powdered wood. The most common form of tobacco in use today, *Nicotiana
tabacum*, was introduced from Mexico by Europeans making settlements on the
eastern seaboard.

From at least as early as 1500 BC the Mayan civilization smoked tobacco as
part of their religious ceremonies. Over the centuries, tobacco use spread through
the Mexico region, the Antilles and beyond – southwards by sea, as far as Brazil,
and northwards via the Mississippi Valley. Native Americans placed enormous
importance on the ceremonial consumption of tobacco; it might be undertaken
communally prior to a battle, hunting expedition or peace talks, or as part of a
sacred ritual to provide a link between the human and divine worlds. The plant's
spiritual associations are reaffirmed in a legend of the Huron people, who
inhabited land between lakes Huron, Erie and Ontario, which tells how, long
before the coming of the white man, there was a great famine. At a council of the
tribes it was decided to call upon the Great Spirit Manitou for help. In response
to their pleas, a beautiful, naked girl descended from the clouds, and, sitting
before the tribes, leaning on her palms, she announced that she was sent to them
to bring food. This said, she returned to the clouds and from where her right
palm had rested, sprouted corn, from where her left palm had been, potatoes.
From the sacred spot where she had sat, however, tobacco appeared – a divine gift
to alleviate the people's distress.

The methods of early tobacco intake were at least as varied as those of today.
The Mayans made primitive cigarettes by rolling tobacco in palm leaves or corn
husks, and equally basic cigars by using tobacco leaf wrappers. The Aztecs and
Incas are known to have ground tobacco and taken it as snuff, while further north
tribes made pipes. The designs of pipes varied from one tribe to another, from
the stone versions of the Hopewell and Adena to birch bark in the northeast and
lobster claws in Maine. Pipe bowls were often symbolic representations of
humans and animals, and were invested with great social significance; important
members of the Hopewell people of Ohio, for example, were buried with their
pipes. As well as stem and bowl designs immediately recognizable to today's pipe
aficionado, Native Americans also used Y-shaped pipes, which fitted neatly over the
nostrils. Elsewhere, tobacco was variously chewed, eaten, drunk as an infusion,
rubbed into the body and even administered as an enema.

ABOVE Tobacco held sacred associations in many Native American tribes, and smoking was an important feature of secular and religious ceremonies. This engraving illustrated an account of explorations in 'Americae' – in effect, the Caribbean – by one Johannes Lerii in 1593.

The smoking of tobacco played a key role in the conducting of negotiations between Europeans and Native Americans. While the Treaty of 1682 was being agreed, for example, when the Delaware people gave land to William Penn for his founding colony, pipes were smoked continuously. Tobacco was to become an essential feature of trade and currency as Europeans moved further into the 'new' continent, and was to prove an invaluable export crop for the early colonists.

THE TRAVELS OF TOBACCO

Europeans first made the acquaintance of tobacco on 12 October 1492 when, after 71 days at sea, Christopher Columbus first sighted the coast of America. He named the island where he landed San Salvador, and here, according to his logbook, the indigenous people 'brought fruit, wooden spears, and certain dried leaves which gave off a distinct fragrance'. The gifts were accepted, the fruit eaten,

TOBACCO PLANT PROFILE

BOTANICAL DETAILS

Tobacco is a member of the *Solanaceae* family, which also includes the tomato (*Lycopersicon*), potato (*Solanum*), peppers (*Capsicum*) and nightshade (*Belladonna*). In 1753 the Swedish botanist Linnaeus named the genus *Nicotiana* and described the two species *N. rustica* and *N. tabacum*. It is the latter species and its varieties that are used in the commercial production of tobacco.

ORIGINS

Tobacco is native to the Americas. The origin of the name 'tobacco' is lost in the mists of time, but may derive either from a place name such as 'Tabasco', 'Tobago' or 'Taboco', or

from a type of pipe used by the Native Americans. It has also been variously been called 'petun(m)' and 'picietl', just two of its Native American names, 'sotweed', the divine or holy herb, *herba regina*, and *herba panacea*.

DESCRIPTION

An annual, tobacco reaches between 20 in (50 cm) and 10 ft (3 m) tall, depending on variety and growing conditions. The large leaves are dark green on top and pale green on the underside, and those of commercial varieties are sessile, that is to say they do not have a stalk. Both insect- and self-pollinating, the fruit capsule contains up to 40,000 tiny brown seeds. These seeds are so small that there are approximately 340,000 to the ounce (12,000 to the gram).

Tobacco smoke contains some 4,000 chemicals, but it was not until 1828 that the alkaloid component of tobacco was isolated and identified. Nicotine is tobacco's strongest psychoactive ingredient. It is a high-powered stimulant and one of the most addictive drugs available, comparable to heroin and cocaine according to the American Surgeon General. It is also a poison, and as early as 1665 Samuel Pepys reported in his *Diary* an experiment conducted by the Royal Society which showed

the toxic effects of tobacco, when it was observed that a cat quickly died when 'fed a drop of distilled oil of tobacco'. It was also regularly used by Victorian gardeners as a fumigant and insecticide.

A direct link between smoking tobacco and the development of lung cancer was made in 1950. Since then further links have been made between smoking and other cancers, as well as respiratory and coronary diseases. Today, as concern grows over the effects of passive smoking, it is increasingly being viewed as a dangerous and antisocial habit.

HABITAT

Tobacco is grown in about 120 countries in latitudes as far north as $50°$. The seed is sown in covered coldframes designed to protect the young plants against strong sunlight. When, after 1 to 1½ months, the plants have reached the four-leaf stage, they are transplanted to their field cropping position. Certain crops are given special treatments in order to achieve a particular result. For example, to produce the large thin leaves required for cigar wrappers, cheesecloth canopies are erected to shade the crop, and to maximize leaf growth the flowers are pinched out.

PROCESSING

Tobacco is harvested when fully ripe in one of two principal methods, by stem or by leaf cropping. Stem cropping cuts the entire plant at ground level, but for some tobaccos, such as the Brazil cigar tobaccos, the plant's individual leaves are gathered as they mature. In this way six to eight croppings can be taken from the same root, maximizing the productivity of each. There are four methods for drying or curing tobacco: air, sun, heat (flue) and smoke, while cigar tobacco requires fermentation. Traditionally, tobacco leaves were hung in well ventilated barns for curing, as a dry yet pliable leaf was required that would last the long Atlantic voyage to England.

but the yellowish leaves were tossed overboard. Columbus sailed on, arriving off the Cuban coast on 28 October, where two conquistadors, Rodriguo de Jerez and Luis de Torres, were sent inland to scout. The natives they encountered wrapped dried tobacco leaves in palm or maize 'in the manner of a musket formed of paper', and after lighting one end, they commenced 'drinking' the smoke through the other. Rodriguo took a hesitant puff and became the first European to smoke tobacco. Columbus returned to Spain with some dried tobacco leaves, and Rodriguo, who by now was an affirmed smoker, took his habit back to his home town, where unwisely he lit up in public. So frightened were his neighbours by the smoke billowing from his nose and mouth that he was imprisoned by the holy inquisitors, only to discover upon his release several years later that smoking had become a national habit.

After this somewhat inauspicious start, tobacco inexorably worked its way across continental Europe, becoming an intrinsic part of many cultures. And, whereas in 1560 a clear distinction existed between those Old World countries that had tobacco and those that had not, a century later this difference had all but disappeared. It was the Portuguese, who at the time were the world's foremost international trading nation, who had much to do with this spread. Already the first to cultivate tobacco outside the Americas in 1512, by 1548 the Portuguese were commercially cultivating tobacco in Brazil and by 1558 snuff was on sale in Lisbon markets. Although tobacco plants had arrived in France in 1556, brought back from Brazil by the revolutionary monk André Thevet of Angoulême, it is the story of his fellow countryman, Jean Nicot de Villemain of Nîmes, that is better remembered. Sent to Lisbon in 1559 to negotiate the royal marriage between the Portuguese king and the French king's sister, he sent back tobacco plants and snuff to Catherine de' Medici, the dowager queen, to treat her son Francis II's migraines. By the 1570s tobacco was known in France as 'nicotiane', the taxonomic name adopted under the Linnaean system. From Portugal tobacco quickly reached Rome, and from there the rest of Italy, Germany, Hungary and other countries of northern and central Europe, its progress hastened by the Thirty Years War (1618–48). Portugal was also indirectly responsible for tobacco's introduction into Turkey (1580) and wholly so into India and Japan, where the word for 'tobacco merchant' appears as early as 1578.

However, it was the Spanish who took the lead in evaluating this new product as a medical resource. The *Aztec Herbal* of 1552 – prepared as a tribute to the son of the then Viceroy of Mexico by Martin de la Cruz and Juan Badinao, two pupils of the college at Tlatilulco – is perhaps the earliest botanical work to refer to tobacco as a medicinal product. Some 19 years later, Monardes, a doctor in Seville, reported that it was the latest craze sweeping his profession and listed 36 maladies cured by tobacco. In 1577 the text of Monardes's *Materia Medica* was translated into English, and across Europe doctors began to view tobacco as a

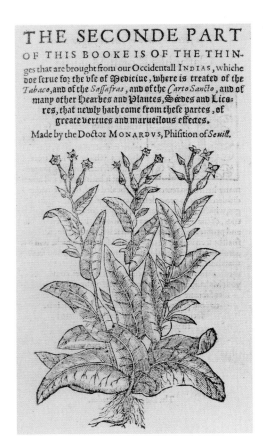

THE SECONDE PART
OF THIS BOOKE IS OF THE THIN-
ges that are brought from our Occidentall INDIAS, whiche
doe serue for the vse of Medicine, where is treated of the
Tabaco, and of the *Saffafras*, and of the *Carto Sancto*, and of
many other Hearbes and Plantes, Séedes and Lico-
res, that newly hath come from these partes, of
greate vertues and maruelous effectes.

Made by the Doctor MONARDVS, Phifition of *Seuill*.

ABOVE One of the earliest drawings of the tobacco plant appeared in the treatise of Monardes, a Spanish doctor, published in 1571. Later translated into English and exuberantly titled 'Joyfull News out of the Newe Founde Worlde', it celebrates tobacco's properties as a miracle cure for several ailments.

'wonder drug' which, it was claimed, would cure ailments as varied as toothache, falling fingernails, worms, halitosis, lockjaw and, ironically, even cancer.

THE TOBACCO HABIT IN BRITAIN

From the first the English seem to have been more concerned with the pleasures offered by tobacco than with its medicinal virtues. By the late 16th century the English were actively exploring the New World and had encountered pipe-smoking Native Americans in what is now Virginia. Since the pipe and not snuff became the favoured method of consumption in England, it seems likely that both pipe and product arrived direct from the Americas. The dubious honour of first introducing tobacco to England in 1564 or 1565 fittingly belongs to a man of somewhat dubious morals – Sir John Hawkins (1532–95), the first English slave trader.

For the next 20 years or so smoking remained predominantly a habit practised by sailors, much to the amazement of crowds who gathered to watch the jack tars billowing out clouds of smoke in ports around England. Sir Francis Drake brought back the consumable *Nicotiana tabacum* in 1575, and was responsible for introducing fellow adventurer – and later pipe smoker *extraordinaire* – Sir Walter Raleigh to smoking in 1585. The following year, Ralph Lane, the first governor of Virginia, taught Sir Walter to smoke the long-stemmed clay pipe, which Lane is credited with inventing and Raleigh claims to have introduced to England. It was also in 1586 that tobacco arrived in English society, when, in July, a group of Virginian colonists returned and caused a sensation in Plymouth when they began 'drinking' tobacco smoke – inhaling and apparently swallowing it.

No bigger boost to the establishment of smoking tobacco (or 'sotweed' as it was then known) as a fashionable pastime was given than by Raleigh, who popularized the practice at the court of Elizabeth I. However, there was the occasional setback, and on one occasion Raleigh was drenched with beer by an over-zealous servant, who, coming upon his master smoking, thought he was ablaze and decided to put him out.

By 1600 the smoking habit had taken society by storm. It became as essential a part of a fashionable gentleman's life as dancing, riding, hunting and card playing – and of a lady's too, with Queen Elizabeth herself sampling the weed in 1601. Although smoking knew no social barriers, it remained an expensive pleasure. As a contemporary merchant, John Aubrey, later wrote: 'It [tobacco] was sold then for its weight in Silver. I have heard some of our old yeomen neighbours say that when they went to Malmesbury or Chippenham market, they culled out their biggest shillings to lay in the Scales against the Tobacco.' Yet, as remains the case 400 years later, the cost does not seem to have deterred the addict significantly; the German traveller, Paul Hentzner, commenting in 1596 on the theatres and other contemporary amusements such as bull-baiting and bear-baiting, observed that:

> [a]t these spectacles, and everywhere else, the English are constantly smoking the Nicotian weed, which in America is called Tobaca — others call it Pætum - and generally in this manner: they have pipes on purpose, made of clay, into the farther end of which they put the herb, so dry that it may be rubbed into powder, and lighting it, they draw the smoke into their mouths, which they puff out again through their nostrils, like funnels, along with it plenty of defluxion and phlegm from the head.

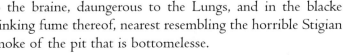

BELOW A tobacco pouch of red leather from the early 17th century. As well as two elegant, silver-mounted clay pipes, the pouch holds a 'stopper' of bone in the shape of a finger. It was used to press tobacco firmly into the pipe bowl.

Even with nothing then known about the relationship between poor health and smoking, many of the criticisms made of the weed still seem very current some four centuries later. One observer at the theatre complained about smokers 'clowding the loathing ayr with foggie fume', while a citizen's wife in a play of the period remarked, 'This stinking tobacco kills men. Would there were none in England.' Yet it is supremely ironic that Britain's most fervent anti-tobacco activist of the early 17th century was also the man who came to rely on tax revenue levied on tobacco in order to support the nation's finances. In 1603 King James VI of Scotland became James I of England; a year later he anonymously published his famous treatise *A Counterblast to Tobacco*, which denounced the habit in strongly religious terms as 'not only a great vanity, but a great contempt of God's good gifts, that the sweetness of man's breath, being a good gift of God, should be wilfully corrupted by this stinking smoke'. The vehement royal revulsion concludes by condemning the practice of smoking as:

> a custome lothsome to the eye, hatefull to the nose, harmefull to the braine, daungerous to the Lungs, and in the blacke stinking fume thereof, nearest resembling the horrible Stigian smoke of the pit that is bottomelesse.

Two Broad-Sides
AGAINST
TOBACCO
The First given by
King JAMES
Of Famous Memory;
HIS
Counterblaſt to TOBACCO.
THE SECOND
Tranſcribed out of that learned PHYSICIA
Dr. EVERARD MAYNWARINGE,
HIS
Treatiſe of the SCURVY.
To which is added,
Serious Cautions againſt Exceſs in Drinking: Taken o
of another Work of the ſame Author, His Preſervation
of Health and Prolongation of Life.
WITH
A ſhort Collection, out of Dr. George Thompſon
Treatiſe of Blood; Againſt ſmoking Tobacco.
Alſo many Examples of God's ſevere Judgments up
notorious Drunkards, who have died ſuddenly,
In a Sermon Preached by Mr. Samuel Ward.
Concluding with Two Poems againſt Tobacco and Coff
Collected and Publiſhed, as very proper for this Age, By J.H.ΦιΛάνθρωπ〇
Animalia omnia ſibi metipſis noſcunt Salutaria, præter Hominem.
Licenſed according to Order, June 6. 1672.

James by the grace of God King of England Scot :
land France and Ireland etc

ABOVE James I's 'Counterblast to Tobacco' sought to discourage his subjects from indulging in the 'tawny weed'. It was first published anonymously in 1604, but his authorship was freely declared in the frontispiece to two anti-smoking 'Broad-Sides' of 1672, almost 50 years after his death.

However, James I — Scottish, malodorous and prone to enriching his male lovers with public money — was not a popular monarch. He was to discover that the pen was not mightier than the sword, and his treatise found very little support. The English just carried on smoking and so, on 17 October 1604, James continued his vendetta by raising import duty payable on tobacco by a staggering 4,000 per cent, from twopence (2d) to six shillings and eightpence (6/8d) per pound. However, this draconian measure was about as effective as his treatise, with the duty being avoided by home-growing and, of course, smuggling, which coincidentally introduced tobacco to those remote parts of England used by the smugglers. Yet, although King James's tax may have been an expression of personal distaste, its long-term impact was more than he could have foreseen. The 'tawny weed', and the customs revenues it generated, were to become a political property throughout the 17th and 18th centuries. Its fortunes were to become entwined with colonial survival, State finances, international destinies and, ultimately, the emergence of a new nation.

TOBACCO AND THE COLONIES

In 1606, James I granted a charter to the Virginia Company to establish settlements in the Caribbean, following exploration of the coast by Elizabethan adventurers. In his *History of the World*, J.M. Roberts has commented that such 'plantations', as the first colonies were known, were initially seen as far more attractive than mainland America; by 1630 St Kitts in the Leeward Islands had 3,000 inhabitants, with another 2,000 in Barbados. The success of their tobacco-growing initiatives, later complemented by sugar as another staple crop (see page 42), brought substantial customs revenue to Britain, and accordingly awarded the Caribbean colonists significant influence in political and economic circles. The primary role of colonies, in their mother country's eyes, was to supply her with crops that could not be cultivated in England, and for which a ready market could be assured. Tobacco fitted the bill to perfection, and was to become even more important to the struggling mainland settlements in the New World.

During the late 16th century England had made various unsuccessful attempts to colonize the North American mainland, notably at the Roanoke Island base established by Sir Walter Raleigh in 1585 and 1587. Sadly, the second group of settlers was lost in 1591 and it was 15 years before the Virginia Company of London attempted colonization again. This time they were better organized and financed, and supported by England's burgeoning naval power. Chesapeake Bay was chosen for its natural advantages and its distance from the Caribbean, which provided a protective barrier against military action by the Spanish. The whole enterprise was a commercial undertaking, the aim being to establish a permanent presence in the New World, rather than merely a trading post or a conduit for trade with the interior.

Peopled by English settlers whom it was assumed could both bring prosperity to the colony and a handsome profit to investors back home, Jamestown was founded in 1607. Initial efforts were poured into creating a diversified economy with the cultivation of a range of crops, including hemp, flax, dye crops, vines and mulberry trees for silk production. Not everything went to plan, however, and if the losses incurred by the Company meant that the project was a financial disaster for investors, then the situation was far worse for the settlers. Life in the male-only colony was often brutal, dangerous and short (51 of the original 104 colonists were dead by 1608). The fragile relationship between the English and Native Americans often broke down and descended into violence; internal strife between settlers was endemic; disease was rife; and the futile search for gold and silver, which took precedence over growing food crops, meant starvation was a constant threat. In fact, famine almost finished the fledgling colony altogether in the horrendous 'starving time' that occurred during the winter of 1609.

It was to this struggling community, a source of increasing anxiety to the Virginia Company which had invested in it, that tobacco came as a saviour. The prosperity it brought would irrevocably change the history of the Chesapeake colony, as a 19th-century historian was to observe:

> So prominent is the place that tobacco occupies in the early records of the middle Southern States, that its cultivation and commercial associations may be said to form the basis of their history. It was the direct source of their wealth, and became for a while the representative of gold and silver; the standard value of other merchantable products; and this tradition was further preserved by the stamping of a tobacco-leaf upon the old continental money used in the Revolution.

Here was a crop that not only seemed ideally suited to the local conditions, had relatively low production costs and a high yield per acre (so could be farmed economically in small quantities), but also one for which there was an apparently bottomless market across the Atlantic. For those colonists, who had suffered so much, it must have been a godsend: they were now literally able to plant money and watch it grow. Tobacco leaf, to the settlers of Virginia, really was 'as good as gold'. It was used as local currency, to extend credit or pay debts, and as one contemporary stated, 'We have [no] trade at home and abroad but that of Tobacco...[it] is our meat, drink, clothes, and monies.' The early settlers even had to pay the passage for their prospective brides in tobacco – some 120 lb (54 kg) for each of the first women who arrived in 1619, and who helped to transform the initial settlements into more permanent agricultural communities. The use of tobacco as currency lasted for 200 years, and was formalized in 1727 with the issuing of Tobacco Notes were issued – pieces of paper testifying to the quality and quantity of the growers' tobacco assets, which were held in a public warehouse.

The first successful commercial crop was cultivated in Virginia in 1612 by Englishman John Rolfe, using *Nicotiana tabacum*, a variety of tobacco from Spanish plantations in the West Indies that was more palatable to Europeans (the first known shipment of tobacco to England had taken place in 1613, but because it was the poor quality *N. rustica*, indigenous to the region, it was badly received). With the development of the sweet *N. tabacum*, however, Virginia's star began to rise. Two varieties were grown in the early Virginian colonies: Oronoco and Sweetscented. The former was stronger and was in demand in continental Europe, while the latter with its milder taste was popular in England. Between 1617 and 1621 exports of tobacco to England increased 1,750 per cent from 20,000 lb (9,072 kg) to 350,000 lb (159,000 kg) – it was the colony's largest export in 1619 – and on 4 December that year in Berkeley, Virginia, Thanksgiving was held for the first time to celebrate the good tobacco harvest. By the late 1660s exports to Britain were approximately 15,000,000 lb (6,804,000 kg) per annum, rising to 28,000,000 lb (12,700,800 kg) by the mid-1680s.

ABOVE An engraving of 1750 illustrates different methods of processing tobacco, depending on its usage. Mature leaves were often hung in airy barns for curing, but exposure to sun, smoke or the heat of a flue were alternative techniques. Tobacco for cigars was fermented in vats.

DEVELOPMENT AND CHANGE

The production of tobacco on the mainland was most intensive from the southern boundary of Pennsylvania to North Carolina. A planter's life was demanding and relentless: forests had to be cleared for tobacco cultivation in Virginia and Maryland and seed sowed in a special bed, to be taken as seedlings to fields of fertile soil with good drainage. The top flower bud was often removed to concentrate growth into the leaves, and mature tobacco leaves were cut and cured in a harvest at the end of summer. Fields were only fertile for a few years, creating a constant pressure for new land, and the intensive work in cultivation meant that labour was also in increasingly short supply. Initially, this was provided by indentured migrants who, having been tempted to the New World by recruiters in England's market towns and ports, worked for a number of years in exchange for their passage. By 1619, however, the first slave ships had cast their shadow, as John Rolfe recorded in his diary, 'About the last of August came in a Dutch man of warre that sold us twenty negars.'

THE ENGLISHMAN AND THE 'INDIAN PRINCESS'

John Rolfe was born in Norfolk, England in 1585. In 1609, aged 24, he set sail from Plymouth in the *Sea Venture*, bound for Virginia, with his new wife. The *Sea Venture* was wrecked and Rolfe was cast onto the shores of Bermuda; the dramatic storm and the remote island refuge are said to have inspired Shakespeare's *The Tempest*. Rolfe's wife gave birth in Bermuda to a child, who sadly soon died; the parents continued to Virginia, but shortly after their arrival Rolfe's wife also perished.

By 1612, Rolfe had established himself as a leading colonist, the first settler to establish the regular cultivation of tobacco in Virginia. In April 1614, the widowed Rolfe made an unprecedented marriage – to a young American Indian princess, Matoaka, nicknamed Pocahontas – 'little wanton' – because of her playful and mischievous nature. Aged only 18 at the time of the marriage, Pocahontas was the daughter of the powerful Chief Powhatan, an Algonquian potentate who was naturally less than enthusiastic about the arrival of the settlers and who had probably been responsible for the extermination of earlier colonists in Virginia.

Pocahontas had already proved herself sympathetic to the colonists, acting as something of a go-between in their negotiations with the Native American tribes. According to legend, in 1608 she saved the life of Captain John Smith, a prominent early colonist and one of the founders of Jamestown. During explorations of the territory around the Chickahominy River, Smith was captured by Native American warriors and brought before Powhatan. According to Smith's version of events, he was at first apparently welcomed, but suddenly the chief appeared to order his execution, and he was forced to lie down on two large flat stones. As warriors stood over him wielding clubs, Pocahontas is said (notably in Smith's own later, more and more elaborate and romantic accounts) to have interposed herself between the captain and the men. Later interpretations have perceived this as a Native American ritual of mock 'execution and salvation', with the implication that Pocahontas's actions were also part of the ceremony. Whatever the truth, Smith claimed he was then raised to his feet by Pocahontas and accepted by Powhatan as a 'son', or form of subordinate chief.

Smith and Pocahontas then became friends and, during a period of good relations between the colonists and the Algonquian, she often visited Jamestown with Native American traders. In 1613, when tensions between the two sides had increased, she was captured and held to ransom by another colonist, Captain Samuel Argall, who hoped to achieve the release of English prisoners and some captured arms from the Algonquians. During her captivity, she met John Rolfe in the settlement of Henrico, and when a meeting was finally arranged with two of her brothers, she told them she loved Rolfe and wished to marry him. Powhatan agreed, but John Rolfe, a devoutly religious man, agonized over his desire to marry a heathen wife. Thus began Pocahontas's Christian instruction and eventual baptism, at which she was given the name Rebecca; Rolfe then married her on 5 April 1614, 'for the good of the plantation, the honour of our country, for the glory of God, for mine own salvation...'. Their wedding was seen to represent a spirit of goodwill between the Native Americans and the colonists, and eight years of peaceful coexistence followed. Their only child – a son named Tom – was born in 1615.

The fame of the compassionate 'Indian Princess' had spread to England, to such a degree that on a visit there in 1616, Rolfe and his wife were received at the court of James I and fêted by London society. Pocahontas also had an emotional reunion with Captain John Smith, whom she had believed killed at Jamestown – a meeting that later storytellers of her life have suggested revealed that it was the exuberant Smith who was her true love. Pocahontas was captivated by her experiences in London, but pined to be back in Virginia. Rolfe and his wife prepared to return, but soon after boarding ship, Pocahontas contracted an illness, probably chickenpox. She was taken off the ship at Gravesend, where she died in 1617 at the tender age of 22. She was buried with little ceremony in the local churchyard.

Rolfe returned to Virginia, leaving young Tom in the care of an uncle in London. He married again to an English colonist, fathered more children and was killed in a massacre in 1622. Tom returned to Virginia in 1640 and the young man himself became an influential settler.

This far less salubrious side to tobacco trade did not generate criticism at the time. It was a response to economic pressures: as the crop's output increased, so did the need for slaves. Some 100,000 were brought from Africa between 1690 and 1770, often as part of the notorious 'triangular' pattern of trade that encompassed Africa, Britain and the New World (see page 54). From the 1660s onwards the Virginian assembly passed a series of stringent racial laws, and in 1705 lifelong slavery was legalized:

> all servants imported and brought into this country, by sea or land, who were not Christians in their native country ... shall be ... slaves, and as such be here bought and sold notwithstanding a conversion to Christianity afterwards.

The relatively 'liberal' slave owners who allowed their slaves any privileges were fined in tobacco, for example 'persons encouraging Negro meetings were to be fined 1,000 pounds [454 kg] of tobacco; owners letting Negroes keep horses were fined 500 pounds [227 kg] tobacco'. By 1700 there were an estimated 13,000 black slaves, equivalent to 13 per cent of the total population. Even the first President of the United States, George Washington, produced tobacco with the aid of 316 slaves on the 17,000 acres (6,880 ha) of land acquired when he married Martha Dandridge Custis.

The requirements of America's growing colonial population created a new and welcome market for European trade and manufactures, as well as a major impact on shipbuilding and the shipping industry. The produce of the colonies, both legal and illegal, had to be conveyed in ships between colony and mother country, and as the colonies grew more prosperous there grew a demand for European furniture and other luxuries. This trade also encouraged the development of unlawful industries, including smuggling and piracy, particularly in the areas around the Caribbean islands such as Jamaica, which offered natural shelters for the pirate vessels to lie in wait for their victims. Such was the notoriety of certain areas that higher insurance premiums were demanded by the marine insurers – another industry to benefit from the new colonial markets and their crops.

THE AMERICAN WAR OF INDEPENDENCE

The new sense of prosperity on the mainland, combined with an increasing antipathy to their British masters, set the colonists on the long road that would eventually lead to the establishment of the United States of America. Much of the dislike for Britain stemmed from the Navigation Act of 1651 and the mercantile system that meant products from America could only be imported on English-owned ships and Virginia was forbidden any production or trade that would reduce English profits. This system kept the growers permanently indebted to their 'masters' and bred resentment, compounded by grievances over taxation:

THE GOLDEN AGE OF PIRACY

The concept of a 'golden age' is deeply ironic, but as the opportunities for the acquisition of wealth by the colonists and the home dealers grew, so too did the financial aspirations of unscrupulous members of European society. The later years of the 17th century and the first 30 years of the 18th century were a boom time for pirates as well as for more conventional traders, but for those who were the victims of this particular brand of seafarer, it was no golden age. Although the lives of pirates are often romanticized in historical fiction, the reality of encounters with men who had everything to lose by capture was extremely barbarous.

The developing American colonies generally lacked strong government, and in consequence their coastlines became a prime hunting ground for pirate sloops. The pirate crews were highly competent, consisting largely of experienced seaman in the prime of life – and they were predominantly Englishmen. Many had served earlier on warships and had become redundant as peace returned to Europe. Although piracy was a dangerous career – capture meant the death penalty – a gamble on its possible rewards was preferable to starvation or a life of crime ashore, and there was no shortage of crews for the pirate ships.

BLACKBEARD

The lives of some of the most brutal and feared pirate captains have often been embellished with the passage of time. Perhaps the most infamous of all was Blackbeard, one Edward Teach (or Thatch), who was active in the West Indies and the Americas from 1717 to 1718. Teach's nickname derived, of course, from his appearance: he sported a long black beard, which he apparently tied up with black ribbons. By all accounts a tall, broad-shouldered man, he was said to wear a sling carrying three brace of pistols, an adornment that must have enhanced his natural abilities as a leader. He is recorded as being intelligent, politically astute and unrelenting.

Born in Bristol, Blackbeard served his piracy apprenticeship in the Bahamas, soon taking charge of his own captured ship and making for the Carolinas with an impressive crew of 400 men. He successfully plundered and pillaged his way along the coastline, ransoming captured ships and gaining several pardons from local governors as a result, a move that effectively legitimized piracy. Resentment grew amongst the more law-abiding members of the colonies, and the Royal Navy – in the form of Lieutenant Maynard and two sloops – was called in to restore order. Maynard forced Blackbeard's ship aground, and in the ensuing vicious fighting, the pirate was decapitated. Maynard returned to England with Blackbeard's skull as proof of his victory.

BUCCANEER WOMEN

Even more horrifying than the likes of Blackbeard in the eyes of contemporary society was the spectacle of swearing, cursing, ferocious female pirates, who appeared to betray the feminine standards of their day. Anne Bonny and Mary Read were pirates on the sloop of 'Calico' Jack Rackam, and took to cruising the Bahamas and Jamaica between 1718 and 1720. Their piracy ended when Rackam's ship was surprised at anchor by a sloop belonging to the governor of Jamaica. Testimony relates that all the men on board, and in particular their captain, were too drunk to fight and that Bonny and Read were the only crew members to offer resistance. They were defeated and stood trial in Port Royal.

The case of the two women, tried separately from their male colleagues, caused a sensation. European and American society was outraged to learn that Bonny and Read had lived most of their lives dressed as, and behaving in a manner similar to, the worst of men. Read was apparently raised as a boy, subsequently married, but returned to a masculine role when widowed – presumably partly in order to make a living. Bonny was also disguised as a boy-child during her infancy in County Cork, Ireland, apparently to fulfil the dictates of an inheritance. The two women met in New Providence and became sufficiently firm friends for Bonny to leave her husband (himself probably a pirate) and join Read in Rackam's pirate crew. Although sentenced to death at their trial, both escaped the gallows because each was found to be pregnant. Mary Read died in a Jamaican prison in 1721, but the eventual fate of Anne Bonny is undocumented.

Thomas Jefferson complained memorably that 'planters were a species of property, annexed to certain mercantile houses in London'. The influence of colonists from the Caribbean also became a source of resentment for some of the northeastern settlers, who, aware of their own economic importance, felt that too many concessions were made to this lobby at their expense. This prompted the beginnings of an internal trading structure between settlements along the seaboard, who, as J.M. Roberts has pointed out, were able to develop different specialisms to their mutual benefit. The middle and southern colonies, for example, grew plantation crops, including rice and tobacco, as well as timber; New England was the source of corn, shipbuilding and the refining and distilling of molasses. These new trading relationships, which encouraged radical questioning of the colonial framework, gave the mainland colonies a troublesome cast in British eyes. Nevertheless, by the 1760s more perceptive British politicians were pointing out the immense value of their mainland colonies, and were keen to resolve the growing challenges to Britain's commercial and political authority.

Relationships between Britain and the colonists, whose numbers between 1700 and 1770 had increased tenfold to 2,500,000, deteriorated as a result of the imposition of the Sugar Act in 1764, the American Stamp Act of 1765, and the Tea Act of 1767 (see page 96). Throughout the early 1770s, when British income from the colony was running at approximately £80,000 per annum, the situation grew worse, and in 1775 the American War of Independence (known as the 'Tobacco War' in Chesapeake) was declared. Britain recognized its former colony as an independent nation in 1783, and ironically trade with the fledgling nation was greater than in colonial times, with total exports rising from £12.5 million in 1782 to £20 million in 1790.

CONSUMPTION AT HOME

As Virginian tobacco production levels rose, so there was a boom in literature, both warning of its deleterious properties when consumed for recreation and praising its perceived medicinal attributes – many of the ailments it was promoted as curing being those it is now widely believed to cause. Into the former group fell Nicholas Boisregard, who warned young people that too much tobacco would cause trembling, staggering and a withering of 'their noble parts'. One of the more spurious medicinal claims was that it prevented the spread of bubonic plague, which devastated London's population in 1665–66, killing an estimated 70,000 of the 5,000,000 population (14 per cent). It was considered so efficacious that, on pain of flogging, boys at Eton were forced to smoke a pipe every morning in order to ward off the plague. This anecdote also underlines the point that tobacco consumption was universal. And it was this mass market – young and old, male and female, nobleman and peasant – that enabled tobacco to become such an important factor in the nation's finances.

Tobacco was the 'golden leaf' for James I. Always short of cash, he quickly recognized the nation's passion for tobacco and the opportunities for raising income by taxing the tobacco import/export trade. Indeed, the tax revenue from tobacco is something that no Government since has been willing to give up. James overcame his prohibitionist scruples and in 1608 reduced his punitive 1604 duty to a realistic one shilling per pound. In 1615 he illegally made the import of tobacco a royal monopoly, selling the privilege for a rent of £14,000 per annum. In 1633 he licensed the retail trade (as early as 1614 there were an estimated 7,000 shops 'in and around London, that doth vent Tobaco') and in 1620 an agreement was reached between the Crown and the Virginia Company that exchanged a ban on tobacco cultivation in England for a 1 shilling per pound duty on Virginian tobacco. So important was the tobacco trade that, even when Britain was at war with the French in the mid-18th century, a special treaty was concluded to allow the lucrative business to continue. Tobacco-laden ships would sail from a named port in Britain to a named port in France, unload and return empty. In part, it was the prospect of direct access to the Virginian tobacco market that persuaded the French to support the colonies in their battle to become independent from British rule, the loan which Benjamin Franklin negotiated being secured on 5,000,000 lb (2,268,000 kg) of Virginian tobacco.

RIGHT The sign of an 18th-century tobacconist's shop includes mention of leaf tobacco (for pipes), snuff and cigars, all popular ways of enjoying the plant. It also features two sides of the cultivation coin: the plantation slave and his wealthy master. By the end of the century, the slave population of Virginia and Maryland had increased from 20,000 to 395,000.

The 17th century was a volatile one. Economic instability was accompanied by high price and tax rises, there were wars, notably with France, Holland and the Civil War at home, the attempted regicide of James I (Guy Fawkes in 1605) and the successful regicide of Charles I (in 1649), a Commonwealth, plague and the Great Fire of London, the Glorious Revolution and Puritanism. Yet throughout this time England was building her naval strength, developing international trade links and acquiring various overseas possessions in Asia, Africa, the West Indies and North America. The income generated by the trade in tobacco and other economic crops such as sugar and cotton helped to swell the royal coffers and provide a degree of national financial stability as well as individual profits. This allowed further speculation and investment in foreign trade, which in turn helped to lay the foundations for the rapid imperial expansion that was to be such a hallmark of the 18th and 19th centuries.

Tobacco wealth also enabled urban and industrial development in Britain. An example is the city of Glasgow, which by the 1720s was handling over half of all the American tobacco brought into Britain. This in turn enabled the city to develop its port at the expense of Port Glasgow further down the River Clyde. The subsequent shipbuilding and engineering industries brought further prosperity and made Glasgow the industrial centre of Scotland, earning it the nickname 'The Second City of the British Empire'. Bristol was another city to benefit significantly from tobacco. It not only played a pivotal role in the Triangular Slave Trade, but was also home to the cigarette and cigar manufacturers W.D. & H.O. Wills, later known as Imperial Tobacco.

FASHIONS IN TOBACCO

Up until the Commonwealth in Britain, the universal form of tobacco consumption was to smoke it in a pipe. However, following the Restoration in 1660, Charles II, who had spent his exile in the French palace at Versailles, brought back with him many French habits, including the taking of snuff – dried tobacco ground into a fine powder and inhaled through the nostrils. The first snuff-takers used strands from the dried tobacco leaves, rolled and knotted like a rope, which was bought in appropriate lengths and ground into powder by the purchaser, using an instrument resembling a nutmeg grater. With the advent of ready-to-use aromatic powders, possessing a finer and more even texture and using recipes jealously guarded by their manufacturers, snuff rapidly became the favoured aristocratic form of tobacco. George III's wife was affectionately known as 'snuffy Charlotte' in recognition of her predilection for the powder, and it marked a class differentiation in tobacco consumption which lasted until the mass production of the cheap cigar and cigarette in the late 19th century. The Regency dandy and wit Beau Brummell made snuff an essential fashion attribute for any man about town, and a keen interest was taken in the individual blends, which

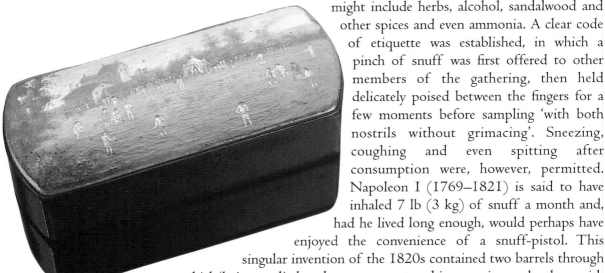

might include herbs, alcohol, sandalwood and other spices and even ammonia. A clear code of etiquette was established, in which a pinch of snuff was first offered to other members of the gathering, then held delicately poised between the fingers for a few moments before sampling 'with both nostrils without grimacing'. Sneezing, coughing and even spitting after consumption were, however, permitted. Napoleon I (1769–1821) is said to have inhaled 7 lb (3 kg) of snuff a month and, had he lived long enough, would perhaps have enjoyed the convenience of a snuff-pistol. This singular invention of the 1820s contained two barrels through which 'being applied to the nose, upon touching a spring under them with the forefinger, both nostrils are instantly filled, and a sufficient quantity driven up the head to last the whole day'!

Two contrasting styles of snuffbox, dating from the 18th century (above) and the middle of the 19th century (opposite). The lacquered wooden box features a scene of early cricket, perhaps painted to reflect an owner's particular interest. The gold enamelled box, made in Geneva, displays a miniature of the Imperial Palace at Cagayan in the Philippines.

Not surprisingly for such a social commodity, snuffboxes became highly fashionable, luxury objects. The first published designs were included among the briefs for goldsmiths and glasscutters of a Nuremberg architect, Paul Decker, in 1710. Those from Parisian jewellers, studded with gems and elaborately carved, were in particular demand in the 18th century and much copied. Shapes became more elaborate, with oval, angular and asymmetrical boxes becoming popular by the middle years of the century.

While the 'genteel' royalty and those with social aspirations snuffed, and 'polite' women eschewed smoking as unladylike, pipe smoking remained popular amongst the remainder of the male population. As Joseph Addison commented in 1714, smoking in the coffee houses (the precursors of gentlemen's clubs) was a way to break the ice and get to know fellow customers — the minor nobility and the mercantile classes. An equally common image of the time was a working man enjoying his pipe with friends in the alehouse. Fashions change, however, and while tobacco-chewing remained popular in the southern states of the USA (reaching a peak consumption of 3 lb [1.4 kg] per capita per annum in 1890) and the Revolutionary French were smoking the cigarito, the least similar form of consumption they could find to the hated nobility, who 'snuffed', a new way of smoking found popularity amongst the upper classes in Britain. The first Briton to smoke a cigar was John Cockburn, while marooned on the island of Honduras in 1731, but for the next century the cigar remained a minority smoke. Between 1826 and 1830, however, cigars imports rose a staggering 9,615 per cent from 26 lb (12 kg) to 250,000 lb (113,400 kg). This may have, in part, been due to royal patronage, Prince Puckler-Muskau having introduced diners to the German habit at a dinner in honour of the Duke of Sussex, brother of George IV, in 1824. Certainly the royal patronage of another German aristocrat, Prince Albert, who married Queen Victoria in 1840, helped the cigar to replace snuff as the choice of the upper classes and those anxious to emulate them. With this new trend there developed a new smoking etiquette – smoking lounges became a feature of hotels, smoking jackets and hats became high fashion for male smokers, and a convention developed that after dinner, once the ladies had retired, the men enjoyed a cigar, port or brandy and nuts before moving on to the smoking room (often also equipped with a billiard table). Furthermore, as Henry Davenport Northrop explained in 1893:

> When the smoker was around a lady, there were certain rules to be followed. A gentleman in meeting a lady acquaintance should remove his cigar from his mouth and hold it down by his side before raising his hat to her. Above all, never smoke while walking or riding with a lady. She may not object to it, but that does not pardon your rudeness.

SMOKING IN STYLE

The 30 Years War (1618–48) assisted the spread of tobacco across Europe, and conflicts throughout the 19th century helped to promote various forms of smoking. The Mexican War (1846–48) exposed United States soldiers to the darker, richer tobacco favoured in the southwest, which led to a massive rise in the popularity of cigarros, cigarillos and cigars. One story of how the paper-rolled cigarette evolved involves the Turkish/Egyptian war. During the siege of Acre in 1832, an Egyptian artilleryman had increased his gun's fire rate by rolling the gunpowder charges in paper tubes. Rewarded with a pound of tobacco, he and his colleagues discovered their sole pipe was broken. Enterprisingly, they reapplied their military discovery to a recreational pastime, and so tobacco rolled in paper was born. This form of consumption became popular with both armies and in 1847 Philip Morris opened a shop in London selling handrolled Turkish cigarettes before launching his own brand in 1854.

It was Turkish troops who also exposed their British allies to the 'advantages' of cigarettes during the Crimean War (1853–56) and it was a Crimean veteran, Robert Gloag, who opened Britain's first cigarette factory in 1856–57, manufacturing 'Sweet Threes'. The match also helped the advance of cigarettes. Matches made from phosphorus and ignited by friction were invented by John Walker in 1827 and the 'lucifer' was constantly improved on. 'Vestas', 'Flamers', 'Vesuvians' and 'Fuzees' followed, but it was not until 1892 that book matches were invented. There were teething problems – the striking surface was inside the book and frequently all the matches caught fire together – but the technology had been perfected by 1912. Another innovation that helped the popularity of cigarettes came from North Carolina, where, in 1839, charcoal was used to cure the thinner, low-nicotine leaves from the Piedmont variety for the first time. This higher temperature process not only cost less, but also produced tobacco with a brilliant golden colour. This is the classic, mild, 'Bright Leaf' form of tobacco, which allows the smoker to inhale the smoke easily – something that was not commonly done up until this point. Further impetus to cigarettes was given by the discovery of a chlorophyll-deficient variety of tobacco named 'White Burley' by an Ohio farmer in the 1860s. This became the staple of American blended tobaccos. Cigarettes were given a boost in France by Napoleon III (1808–73) who smoked 50 a day, and newly sophisticated advertising techniques emphasized the associations of sensuality and freedom that accompanied the experience. A significant indication of their effect was Prosper Mérimée's decision to cast the heroine of his novel, *Carmen* (1845), made into a celebrated opera by Georges Bizet in 1875, as a sultry cigarette girl in an Andalusian factory.

Cigarettes became popular relatively late in the USA, but rapidly established themselves in the early 20th century. In 1865, fewer than 20 million cigarettes were produced, but by 1928 the number had reached 100 billion. The reason for this growth, apart from the First World War, was that cigarettes were cheap and convenient both to consume and to manufacture. This became particularly true with the patent of the Bonsack machine, the first practical cigarette-making machine, in 1881; it was sponsored by the tobacco baron, James Buchanan 'Buck' Duke. As cigarette production grew, skilful marketing strategies sought to identify them with the spirit of a new, more hedonistic age.

Today, the global tobacco industry is big business on which the revenues of many of the world's governments continue to depend. The British Government, which first used tobacco revenues from newly independent American colonies to fund further expansion of its empire, raised £5,775 million in taxes from tobacco products during 1987–88. And while the apparent connections between tobacco smoking and life-threatening illnesses has left a legacy of complex law suits in the United States, it is ironic that the nation's founding colonies were largely sustained by the profits from the 'tawny weed' itself.

OPPOSITE A sheet music cover of the 1920s, with its echo of Dorothy Parker and Sally Bowles, encapsulates the decade's mood of social liberation, exploration and change. As cigarette sales soared in Europe and the USA, they became a statement of contemporary sophistication which advertisers continue to exploit.

CUTTING THE CANE

THE EUROPEAN TASTE FOR SUGAR created a highly influential industry in the Caribbean in the 17th and 18th centuries. Sugar cane became a staple crop for many fledgling colonies, notably those of Britain and France, who began to dominate the region as the Spanish and Portuguese presence declined. From St Kitts, the first British settlement in 1632, to Barbados, Antigua, Jamaica and the British Virgin Islands, the islands generated considerable wealth, yet sugar's influence was pernicious for the majority of those involved in its production. Labour-intensive in its cultivation, sugar cane gave rise to vast plantations worked by African slaves, radically changing the Caribbean's culture and demography. The notorious 'triangular trade' brought West Africa, the New World and Britain into a profitable economic nexus, but its human consequences have still to be resolved.

Discovery and Early Use

Even more than tobacco, sugar cultivation has left a highly ambivalent economic legacy. For the Caribbean islands in the 17th and 18th centuries, as Henry Hobhouse has perceived, it provided the 'supreme cash crop' requiring intensive, large-scale farming and fuelling the slave trade. As sugar plantations increasingly replaced tobacco, the population balance shifted dramatically; Barbados, for example, contained only 6,000 African slaves and 37,000 white inhabitants in 1643, but by 1660 the number of slaves had grown to over 50,000. In the 19th century, the major plantations were to become victims of the slave trade's decline, but its impact remains manifest. Few industries have so materially influenced their locations as sugar, transforming their human profile, environment and economy; it is also one of the world's most indulgent and least necessary crops.

Sugar cane is essentially an adaptable plant, which has prospered in many parts of the world. Believed to have been first harvested in the Pacific Islands about 5,000 years ago, sugar cane then spread to China and India. Fascination about the mysteries of extracting its sweetness has long surrounded the crop; the Emperor Darius of Persia, invading the Indian subcontinent in 510 BC, described it as 'the reed that gives honey without bees'. For most Europeans, only the establishment of sugar cane plantations in Madeira and the Canary islands, followed by those in the New World, brought this seductive commodity within their grasp.

It was the major expansion of the Arab peoples in the seventh century AD that spread sugar cane across the whole of the Mediterranean, following their invasion of Persia in 642. The Arabs proceeded to establish forms of sugar plantation in Syria, Palestine, Morocco, Spain, Sicily, Cyprus, Crete, North Africa and Egypt, yet for most people in Europe honey remained the main sweetener. Sugar was first tasted by Western Europeans when knights of the first Crusades of the 11th century AD encountered it in Syria and brought back small quantities to England in 1099. Throughout the Middle Ages a small amount of sugar trickled into Britain via Mediterranean trading ports such as Venice and Genoa, and North Africa, but the prohibitive cost of this new luxury restricted its use to the tables of royalty, aristocrats and important members of the clergy. A record from the household of Henry III in 1226 refers to the procurement of 3 lb (1.4 kg) of sugar from the Mayor of Winchester, and by 1288 the Royal Household was consuming 6,000 lb (2,700 kg) per year. In 1319 sugar was available in London at 'two shillings a pound' – a veritable fortune. As with many expensive imports sugar consumption became an ostentatious display of wealth, used to impress.

Over the next 200 years the price of sugar was significantly to decline, primarily due to the arrival of non-Mediterranean-grown sugar in Western Europe. In the early to mid-15th century sugar plantations on the Portuguese-occupied islands of Madeira, the Azores and São Tomé began to challenge their Mediterranean rivals, followed by Spanish plantations on the Canary Islands in

ABOVE First brought to the New World by Columbus, sugar cultivation remained under Spanish and Portuguese control in the region throughout the 16th century. This engraving, dating from *c.*1600, depicts an early sugar mill in which the stems are crushed, boiled to distil the sap and shaped into sugar 'loaves' in helmet-shaped moulds (right).

1480. (These new plantations were the first to use slaves outside Europe, setting the trend for the later evils of the Atlantic slave trade.) For 100 years the sugar trade was dominated by the Atlantic islands, eventually to be superseded by sugar plantations in the New World. As a consequence, good quality sugar became cheaper and more available throughout the 17th century (the price halved over the 100 years and fell by another third by 1750, despite intermittent sharp price rises) and was to become viewed as an essential, although potentially damaging, feature of the European diet.

By 1700 sugar was still expensive in Europe, but it was now considered to be a core ingredient in everyday meals. The value of sugar to the Caribbean islands was proportionately high; although other crops, especially tobacco, hardwoods and coffee, also contributed to the islands' standing, sugar served to crystallize the region's importance and to strengthen the influence of its planters in their mother country's economic affairs.

In 1494 Christopher Columbus was able to inform Ferdinand and Isabella of Spain that on the island of Hispaniola (now split between Haiti and the Dominican Republic) 'the small quantity [of sugar] we have planted has

SUGAR CANE PROFILE

BOTANICAL DETAILS

Sugar cane is one of the biggest members of the tropical grass family, growing to a height of 16 ft (5 m). Latin names for the species include *Saccharum officinarum, S. spontaneum, S. barberi* and *S. sinense*. There are now many cultivars available to the cane farmers. Today, sugar cane provides three-fifths of the world's sugar (the remainder being extracted from sugar beet) and is so common a commodity that it would be virtually impossible to avoid coming into contact with it.

ORIGINS

Sugar cane originated in Asia, probably as the result of a hybridization of wild varieties. Sugar cane was introduced to the Caribbean by Christopher Columbus, who took the plant with him on his second voyage of discovery in 1493.

DESCRIPTION

The cane, which resembles bamboo, takes 12 months until it is fully grown and, once chopped down to the stem, will re-grow in 12 months provided that the roots are not damaged.

HABITAT

Sugar cane is an easy plant to grow – it just needs a deep, rich, well-drained soil and a hot, moist climate with strong sunlight. A typical sugar content for mature cane is 10 per cent by weight and 2½ acres (1 ha) of land will yield about 10 tons of sugar. These figures are variable according to the variety of cane, the location and the weather.

PROCESSING

Harvesting tends to occur during the dry season and can last up to a month. Extracting the sugar is a fairly simple process: the plant is harvested before it runs to seed; the stem, which contains the majority of the sugar, is crushed; and the sap is boiled into a thick syrup. The primary problem with harvesting sugar cane is that it needs to be processed within approximately 24 hours or else fermentation sets in.

succeeded very well'. Although Columbus had failed to reach China, his discovery of the New World would prove to be far more bountiful than a direct trade route to the Orient. The strange dried and living plants, unknown animals and birds and the five Native Americans he brought back to Spain were a taste of the wonders and riches waiting to be discovered in the new lands.

Soon after settling in Hispaniola Christopher Columbus offered to send native West Indians back to Spain. Isabella refused the offer, and when Columbus sent over two shiploads of Native Americans, she ordered their immediate return. The indigenous people of the West Indies were split into two tribes: the Arawaks and the Caribs. The peaceful Arawaks, who were vegetarians, had been displaced from many of the islands by the more warlike Caribs, who were confirmed meat eaters (the word 'cannibal' is a corruption of Carib). Early settlers at first used the Caribs for labouring, but they were found to be unsuitable as they understandably resented the enforced workload. Far more devastating for the Caribs were the diseases that Europeans brought with them to the New World. Influenza (which was introduced into Hispaniola through pigs on Columbus's boats) was followed by typhus, chickenpox, typhoid, scarlet fever, whooping cough, bubonic plague and smallpox. This last disease in particular decimated the Native American population, both in the Caribbean and on the mainland. By 1508 Hispaniola's population is reckoned to have dropped by over 95 per cent to about 100,000. A new source of labour was sought and in 1510 the first large consignment of African slaves was exported from Spain across the Atlantic. Within 20 years direct commercial traffic with the countries of West Africa had been established, laying the foundations for the triangular trade (see page 54).

DEVELOPMENT AND CHANGE

The sugar cane planted by Columbus prospered and a cargo of sugar was brought back from Hispaniola to Seville as early as 1515. The first New World sugar to reach England came from the same island and was procured by John Hawkins, father of Richard, through the exchange of African slaves brought across the Atlantic – a portent of the human atrocities that were to come. By 1530 there were over 12 Spanish- or Portuguese-controlled plantations in operation in the West Indies. The two countries owned the majority of the islands of the West Indies after Pope Alexander VI had split the region between them, but their tenure became increasingly unstable as England, France and Holland showed an interest in the potential wealth to be gleaned from this new land. Initially this interest took the form of privateering raids on the territories and shipping out of the Caribbean, then, following the decline of Portugal's empire and the Spanish defeat by England in 1588, attention was focused on developing the disputed territories economically. Companies were established to exploit the sparsely populated lands and England began acquiring islands in the Lesser Antilles.

RIGHT One of a sequence of paintings of sugar production in Antigua, made by the artist William Clark in 1823. The workforce on the Weatherall plantation is shown placing cuttings of stalk in rows of holes, a traditional cultivation method that was labour intensive.

The first English settlement was on St Kitts in 1624, then Barbados in 1627, Nevis in 1628, Antigua in 1632 (its first plantation was founded in 1650) and Montserrat in 1632. The capture of Jamaica from the Spanish in 1655, achieved with only 5,000 soldiers, was to have a profound effect on the power struggle in the Caribbean in favour of the English; together with Barbados, it retained the strongest British influence in society and architecture. The changing ownership of Caribbean islands reflected the importance with which they were viewed by European powers. The British Virgin Islands, for example, were first claimed by Columbus for Spain in 1493, then taken by the Dutch in the 17th century, before being claimed shortly afterwards by the British, who proceeded to develop a sugar industry that shaped the island's fortunes for the next 150 years. France took possession of Guadeloupe in 1634, evicting the native Carib population, and of Martinique in 1635, whilst the Dutch obtained Curaçao in 1634.

By the mid-17th century the English sugar trade in the New World had begun after the settlers had tried a variety of other crops, including tobacco, cotton, indigo, limes and ginger. Sugar cane proved to be the most successful and financially rewarding crop, for it commanded the highest price per acre, paid lower English import duties and, with the insatiable appetite of the English for sweetness, had a guaranteed market. The conditions in the New World were perfect for the cultivation of sugar cane and, initially at least, were ideal for the 'slash and burn' technique of farming that was prevalent before plant nutrition was understood. Being well wooded and with a low population density it was possible to burn an area of scrub or forest, grow a crop on the richer soil and then move on to another site a couple of years later. This technique did away with the need to leave areas fallow every two or three years. Poor land management was to prove problematical later in the colonization of the West Indies, however, and was put forward as one of reasons why French sugar became cheaper than British (their islands had fresher and more productive soil).

EXTRACTING SUGAR

Sugar cane was grown in one of two ways: either by digging a row of holes and inserting 2-ft (60-cm) cuttings of old cane stalk, or by digging a series of trenches and placing the cuttings end to end. The latter 'Jamaica' method made weeding much easier. A gang of 15 slaves could plant a plot of 1 acre (0.4 ha) in a single day. This would yield a ton of sugar when harvested between January and May. The slaves cut the cane by hand, stripped off the outer leaves and transported the bundles of stalks to the sugar mill. The sugar cane was ground by mills powered by water, wind or oxen. In the 17th century a three-roller mill was used, with a central roller turning against the two outer ones. The stalks were passed through one set of rollers and back through the opposing pair. It was a

BELOW Harvested cane, bound in bundles, is brought to an Antiguan windmill for processing. Cane stalks had to be ground between rollers to extract the juice within 24–48 hours of harvesting, to avoid fermentation. The diagonal structure and small wheel enabled the sails to be adjusted in order to catch the prevailing wind.

ABOVE A boiling house in Antigua, painted by William Clark in 1823. In almost incredible heat and humidity, the cane juice was boiled in a sequence of vats, until solid crystallized sugar was formed.

dangerous operation and there were many cases of workers getting caught up in the rollers. The brown cane juice was piped down to a cistern in the boiling house, from where it was ladled into copper kettles above a furnace. The searing heat of the boiling house, with no ventilation and high humidity, must have been virtually unbearable – temperatures of 140°F (60°C) were recorded during the day and 120°F (49°C) at night. The cane juice was boiled to remove impurities and to evaporate it into crude crystallized sugar, which could be exported and refined. There were usually five coppers of diminishing size, but with increasing temperatures, which the sugar boiler decanted the ever-thickening brown liquid

into one by one. When the cane juice was placed in the smallest, hottest kettle, lime was added to help crystallization, and when the boilerman thought that the time was right, the sugar was doused in a cooling cistern. From 1 gal (4.5 l) of sugar cane juice came 1 lb (0.45 kg) of muscovado sugar. The sugar was then put into earthenware pots and placed in the hot curing house to dry out. The bottoms of the pots had a number of holes, which were corked for the first two days and then unplugged to allow the liquid molasses to be collected and distilled into rum. This process was repeated for about a month, after which the sugar was removed from the pot, the top and bottom of the sugar loaf cut off and the remaining 'dry' sugar reboiled and then placed in the sun. The sugar was finally packed into a large, 1,800 lb (816 kg) cask known as a hogshead ready for shipment to Europe. The muscovado sugar travelled better than other types of sugar, but was not ready for public consumption and had to be refined when it reached its destination.

Refining required a source of clean water and a sustainable fuel supply, both of which were more readily available in Europe than the colonies. Added to this, the more salubrious climate meant that it made sense to build sugar refineries in port towns. By the end of the 18th century there were 150 refineries operating in towns and cities such as Bristol, Southampton, Whitehaven, Kingston-upon-Hull and Newcastle. From the refinery sugar found its way into the ever-eager mouths of the British public via numerous shops, stalls and other retail outlets.

CULTIVATING THE CARIBBEAN

Barbados was the first English-controlled island to produce large quantities of sugar, yet it was 20 years after the seizure of the island before any significant amount was exported. This was due to a number of factors, including the unstable nature of the region and disputed land rights. The first settlers were more concerned with growing subsistence crops such as plantain, beans and corn, and it took some time for them to diversify to export crops such as indigo, tobacco, ginger and, of course, sugar. However, as Sir Dalby Thomas, Governor of Barbados, noted in 1690, the first English settlers were inexperienced in cultivating the crop and needed a helping hand:

A Hollander happened to arrive from Brazil, upon our island Barbados where, though there were good sugar-canes, the English knew of no other use for them than to make refreshing drinks for that hot climate. Since which time, by the many ingenious men the last civil war necessitated to seek their fortune in the New World, there has been so many several sorts of coppers, mills, boilers, stoves, pots and other tools of engineering for planting and pressing the canes, boiling up, separating, cleansing and purifying the sugar, as well as drawing spirits of admirable use from the molasses, that we at present exceed all the nations of the world in the true improvement of that noble juice of the cane, which next to that of the vine exceeds all the liquors of the world.

Small plantations of 5 to 30 acres (2 to 12 ha), which came to characterize Barbados's sugar industry, started to appear, complete with basic sugar mills (these were required as sugar cane juice had to be boiled between 24 and 48 hours after harvesting to prevent fermentation). In the early years of colonization white indentured servants travailed alongside the newly imported slaves. These labourers were contracted to work for a period of between 3 and 10 years, in return for which their passage costs were paid for and they were provided with some land at the end of the work term. Indentured labourers came from a variety of different backgrounds – they were criminals, debtors, political casualties and dropouts. Many of them had disreputable reputations, as Josiah Child recorded in 1668:

> Virginia and Barbados were first peopled by a loose vagrante People, vicious and destitute of means to live at home (being either unfit for Labour, or such as could find none to employ themselves about, or had so misbehaved themselves by Whoreing, Thieving, or other Debauchery, that none would set them on work) which Merchants and Masters of Ships by their Agents (or Spirits, as they were called) gathered up about the Streets of London, and other places, cloathed and transported to be employed upon Plantations; and these, I say, were such as, had there been no English Foreign Plantation in the World, could probably never have lived at home to do service for their Country, but must have come to be hanged or starved, or dyed untimely of some of those miserable Diseases, that proceed from want and vice; or else have sold themselves for Soldiers, to be knocked on the Head, or starved, in the Quarrels of our Neighbours, ... or else, if they could, by begging or otherwise, arrive to the Stock of 2s. 6d. to waft them over to Holland, become servants to the Dutch, who refuse none.

Indentured workers were soon phased out with the increased access to supplies of slaves in the late 17th century. Gradually the number and size of the plantations increased and the workforce rose correspondingly, so that by 1660 Barbados had become one of the world's most densely populated agricultural areas. It was the greatest sugar producer in the trade over the next decade, supporting 40,000 people, two-thirds of whom were white. For an island of just 166 square miles (430 square km) this dramatic growth inevitably led to problems, and poor land management resulted in a sharp decline in the fertility of the soil. In an attempt

ABOVE This delightful naïve painting of a Barbados plantation owner and his slave dates from around 1830. In the distance appear the sails of the sugar mill, smoke from the distillery and the master's elegant mansion. Once a highly prosperous sugar island, Barbados became less important in the 18th century, due to problems of soil exhaustion and competition from larger Jamaican estates.

to rectify this, terraces were constructed to prevent valuable soil being washed away by rainwater and slaves were employed collecting overspill that had accumulated in gullies. Barbados was the first island to introduce cattle for the express purpose of using the resulting dung to regenerate the exhausted land. In 1689 the Barbadian sugar planter Edward Littleton records in his pamphlet *The Groans of the Plantations* that 'some save the Urine of their People to increase and enrich their dung'. By around 1700 the number of sugar plantations on Barbados had reached about 900 and they covered 80 per cent of the island's arable land. Celebrated Americans such as George Washington and William Jefferson had interests in Barbados that helped to fund their political and artistic aspirations. Some 25 years later it was reported that there was no uncultivated land left and what land there was required the attention of four to five times the amount of slaves per acre than the French-owned islands. At the turn of the 18th century Barbados exported 10,099 tons of sugar to England and Wales (approximately half the total amount exported from the British West Indies) but by around 1748 the amount had dropped to 6,442 tons.

While Barbados was at the vanguard of British expansion and exploitation in the Caribbean, the inhabitants of the Leeward Islands of St Kitts (St Christopher), Nevis, Antigua and Montserrat were making slower and more unsteady progress towards economic prosperity. Although sugar cane cultivation was attempted as early as 1643 on St Kitts, it was not until the Royal African

Company transported about 8,000 slaves to the islands between 1674 and 1686 that sugar began to be produced in significant quantities. The islands were hampered by numerous difficulties and they could not compete with their neighbours until the mid-18th century. The situation of the Leeward Islands and their lack of garrisons and fortifications left them vulnerable to raids by privateers from nearby French islands. They were also caught up in the middle of the Anglo-French conflicts that dogged the end of the 17th and beginning of the 18th centuries. The islanders preferred to pursue a policy of fleeing from attack and then demand compensation for the resultant damage from their own government. This understandably did not go down well with the governors of the islands, who tried to bully the inhabitants into constructing some sort of defence for themselves. Things came to a head in 1710 when Governor Daniel Park was shot dead for interfering too much.

The 18th century saw an upswing in fortune for the Leeward Islands. The small plantations had been transformed into profitable concerns and the

WILLIAM BECKFORD AND JAMAICA

William Beckford was an English historian who spent much of his life in Jamaica, where he made observations on the country and, particularly, on the cultivation of sugar cane and the conditions of the black slaves working on the plantations. In 1790, he published *A descriptive account of the island of Jamaica, with remarks upon the cultivation of sugar cane throughout the different seasons of the year, and chiefly considered in a picturesque point of view.* His efforts to be 'picturesque' and his religiosity produced an account that gives us some insight into the quality and prejudices of an 18th-century European. For example, he writes:

An European, who would be almost dissolved were he to work beneath the vertical ardours of a tropic sun, does not always consider, when he expresses his surprise that the negroes should be obliged to labour in such an intensity of heat, that the climate is congenial to their natural feelings, and that the careful benevolence of Providence has thickened their skins, to enable them to bear what would otherwise be insufferable ... A person who has not been used to the labour of negroes in our colonies, would be at first surprised to observe in how short

a space of time a good gang of able labourers will get through a piece of standing canes...

Elsewhere in his account, Beckford provides a very clear description of how sugar was harvested, remaining almost oblivious to the slaves who implemented it:

This valuable plant requires great care and labour to cut ... The first cut is made at the top of the plant, if it be not out of reach on account of its height ... So soon as the canes are cut and tied, they are carried upon very hilly and steep estates, by mules; upon flat land and easy elevations, by wains: the burdens are deposited at the front of the mill-house, into which two or three weakly or new negroes convey them, and where they are placed upon a table, or frame, from which the feeders can with conveniency remove them, and afterwards insert between the canes of the mill, by which, and the revolution of the rollers, their juice is expressed.

William Beckford returned home to England, settled in Suffolk, and died in London in 1799.

ABOVE The wealth
generated by successful
plantation owners left
its legacy in their
magnificent houses,
full of imported
luxuries such as fine
china and elegant
furniture. This
example of a genre
found throughout the
American South and
Caribbean islands is
the Jackson plantation
house, near Schiever,
Louisiana.

abundant arable land had finally been put into service. By the middle of the century, St Kitts shipped more sugar than Barbados, and the four islands put together exported 42 per cent of all the sugar to England and Wales (three times Barbados's total). The Leeward Islands only covered 5 per cent of the British West Indies, but in 1748 they accounted for 18 per cent of the white population and 24 per cent of the slaves.

The growth of the sugar industry was an unusual and dynamic mixture of Asian plant, American soil, European technology and management and African toil. It soon eclipsed all other exports from the New World, including tobacco from the Chesapeake colony, and created an important role for merchants in the exchange of sugar for slaves, machinery, financial credit and the import of home commodities. This final process was to be a highly profitable yet often overlooked aspect of the Caribbean trade network. As with tobacco (see page 23), the colonial populations helped to stimulate demand for British exports and manufactured goods. By the 18th century the islands were great consumers of British goods, for by concentrating on the production of one or two key crops the inhabitants of the West Indies were forced to import all necessary and personal goods (specifically from Britain). A list of requirements at the time included 'woollen, linen, silk, iron, brass, copper, leather, glass, chinaware, clocks, watches, jewels, wrought plate, gold and silver lace, medicines … gunpowder … brickes, paint, oil, cordage, sugar pots, drips, hoops, candles … pipes … cards, swords, pistols, walking canes … grindstones, paving stones, books, toys, stationery, cutlery, Birmingham and haberdashery wares, all sorts of household goods and furniture; wearing apparel, cabinet ware, chariots, chaises, coppers … in short all things necessary for life, and almost the whole consumption … is British manufacture.' The slave population required 'vast quantities of check linen, striped hollands, fustian, blankets for their bedding, long ells and bays for warm clothing, coarse hats, woollen caps, cotton and silk handkerchiefs, knives, razors, buckles, buttons, tobacco pipes, fishing tackle, small glasses, thread, needles, pins and innumerable other items, all of British growth or manufacture.' Many of these goods would have been manufactured close to the British port involved in the transaction, resulting in a profitable local industrial infrastructure.

The value placed upon the sugar islands – considered greater than British or French Canada and (by some) the mainland American colonies too – is reflected in the large force of troops dispatched to the region by William Pitt the Younger in 1793. His disastrous attempt to emulate his father's achievement in Canada resulted in the death of over 40,000 British troops in three years (amounting to

BELOW A map of the West Indies from the *New History of Jamaica*, published in London in 1740, the time of greatest prosperity for the island. It acknowledges the role of Spanish explorers and cartographers, but colonial control of the Caribbean was by now firmly in British (and some French) hands.

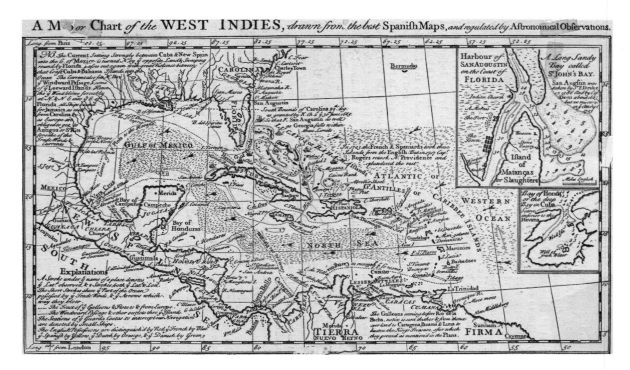

nearly half of those killed in the entire Napoleonic struggle). Interestingly, given this investment of military might, the islands were not unproblematic territories: even the rich and verdant island of Jamaica was a slow colony to evolve. For many of its formative years Jamaica had the reputation of being the most debauched and disorderly English Caribbean island. It was renowned as a hotbed of buccaneers and undesirables who, when not robbing Spanish ships, spent their free time in the inns and brothels of Port Royal. Jamaica was perfectly situated for attacks on Cuba, Hispaniola and Central America and its multitude of secluded bays offered ideal hideaways.

However, vice was not the only thing Jamaica had to offer. Covering 4,181 square miles (10,830 square km) it possessed far more arable land than all the other English Caribbean islands put together. From 1665 onwards, small and large landowners began establishing cotton, cocoa, indigo and sugar plantations in the fertile valleys and coastal plains. Henry Hobhouse has noted that by 1720 it had overtaken the sugar production of Barbados, its plantations characterized by much larger estates with 500 slaves. The 18th century became the era of the sugar barons, whose magnificent plantation houses and luxurious lifestyles were founded upon the corruption of the slave trade. The Greenwood Great House, once owned by the Barrett family (of Elizabeth Barrett Browning fame), remains full of desirable objects: oil paintings, specially commissioned Wedgwood china, a library of rare books, fine antique furniture and exotic musical instruments.

There were inherent dangers for the new plantation owners, however. A crop could be destroyed by a tropical storm, and there was a constant threat of drought, fire, disease, slave insurrection, native West Indian attack and invasion by another European country. Sugar planters also had to rely on military and naval protection from their native country; the young Horatio Nelson arrived to become second in command on the Leeward Islands in 1784.

Buccaneering and farming proved to be incompatible bedfellows in Jamaica — smallholders found the allure of piracy too much and many indentured white servants decided to run away to sea rather than work out their contract. Trading was problematic as African slavers and vessels containing English goods were extremely cautious about dealing with the notorious island and charged well above the market rate for the risk involved. A 20-year war of attrition finally saw the planters drive out the buccaneers, yet there were more obstacles and misfortunes to be overcome before Jamaica could fulfil its promise.

Along with the other British Caribbean islands, Jamaica found the Acts of Trade and Navigation, established in the mid-17th century, a hindrance to profitable trade. The act decreed that all British colonies must trade with and import from the home country. Likewise the *asiento* of 1713, which gave Britain, under the South Seas Company, the monopoly supply of slaves to the Spanish American colonies, resulted in the curtailment of the lucrative free trade from

Kingston with the Spanish. Jamaica's sugar production steadily increased in the first half of the 18th century from 4,874 tons exported to England and Wales to 17,399 tons in around 1748. What is more telling is the rise of slaves compared with whites. Around 1700 there were 42,000 slaves to 7,300 whites, but by the middle of the century slave numbers had shot up to 118,100 while there were only 3,000 more whites than 50 years previously. Production of sugar increased accordingly: by 1815 Jamaica was exporting 73,489 tons of sugar through the toil of 339,800 slaves. At the same time there were just 27,900 whites on the island. These figures are explained by the proliferation of vast plantations with large armies of slaves and the trend for wealthy planters to turn their backs on the New World and watch the profits role in from the comfort of the Old.

SUGAR AND SLAVERY

The initial prosperity of the sugar industry of Barbados and continued growth of the industry in the New World was made possible by the use of slave labour. By the end of the 17th century over 250,000 Africans had been forcibly brought over to the English Caribbean islands to spend their lives in slavery. Millions more would follow the deadly route to the Americas. There has been much debate about the origins and nature of Afro-American slavery and all that can be said with any certainty is that it was a wholly reprehensible business.

It was not in itself a new phenomenon: African servants and bodyguards had long been popular among wealthy Arabs and their merchants made sizeable profits exploring and trading along the west coast of Africa. Portuguese exploration of the same area in the 15th century brought them into contact with Arab slave traders. One Portuguese ship returning from Africa captured and enslaved a galley with a crew of Black Muslim Arabs. The crew railed at their treatment and informed the Portuguese that there were many more suitable servile heathens to be found in the interior of Africa. In exchange for their freedom they offered to capture some of the 'godless' people. Soon there was a regular trade between Spain and Portugal and West Africa. In 1444, 235 slaves from Lagos arrived at Seville on board one of Henry the Navigator's boats. They were sold on to Spanish sugar growers, whose inefficient methods of production meant that extra workers were required for the industry to remain competitive. Seville quickly became the European centre for the slave trade with 100 ships landing at her port each year, and by 1454 slaves were distributed over Castille, Aragon, Portugal, the Canary Islands and Madeira. This resumption of slavery in mainland Europe seems not to have troubled the consciences of many Christians: papal complicity in the trade was given with the authorization 'to attack, subjects and reduce to slavery the Saracens, Pagans and other enemies of Christ'.

The modern slave trade, with its origins in the Iberian/West African exchange, is a contentious and emotive subject. The explosive speed with which the

RIGHT A sale poster for a plantation estate in 1850 lists domestic and agricultural slaves among the disposable possessions. Although all are identified by function, significantly the plantation workers are without names.

SALE

The Estate in Block, Sugar Houses, Stock, Implements, &c.,

SLAVES

Lot 1. Solon, Griff Boy, good waiter
2. Yellow Girl, Grace and Two Children, Saul and Louise
3. Pete, house servant
4. Octoroon Girl, Zoe
5. Plantation Slave
6.　　ditto　　ditto
7.　　ditto　　ditto
8.　　ditto　　ditto

Afro-American slave trade took off, the extraordinarily harsh subjugation of the slave population and the sheer numbers involved have no obvious comparisons with older forms of bondage from antiquity and the Arab world. It is true that in the ancient world a large percentage of the population lived in a state of servitude, but there were many different types of slavery, some onerous and some less so. The nature of the modern slave trade was in part racially inspired, and some Europeans attempted to justify their iniquitous activities by promulgating the idea of their innate superiority. However, this can also be seen as expediency – the colonists and merchants needed a workforce to enable them to prosper, and racism was a useful means to aid economic exploitation. It was Africa's misfortune that her inhabitants fitted the bill.

England was a relative latecomer to the slave trade, but by 1650 had caught up with its European rivals in carrying slaves across the Atlantic. By 1670 England had overtaken both the Portuguese and Dutch to become the most prolific shipper of slaves (in the next 100 years its annual shipment of slaves rose sixfold). This dubious honour was to be upheld until 1807 when Parliament outlawed British involvement in the transportation of slaves. The exact number of slaves transported to the Americas from the 16th to the 19th century is hard to determine. Recent revisions have placed the figure at about 11.7 million exported and 9.8 million imported between 1500 and 1900 (the difference between export and import is a chilling testament to the loss of life that occurred in transit). What is clearer is that England carried over 3.4 million slaves out of Africa between 1662 and 1807.

THE TRIANGULAR TRADE

The growth of Britain's sugar and slave trade (they are inextricably linked) was reflected in the development of the triangular trade. Working on the principle that empty ships do not make a profit, English merchants devised a way of profiting from the transportation of slaves to the New World and the importation of its produce to England. There were three stages to the endeavour, hence the name. Firstly, goods such as firearms, iron and salt were shipped from England to the west coast of Africa, where they were exchanged for slaves. These slaves were then transported across the Atlantic to the West Indies to be sold to plantation owners. Finally the ships were loaded up with sugar and rum for the home journey. Following the precedent of granting chartered companies monopoly rights, Charles II gave the Company of Royal Adventurers of England into Africa the right of 'the sole and entire trade in Negroes on the African Coast' in 1660. In 1672 the company was re-formed as the Royal African Company, with a list of shareholders headed by the king and queen. Its monopoly only lasted until 1698 when trade with Africa was opened up to all merchants on the payment of a 10 per cent duty on exports to Africa. This was abolished 14 years

later as it was being blatantly flouted. Groups of
investors – local merchants, seafarers and speculators – clubbed
together to spread the cost and risk of a round voyage. Profits could
be handsome and in the 18th century cities such as London, Bristol and
Liverpool prospered on the trade. In 1725 London sent out 87 vessels carrying
26,440 slaves; in the same year Bristol saw 63 ships leave its port to carry 16,950
slaves to the West Indies. Exact profit margins are difficult to determine, but
towards the end of the century a 10 per cent return on the initial investment
appears to have been common. However, profits fluctuated according to the
success of the voyage and there was no guarantee of any financial gain.

Taking between 12 to 18 months to complete, the voyage was fraught with
potential dangers and problems. The middle passage from Africa to the West
Indies was the most hazardous and remains one of the starkest images of the slave
trade. Slaves were bought from African chiefs, merchants and traders on the
coastal region from Senegal to Angola (the British took most of their slaves from
the Bight of Biafra). The chiefs and merchants traded inland for captured slaves
and as the price for slaves rose so the boundaries of slaving were pushed further
into the heart of Africa. The number of fatalities among captives before they even
reached the markets on the coast is unknown, but was likely to be high. They were
invariably the victims of slave raiding, kidnapping and wars (some of which were
started specifically in order to get more slaves). Slave traders usually bought twice
as many men as women, and boys and girls in smaller numbers. The men were on
average 4 ft 6 in (1.4 m) tall and between 16 to 30 years old. They were shackled
together by hand and foot during the entire crossing. The extraordinarily cramped
conditions, the heat, the smell of faeces, sickness, shock, despair and the terror of
the unknown took their toll and about 1 in 10 slaves died on the three-month
transatlantic crossing. This figure would significantly rise if the boat was manned

by an inept crew or if it was becalmed in the dreaded Doldrums. Of the 3,400,000 Africans shipped by British merchants between 1662 and 1807 approximately 450,000 or 13.2 per cent died *en route*. When the deaths before embarking and during the 'seasoning' on arrival are included, the figure takes on an even worse dimension. During seasoning slaves were taught the rudiments of English and drilled in the routines and disciplines of life on a plantation.

THE EXPERIENCE OF PLANTATION LIFE

Conditions for the seasoned slaves did not improve much – indeed, the life expectancy for sugar slavery was only half that of other forms of field slavery. The work was exceptionally gruelling, and Edward Littleton recorded that, even with a prime selection of slaves, a sugar planter would 'lose a full third of them, before they ever come to do him service. When they are season'd and used to the Country, they stand much better, but to how many Mischances are they subject … he that hath but a hundred *Negroes,* should buy eight or ten every year to keep up the stock.' The death rate on plantations in the British West Indies was about 10 per cent per year in the first half of the 18th century. The reason for this high mortality rate was a combination of overwork, brutality, a low-protein diet, disease, poor medical treatment, unsanitary housing and poor clothing. Fertility was unusually low with only half of British West Indian slave women giving birth in the mid-18th century. Mainland slaves with a similar mortality level had an 80 per cent higher birth rate. The overriding reason for low life expectancy was the extremely arduous working conditions. Sugar cane was the most exacting crop to cultivate, with each stage of production involving arduous labour. The tropical sun beat down incessantly, wearying even those used to extreme heat. Ploughs were rarely used because the planters wanted to keep their slaves occupied throughout the year and not just during the busy harvest period. The regime of the plantation was a violent and ruthless one, aimed at intimidating the slaves into working.

Plantation owners were an unusual breed of men who were prepared to risk their health and happiness for the potential fortune that could be made in the New World. Many were aggressively acquisitive, prone to drunkenness and unruly behaviour, but also courageous and ambitious. Obviously it is wrong to tar all planters with the same brush and a number of them were careful, civilized and conscientious, but the defining characteristic among them was their determination to earn a fortune as swiftly as possible, at whatever cost. Slavery in the West Indies had a particularly bad reputation for cruelty. One reason for this might be the perceived threat of high numbers of black slaves compared to whites. In 1748 there were six slaves to every white, while in 1815 the ratio had risen to 12 to 1 (see page 52). It has been suggested that a feeling of isolation could have contributed to the Caribbean planters' desire for strict control.

PLANTATIONS IN JAMAICA

The plantation system evolved to supply the demands of Western Europe for exotic produce, and to make the newly acquired territories thousands of miles away from home an economic success. It was responsible for the largest body of forced labour in history, simultaneously establishing control of the new land and its people while creating a profit. A hierarchy of labour was imposed by the European owners, who set the indigenous population to work clearing land and planting crops. This was to have a profound effect on the landscape as vast swathes of forest and undergrowth were cut back and burnt, and plantation houses, stockades, boundary fences, roads and bridges were constructed in their place. Alien plant species, such as banana and sugar cane, began to dominate the scenery and eventually became synonymous with the Caribbean landscape.

One of the striking features of plantations was the disparity of working conditions endured by the slaves. Crops such as sugar, which were grown in humid conditions in a labour intensive manner, exacted a particularly horrific toll on the labourers. In contrast, the tobacco plantations of the American mainland had proportionately smaller numbers of slaves per plantation working in a more salubrious climate. Such differences, of course, were of little relevance if the plantation was run by a brutal overseer. The relationship between slave and master was often a fine balance between veiled insubordination and excessive retaliatory force. Slaves vented their resentment through petty acts of vandalism such as breaking tools, injuring work animals, stealing, planting crops incorrectly and by running away. Punishments were severe, with beatings commonplace.

A fascinating record of daily plantation life in the mid-18th century is found in the diaries of Thomas Thistlewood. Born in 1721, Thistlewood arrived in Jamaica in 1750 and remained on the island until his death 36 years later. Thistlewood was initially employed as penkeeper on a timber and livestock estate, but a year later he was made overseer of a sugar plantation. Eventually, in 1767, he purchased an 160-acre (65-ha) plot, which he turned into a livestock, vegetable and flower estate. Lacking the necessary financial resources to

establish a profitable sugar plantation, Thistlewood never made the fortune of which he had dreamed, but he did achieve respectability among the island's plantocracy class. One of the key strengths of Thistlewood's diary is the detached manner in which he records events such as beatings without comment. Other details, including sexual relationships, are recorded in the same matter-of-fact manner, although Thistlewood reverted to abbreviated Latin to describe his liaisons with the female slaves. Thistlewood does not question the morality of such relationships, and we can infer that they were not uncommon. He became extremely attached to a slave called Phibbah (who became his *de facto* wife and bore him a son, John), paying for her manumission and setting up an annuity for her in his will. However, Thistlewood continued to take other women, suffering consequent bouts of venereal disease.

Thistlewood's diary illustrates the tension and dynamics between plantation owner and the slave workforce. Severe punishment was meted out as a normal response to misdemeanours, although the influence of Phibbah may have persuaded him to stop the more excessive practices – he was by no means the worst of the plantation owners, but his treatment of the slaves under his jurisdiction seems to be on a par with that of his oxen and horses. Thistlewood may have felt it was necessary to subjugate the slaves by force for his own safety as much as to encourage them to work. Plantation overseers were occasionally killed by slaves; Thistlewood himself was attacked by a machete-wielding runaway while walking around the estate. The fight lasted about 20 minutes and he was lucky to emerge unharmed. The slave was charged with attempted murder, but was acquitted when another slave refused to give evidence. In 1760 a major slave rebellion erupted on Jamaica; those involved were intent on freeing the island's slaves and were killing and burning all in their path. Thistlewood records the nerve-racking night watches and the high anxiety felt by the plantation owners and white workers as the rebellion spread. The slaves on his plantation appeared restive and Thistlewood was sure that given the opportunity they would join the uprising (which eventually failed).

THE MAROONS OF JAMAICA

The Spaniards occupied Jamaica in 1509, initially enslaving the native Arawaks, whose population at that time is estimated at anywhere between 6,000 and 60,000. By 1655, when the British captured the island from the Spaniards, not a single Arawak remained — introduced diseases, brutality and the confiscation of agricultural land used for growing food had destroyed an entire people. Plantation owners therefore looked to Africa for slaves to work the land.

The British conquest of Jamaica provided the opportunity for the black slaves of the Spaniards to escape, take to the hills and form the basis of the first Maroon society in Jamaica. (The title 'Maroon' is said to derive from the Spanish *cimarron*, meaning 'wild and unruly'.) Most of these 'Spanish' slaves originated from northern West Africa and Angola, but during the 150 years of Spanish occupation, their ethnicity had become substantially mixed.

The white Spanish occupiers were, of course, reluctant to leave the island, as they were instructed to do by the British, and a complex society developed in Jamaica. The resident groups included the ruling British, white Spanish guerrillas, former slaves — many creoles — with loyalty to the Spanish, former slaves revolting against any white domination, and newly arrived African slaves.

The British were more than a little unnerved, realizing that the Maroon groups of escaped slaves in particular were extremely powerful on the island. The Maroons had, of course, substantial knowledge of the terrain that they had once worked, and they were also skilled fighters. They achieved substantive success in plundering and burning plantations, killing British soldiers who moved outside the white settlements and capturing slaves to join their numbers.

CUDJOE

In 1668, the inferior local sugar cane of Jamaica which the Spanish had been unproductively farming was replaced by high-quality cane plants from Barbados. The sugar estates grew to proportions that took over the vast majority of the agricultural land on the island. Larger numbers of slaves were required and duly imported, including Coromantees from the African Gold Coast. In 1690, a dangerous insurrection took place: slaves on an estate killed their brutal 'governor' and seized arms and ammunition. Although the leaders of the revolt were captured and executed, a young Coromantee, Cudjoe, and his two brothers, Johnny and Accompong, escaped and established the first of a number of Maroon gangs in the nearby hills.

The confidence of the gangs increased with the success of their raids upon the white colonists. Cudjoe emerged as the gang leader, styled, paradoxically, 'General Cudjoe', with his brothers as 'Captains', titles reminiscent of European military structures. Cudjoe organized the gangs in military style so that they developed into a well-disciplined and formidable force. By maintaining contact with the slaves on plantations, many of whom knew individual gang members personally, they could obtain food supplies in difficult times and even intelligence regarding armed militia movements. Cudjoe was to inflict numerous and devastating defeats upon the British, and his genius in tactical warfare was such that even Western observers were obliged to acknowledge his skill — and to take his presence seriously. Interestingly, his success was in part due to the fact that the British were reluctant to exercise military tactics appropriate to the situation: guerrilla warfare was seen by them as an inferior brand of engagement, and they adhered to inept European practices.

Cudjoe defeated all the British colonial forces set against the Maroons. In 1738 a treaty was drawn up granting the Maroons all the rights of freedom that they sought (apart from repatriation). In a dignified gesture of retributive humiliation, Cudjoe would not sign the treaty until the British governor's signatory — Captain John Guthrie — agreed to sign his name in his own blood, as Cudjoe was willing to do. Guthrie was eventually forced to comply.

A slave owner, as shown by the Barbados slave act of 1661, had almost complete authority over his slaves and could mete out whatever punishment he wanted. Technically he could be fined 3,000 lb (1,360 kg) of sugar or £25 for killing one of his slaves, but he could avoid payment by claiming that he was disciplining the errant person. Crimes right down to theft of anything worth more than a shilling were capital offences. Plantation overseers searched the slave cabins twice a month for stolen property and weapons. Of course slaves resented their harsh treatment and responded by breaking tools, burning down cane, mutilating livestock, running away and rebelling. This final act of defiance was a perennial worry, especially in Jamaica, where communities of ex-slaves known as Maroons had escaped the plantations and found sanctuary in the mountainous interior of the island. The terrifying Cockpit County was unaffectionately known as the 'Land of Look Behind', and any British soldiers who ventured there rode back to back in pairs, to literally 'cover one another's back'.

The Maroon War troubled the white inhabitants of the island between 1729 and 1739, but the treaty that ended the conflict ensured Maroons returned runaway slaves in exchange for autonomy and 1,500 acres (600 ha) of land. Slavery conditions did improve gradually toward the end of the 18th century. Rewards and incentives such as granting slaves a half or full day's leave to tend their own small plots of land and special treats such as tobacco or rum rations were introduced with some success. Investment in agricultural techniques and health care helped to increase the birth rate and diminish the reliance on the slave trade. However, it was still to be many decades before the slaves of the sugar plantations were emancipated.

There was thus an immense human price to be paid for the affordable enjoyment of an Englishman adding a couple of teaspoons of sugar to his cup of tea. During the three centuries of plantation expansion millions of Africans were sold into slavery and shipped across the Atlantic to a life of abject misery. From the late 17th century onwards the Quakers had vociferously denounced the slave trade, but it took another 100 years for popular support to manifest itself in an abolitionist movement. Moral repugnance for slavery was fostered by the Enlightenment and its belief in the rights of man. The biblical interpretation of the acceptability of slavery was re-evaluated by theologians. They argued that God revealed his purpose to humankind in stages and while previously slavery had been condoned by Christians, with the dawn of a more enlightened time slavery should be reassessed.

CONSUMPTION AT HOME

The curious aspect to the story of sugar is that it was all unnecessary. Refined sugar is not an essential part of the diet, indeed if taken in significant quantities it is positively harmful to health. It is not even an economical source of energy.

So why did the British, and it was the British in particular, become so enamoured of this superfluous sweetener? An addiction to sugar was established early on as a national weakness – the mediaeval palate found nothing incongruous in serving pork, chicken, rabbit or haddock with a sweet sauce. It was an expensive luxury until large shipments started returning from the New World, however, and sugar's usage as a culinary ingredient was restricted to the kitchens and tables of the rich and powerful.

The possible medicinal properties of sugar (as with many other exotic goods such as tobacco) had been fiercely argued over since the 14th century when Arab doctors used sugar to cure chest ailments. It was subsequently found in European apothecaries for the treatment of anything from constipation to an upset stomach. Unsurprisingly, those with investments in the New World were happy to proclaim sugar a veritable panacea. The one feature of sugar culture that was constant from the time it first appeared in England was that of conspicuous consumption. In the 15th century, for example, exotically shaped dishes carved from marzipan sat on the tables of the socially ambitious, while during the Tudor period special sugar containers and matching spoons were used to add sugar to wine (with the growth of tea consumption these were converted into sugar bowls and tongs). By 1720 the fashion had extended to a complete tea service, including silver tea caddy, teapot, kettle, spirit burner, sugar bowl and tongs.

Sugar prices dropped dramatically from the mid-17th to the mid-18th centuries, while the amount of sugar imported between 1700 and 1748 doubled. Consumption per capita rose accordingly from 4 lb (1.8 kg) in 1700, to 10 lb (4.5 kg) in 1748 up to 20 lb (9 kg) in 1800. The last sharp rise was caused in part by the widespread adoption of tea drinking.

Unlike the Chinese, the British had a penchant for sweetened tea and soon even the lowest members of society were imbibing the hot, sweet liquid. With the consumption of sugar no longer the mark of social superiority, the genteel classes devised elaborate tea ceremonies and etiquettes to try to differentiate themselves from those they deemed to be their inferiors.

The miserably inadequate justifications for the need of slavery fuelled the movement for a more egalitarian and moral system of trade.

BELOW An elegant silver porringer made in London in 1657. Initially an exotic luxury suited to such a container, sugar became increasingly available during the century as plantations in the New World began to deliver. The burgeoning domestic market was also linked to an expanding consumption of tea.

THE EFFECT OF EMANCIPATION

Adam Smith contributed to the emancipation debate in his *Wealth of Nations*, in which he appraised the economic disadvantages of slavery. The Tories under Pitt the Younger and the Abolition Society led by Thomas Clarkson and William Wilberforce joined forces to pressure Parliament into banning slavery. Wilberforce urged a practical as well as a moral imperative in his memorable address to Parliament in 1792: 'Consider the immense disproportion of numbers; there are now in Jamaica near 300,000 slaves, and but about 20,000 whites of all ages and descriptions. We are every year importing into that island a greater strength of blacks than there is of whites to be opposed to them. Where is this to stop?' However, Parliament was not riven with evangelical vigour and its 1807 Abolition of Slavery Act had more to do with changing circumstances than religious zeal. In 1944 Eric Williams asserted in *Capitalism and Slavery* that abolition was a result of economic expediency – the British West Indies sugar trade was being destroyed by the French and a worldwide ban on the slave trade would be beneficial to British merchants.

The abolition of slavery was actually economically damaging, for England had just gained Trinidad and Demerara, both of which were prime islands for slave-worked plantations: abolition occurred because the British Government believed that it was financially possible to survive without slavery. The growth of the manufacturing industry and the ascendancy of the sugar trade gave the impression that the slave trade, long viewed as a necessary evil, could finally be wound up. Change did not occur overnight, however, and the slaves of the British Empire had to wait until 1833 for their emancipation. Some Caribbean islands, such as Cuba, quickly mechanized to compensate for the end of slave labour; crushing rollers and copper boilers were steam-driven, using bagasse, a cane residue, as fuel. A railway appeared in 1845, and in 1855 a centralized sugar mill under private American ownership was developed. Productivity undoubtedly increased – as Henry Hobhouse has observed, by the end of the 19th century Cuba was harvesting 10 times as much sugar as Jamaica was at the beginning of it – but by then the sugar cane markets had changed out of all recognition.

The decline of the sugar industry in the New World was widely blamed on the ending of slavery. In reality, however, it was affected more by the introduction of free trade practices (primarily abolition of tariffs and the Navigation Act to enhance Britain's advantages as a clearing house for international trade) and the commercial introduction of sugar beet. The latter, a biennial root crop with a strong resemblance to a turnip, is suited to a temperate climate; the sugar is contained in its bulbous roots. It offered a source of sugar not dependent on tropical conditions and which could be cultivated at home in sufficient quantities to negate the need for expensive imports. Within 30 years beet sugar dominated the European market and ultimately threatened the hegemony of sugar cane.

THE KINGS OF COTTON

THE STORY OF COTTON provides a powerful example of colonial trade, and the economic beliefs that drove it, for over three centuries. In the form of high quality calico and delicately woven muslins, it provided a major Indian export for the East India Company in the 17th and 18th centuries, but as Europe became increasingly industrialized America became the primary source of raw cotton for processing. This single crop sustained a whole way of life in the American South, embracing planters, merchants and riverboatmen, but it also fostered the slavery on large-scale plantations, one of the key causes of the American Civil War. By imposing heavy taxes and tariffs on Indian cloth, Britain ensured a market for her own manufactured products at the expense of the native cotton industry. This political manipulation greatly angered the Indian independence movement.

DISCOVERY AND EARLY USE

Cotton is one of the four great natural raw materials from which we make fabrics and textiles. Of the other three, flax, the source of linen, is also from the vegetable world, while wool and silk are animal products. Cotton's mass of white fibres, contained until maturity within the green fruit or boll, has often evoked comparisons with the animal world; a strange Northern European myth describes cotton as a plant that was part animal, part bush. On the end of the plant stems were fixed Scythian lambs, which bent down to graze the grass within reach. Once this was exhausted the lambs starved to death, making the 'wool' accessible for easy harvest. The exact origins of this story are unknown, but it was still being promulgated as late as the mid-14th century by the anonymous compiler of *The Voyage and Travels of Sir John Mandeville, Knight*, a travel book published between 1357 and 1371. Even today the Germans continue to use the word *baumwolle* for cotton, which literally translated means 'tree-wool'.

As early as 450 BC the Greek historian Herodotus described the trees of India as bearing fleeces more delicate and beautiful than those of sheep, and noted the Indians' custom of spinning the fibres into cloth. By 169 BC the Greek word *carabasina* occurs in literature, derived from the Sanskrit *karpasi* and translated as 'cotton' (in modern Hindi, the word is *kapas*). The cultivation of cotton was subsequently brought west; although the ancient world thought of cotton as an Indian product, by the 10th century it was considered to be an Arab one, part of the inheritance from the Moors, Berber-Arab Muslims who invaded and subjugated much of Spain. Naturalized in Spain, cotton was cultivated and processed (for paper as well as fabric) alongside sugar cane, silkworms and rice in the centres of Granada, Seville and Cordoba. From the evidence available, it appears that with the possible exception of Moorish southern Spain, Europe did not manufacture calicoes, muslins and other fine cottons until the invention of spinning machinery in England in the late 18th century.

The exact date of cotton's first arrival in England is unknown, but by the early 16th century records show regular imports of 'cotton wool'. Small quantities had been imported for centuries before this, however, for use as padding or wadding in clothing such as doublets, for candlewicks and as a thread for embroidery. In 1554, Dutch and Walloon immigrants to England introduced the manufacture of 'fustians of Naples', a fabric that was most probably a cotton/linen mix, for a 1601 text describes fustians as 'of Bombast or Downe, being a fruit of the earth growing upon little shrubs or bushes ... commonly called Cotton Wooll; and also of Lynnen yarn most part brought out of Scotland.'

The first evidence for English cotton manufacture is dated 1641; Lewis Roberts's 'Treasury of Traffic' states that the Manchester Company 'buy cotton wool in London that comes from Cyprus and Smyrna, and at home worke the same and perfect it into fustians, vermillions, dimities and other stuffes'.

COTTON PLANT PROFILE

BOTANICAL DETAILS

The genus *Gossypium* is a member of the *Malvaceae* or mallow family, which also contains okra and hibiscus. *Gossypium* has 39 species, of which four are cotton: *G. hirsutum*, known as 'American upland' cotton; *G. barbadense*, or 'Sea Island' cotton; *G. arboreum* and *G. herbaceum*.

G. *hirsutum* is the Central American species, now very common in the United States. *G. barbadense*, of South American origin, was transported to the West Indies, then to coastal South Carolina and Georgia, before recrossing the Atlantic to Africa, where it became 'Egyptian' cotton. Both *G. arboreum* and *G. herbaceum* are Asiatic cottons.

ORIGINS

The early forms of cotton cultivated in Asia, which were first spun in India, most likely came from a wild tree native to Africa. Geneticists have established that the presence of wild and cultivated cotton in the pre-Columbian Americas is due to a very early flotation of seed across the oceans, rather than human contact.

DESCRIPTION

Cotton is a shrubby herbaceous plant, which in the wild will reach 20 ft (6 m). As a commercial crop it is grown as an annual and rarely exceeds 6 ft (2 m). The green, downy leaves (some species have red leaves) arise on the main stem in a regular spiral arrangement, and the creamy-white flowers, which turn pink as they mature, appear on alternate sides of the fruiting branch some 8–11 weeks after planting. Cotton readily self-pollinates and 6–8 weeks after flowering the green seed pod or 'boll' splits open (dehisces) naturally. Each boll contains between 27 and 47 seeds, and growing out from certain epidermal cells on the seed are the slender, hollow, single cell hairs.

In harvesting, the seeds are separated from the hairs, the latter composed of 87–90 per cent cellulose, 5–8 per cent water and 4–6 per cent natural impurities, and are ¾–2½ in (2–6.5 cm) in length. When dried, the hairs twist so that fine, strong threads can be spun from them.

HABITAT

Cotton grows best in deep, humus-rich soil. It requires a water regime equivalent to 4 in (10 cm) per month for the first three months, followed by a dry spell during harvest period (also about three months long). The highest quality cotton is grown in a coastal location. 'Sea Island' cotton from South Carolina and Georgia is the most valuable because the fibres are much longer and softer, resulting in a finer yarn and a silky quality of cloth.

PROCESSING

Many of the techniques that convert cotton fibres into yarn have not changed significantly since the Industrial Revolution. Mechanically harvested cotton is sprayed with a defoliant to encourage all the cotton bolls to mature at the same time. Once picked, the fibre is removed from the seed (or 'ginned') and baled for distribution to a textile mill. The by-product of ginning, cottonseed, is fed to livestock as a protein feed, while oil from the seed has industrial uses. At the mill, the 'lint' or 'raw cotton' is 'ring spun'. Fibres are mechanically raked to remove foreign matter. A picking machine wraps the fibres into a 'lap' and a carding machine brushes loose fibres into rows, which are then joined to create a soft sheet or 'web'. Finally, the webs are formed into an untwisted rope or 'card sliver'.

For higher quality yarns, the card sliver is put through a combing machine, which removes unwanted short lengths. The sliver is 'drawn' by a series of rollers to create firm, uniform strands of usable size. For thinner strands, the sliver is pulled and slightly twisted, converting it to 'roving'. The roving is transferred to a spinning frame, where it is drawn further, twisted on a ring spinner, and wound on a bobbin as yarn.

However, it seems that by this time the industry was well established, and it is likely that, like fustians, it owed its introduction to immigrants – this time clothiers and artisans who fled the capture and destruction of Antwerp in 1585 by the Duke of Parma. It is hypothesized that the immigrants who settled in Manchester began this new industry because there were stringent restrictions precluding foreigners from setting up in trades already established in Britain, but none preventing the establishment of new arts. The 'cotton wool' (raw cotton) used by the early spinners was imported into London from the Levant and Syria by the Levant Company. The whole process was hand-powered and labour intensive, and because the technology available did not facilitate the spinning of fine yarn, the main output of the weavers was strong fabrics such as fustians and dimities. Throughout the 17th century the cotton weaving industry expanded slowly, keeping within Lancashire, not least because England's poor communication and transport network meant good trade links were hard to establish. So it is quite an achievement, and a reflection upon the importance of its overseas colonies and trading links, that one of the last countries to gain cotton manufacture came to dominate the world market within the space of only 150 years, and to hold this position for a further century.

COTTON FROM INDIA

It is in some ways ironic that the first exposure to fine cotton fabrics for the majority of British citizens was not homespun cloth, but imports from the Indian sub-continent. Until the 19th century this long established and productive industry relied entirely on hand spinning and weaving techniques, achieving a remarkable quality of fabric. Individual regions developed their own styles and designs, the check cotton *lunghis* of the south, for example, corresponding to the plain white *dhotis* of the north of the country. Traditional methods of producing cotton can still be witnessed in key textile states such as Gujarat; weavers work alone or in small groups at looms placed over small pits, using foot pedals to control the movement of the shuttle and warp (lengthwise) threads. The number of weft threads (woven across the width of the fabric) determines the quality and price of the cotton material, and varies from about 20 threads in the coarsest cloth to nearer 100 in very fine fabric. The delicacy of Indian muslin was particularly prized in late 18th-century Europe, and those woven at Dacca (now Dhaka, in Bangladesh) were given appropriately evocative names – 'Running Water', 'Evening Dew' and 'Textile Breezes'.

The mass marketing of finely woven cottons was the brainchild of the East India Company. It drew upon a well-organized textile industry producing calicoes in a wide range of dramatic colours and patterns, and imported vast quantities of inexpensive cloth that was either already coloured or dyed upon its arrival. This 'pile it high and sell it (relatively) cheap' policy meant that calicoes became widely

THE EAST INDIA COMPANY

In the early days of international trade, the English were not colonizers. They rather relied on the Portuguese, who had built fortified trading posts in many of the countries that they were the first to reach. However, the English did introduce a new form of organized trade monopoly – the Chartered Trading Company – which was essentially a group of merchant venturers who invested in a company that traded with a particular area in the world. Each Company was independent, but Government underwrote its power. There were several English Trading Companies, including the Muscovy Company (1555), the Levant Company (1581), the Virginia Company (1607), which established Jamestown in Virginia (see page 23) and the Royal African Company (1660), integral to the slave trade (see page 52). But the most successful of all these Companies was the English East India Company, which received its Charter on 31 December 1600.

'The Company' was formed to attempt to get a share of the East Indian spice trade by purchasing at source on the coast of India and the Spice Islands – Sumatra, Java and southern Borneo. However, it quickly diversified from importing spices into England to trading between Asian ports, a move that extended its sphere of influence from China to the Red Sea. The Company was particularly attracted by the Persian silks trade, the Indonesia/India exchange of spices for silks and cottons, and the opportunities of China and Japan. Trade with these last two countries took place indirectly through 'factories' (fortified trading posts) in Siam (Thailand), with no direct access to mainland China until the Portuguese let an English ship from Surat call at Macao in 1635.

English ventures into the Dutch-controlled spice market brought the two nations into conflict, after which the Dutch virtually excluded Company members from the East Indies. As the Dutch tightened their grip on the spice trade, the East India Company was forced to seek new markets. Ironically, the Dutch policy backfired in some ways; European demand for spices and pepper, unlike the dramatic increase in that for sugar and cotton, remained fairly constant – increased exports from the Spice Islands simply deflated prices in Europe.

The Portuguese did not respond favourably to the Company's attempts to gain permission from the Mogul Emperor Jahangir (1569–1627) to open factories on the east coast of India. Indeed, several attacks were made on East India Company ships off Surat in 1612 and 1615 before an end to hostilities was reached in 1635; by this time the Company had already established itself at Surat on a permanent footing, with subordinate factories in the main commercial centres of Gujarat and north Indian cities such as Agra and Lahore. It was these inland factories that provided cotton cloth, initially for the Indonesian market, but increasingly for the London market, along with another plant product, indigo, a blue dye for textiles, which became Surat's most valuable export to Britain in the 17th century before suffering from cheap imports. Yet despite all the advances, the 17th century was a volatile one for the Company and from the 1620s it went into a period of contraction that lasted until the 1660s, divesting itself of outlying factories and concentrating on the Indonesian archipelago and India.

Fortunately for the East India Company, Indian cotton cloth had no competition in Europe until the late 18th century. The immediate success of the Company thus depended on textiles, in particular calicoes – all-cotton fabrics woven in plain weave and printed with simple designs in one or more colours. By the late 17th century India and cotton had become very important to the Company as the source of the greater part of its income; and in order to increase further the export of calicoes from India, the Company established more factories: at Madras in 1639, in Hooghly in the new Mogul province of Bengal in 1651, and 10 years later at Bombay, which the English Crown acquired from the Portuguese as part of Charles II's marriage agreement. By the 1680s Bengal was almost as important as Gujarat and Coromandel as a centre of trade, and after an unsuccessful military campaign against the Moguls (1686–89), the Company established a new secure base for their operations at Calcutta in 1691. Administratively, India was divided into three areas – Calcutta (then Fort William), Bombay and Madras. Each raised its own army from local people, commanded by British officers trained at the Company's military academy in Addiscombe, Surrey. This army was collectively called 'John Company' and at its peak numbered some 100,000 men.

available to those who were not sufficiently wealthy to afford linen or silk, and and who until this time had no option other than woollen cloth.

Trade in calicoes was brisk and by 1625 the East India Company was importing over 220,000 pieces of Indian cotton cloth from Gujarat. But when a famine devastated the weaving districts in the 1630s, the Company shifted to importing Coromandel cloth and focused its attentions on Bengal. The English economic depression of the 1620s temporarily limited expansion, as did the Civil War. However, the Restoration of Charles II in 1660 marked the beginnings of a cotton boom. This lightweight, washable and absorbent material had so many uses that one late-17th-century observer noted:

> now few feel themselves well dresst [sic] thill they are made up in Calicoes, both men and women, Calico shorts, Neckcloths, Cuffs, Pocket-handkerchiefs for the former, Headdresses, Nightroyls, Hoods, Sleeves, Aprons, Gowns, Petticoats, and what not for the latter, besides India-stockings for both Sexes.

Shipments of Indian patterned calicoes had reached approximately 1,000,000 by the early 1680s, and accounted for two-thirds of the Company's imports. Indeed,

BELOW Founded on traditional skills of hand spinning and weaving, the Indian cotton industry was almost completely unmechanized until the middle of the 19th century. By 1873, innovations in Europe and the USA were beginning to appear, such as Eli Whitney's 'cotton gin'. This imitated – and greatly speeded up – the process of extracting seed from cotton bolls by hand.

so successful was the Company that at home domestic textile manufacturers – silk weavers, objecting to the import of cloth rather than raw silk to be woven in Britain, and woollen manufacturers, who were seeing rising unemployment as cotton superseded wool – successfully petitioned Parliament. In 1721 an Act was passed that banned the sale of Indian coloured calicoes and silks to the domestic market, although plain white imports were permitted.

Further east, the Company had obtained permission to station agents in Amoy in 1676, and in 1699 moved their operations to Canton, the only point of access for European trade with China throughout the 18th century. It was from Canton that the Company began its import of tea to India and Europe (see pages 93–94). The original Company faced opposition to its monopoly and a rival Company was established. The two merged in 1708 and became the United Company of Merchants of England trading to the East Indies. The United Company had a court of 24 directors, annually elected by the Court of Proprietors (shareholders), who worked through various committees.

By the late 17th and early 18th centuries, the East India Company was trading regularly with the Mogul empire from stations at Madras, Bombay and Fort William in the Hooghly delta (the future city of Calcutta). Demand for tea, spices, shawls and cotton goods continued to increase, and demand for shares in the Company was high (although it was also criticized for exporting bullion to bring back mere luxuries). The Company was seen as a conduit for the riches of the East – no longer an Arabian tale, but solid wealth on which careers and City fortunes could be built. G.M. Trevelyan cites the example of Thomas Pitt, grandfather of the 1st Earl of Chatham and owner of the Pitt diamond. He made substantial wealth in India, first as an 'interloping trader' then (in a 'poacher turned gamekeeper' role reversal) as the Company's governor of Madras.

DEVELOPMENT AND CHANGE

From the end of the Stuart period onwards, London became a great emporium and effectively took over from Amsterdam as the economic hub of Europe. The buoyant textile market had already expanded beyond the domestic market, with much cotton re-exported from London to Europe, America and Africa, and the Act banning imports of coloured calico had little impact on the trade. In fact, as early as 1701 the shape of British trade was itself changing, recognising the importance of the east. Imports from Asia were on a par with those from the West Indies and twice those from North America. The success of the Company in importing pepper, cotton and then tea, was demonstrating the increasing importance of Asia to the British import and re-export markets.

However, cotton's early role in the slave trade was as a commodity. With the seizure of Jamaica in 1655, the English had the opportunity to acquire direct from the Spanish colonists the bullion needed to purchase calicoes and other

ABOVE A view of Calcutta and the River Hooghly in Bengal, painted *c*.1850. The city became a major trading nexus for the East India Company, who founded the settlement of Fort William, from which the city developed, in 1699. Buildings such as Government House, St Paul's Cathedral and the High Court earned Calcutta the sobriquet of 'City of Palaces', but extreme poverty and disease were also widespread.

cotton fabrics in India. The trade was Spanish bullion for African slaves, who were transported across the Atlantic by British slavers. And one of the most significant commodities these slavers used to trade for slaves in West Africa was Indian cottons re-exported from London. So important was this trade that in the 42 years between 1750 and 1792 the value of cotton exports to Africa rose from £7,839 to £437,370, a 55-fold increase. It is a sad irony that materials such as tobacco, sugar and a sugar by-product, rum, that were produced by slaves on plantations were then shipped back to Africa to purchase more slaves, and the slaves themselves aboard ship were issued a tobacco ration to 'pacify' them.

Throughout the first half of the 18th century the Company maintained its monopoly on the import of cotton and tea. As control of India came to be seen more and more as a priority, however, the British (and the French) began to manipulate indigenous rivalries in the region for their own ends. This policy culminated with the battles of Plassey in 1757, at which Clive of India brought down the Nawab of Bengal, and Wandewash in 1760, where Sir Eyre Coote defeated the French forces in south India. These victories together created the first extensive area of British-ruled territory in India, as the conquered Nawab granted the powers of revenue management (*diwani*) in Bengal, Bihar and Orissa to Clive and the East India Company. In effect, this recognized the Company as a European version of a native potentate and set the stage for the future British Raj.

Over the next century, British-ruled territory in the subcontinent continued to expand and to play a major role in shaping Britain's economy and trading patterns. With the absorption of Sind, Kashmir, Assam and Lower Burma, plus the annexation of the Sikh kingdom of the Punjab in 1852, Britain had effectively replaced the Mogul empire as the major power in the subcontinent.

Yet it was not primarily by military might that the British came to control India, but rather by a technique of infiltration and control using native chiefs and government. When the Company gained control of Bengal in 1757, shareholders' meetings decided Indian policy, which meant that votes could be bought by the purchase of shares. When the Company came into conflict with the British Government, Parliament intervened and brought in two Acts – the Regulation Act (1773) and Pitt's India Act (1784). These established practical Cabinet control over the East India Company, whose Council took on a purely advisory rule to the Government-backed Governor-General. From the loss of its commercial monopoly in the early 18th century until the Indian Mutiny of 1857 (when the British Government assumed formal control), the East India Company had become in essence a managing agency for the British Government of India. Even so, before it finally ceased to exist in 1873, the Company continued to turn in huge profits and contribute between £2,000,000 and £4,000,000 to the British economy every year.

RIGHT A cotton fleet setting sail at first light from Mizrapur on the Ganges in 1862. The bales, destined for the Bay of Bengal and the markets of Calcutta, are stacked under protective awnings. Exports of Indian cotton to Britain increased significantly at this time, as a consequence of the American Civil War (1861–65).

At the same time as the cotton industry was beginning to expand in the late 18th century, so was the British empire. In some ways the shock and national feeling of shame at the loss of the 13 American colonies in the early 1780s, which caused George III to contemplate abdication, served to firm British resolve. Britain continued to be the hub to which products such as sugar, tobacco, tea and cotton poured in from non-European countries and from where they were re-exported, and the export trade to the USA in fact became more profitable post-Independence. The momentum behind the Britain's overseas expansion and trade was too strong to be derailed by the loss of America and it carried her onwards to become Europe's pre-eminent imperial power for the next century-and-a-half. The colonies in the West Indies and what was to become Canada did not revolt, and 30 million Indians were living under British control, specifically that of the East India Company.

INDUSTRIAL EXPANSION

Colonial expansion went hand-in-glove with advances made in manufacturing industries, which, from the middle of the 17th century onwards, began to boom. The early part of the 18th century saw Manchester and many other industrial towns take great steps forward in terms of wealth, population and manufacturing. In 1727 Daniel Defoe (of *Robinson Crusoe* fame) noted in his *Tour Through the Whole Island of Great Britain* that Manchester had doubled in size in the previous few years and now had a population of over 50,000. This expansion was reflected in the quantity of cotton wool imported into Britain, which rose from 1,976,359 lb (896,476 kg) in 1697 to 3,870,392 lb (1,755,610 kg) in 1764. The raw cotton continued to come from established sources in the Levant and Syria, but was supplemented by imports from the West Indies, Brazil and India. Yet, although output rose, the product continued to be the heavy cottons; fine fabrics continued to be imported from India. Henry Hobhouse cites a quotation of 1770 for the finest Damascus muslin, made from a pound of cotton wool costing fourpence, but which if 'ornamented by the children in the Tambour' would retail at £15, yielding a return of 900 times the cost of the lint.

It was this vast profit margin that forced the pace of innovation and investigation into ways of manufacturing fine fabrics quickly and efficiently. The subsequent Industrial Revolution achieved these aims and brought factory owners huge profits. Ironically, however, their money was to come from manufacturing huge quantities of machine-woven cloth, sold at affordable prices, not small amounts of handmade works of art.

Until 1760 the British cotton industry relied on 'cottage industries', where every thread was spun singly by the fingers of a spinner with the aid of the spinning wheel, machinery nearly as simple as that used for millennia in India. Fustians and other strong cottons continued to be the weaver's staple output, and

although on the increase, cotton manufacture could never have become of such great national importance unless a way to compete with the cheap, fine Indian calico imports could be found. Therefore the industry needed to develop processes that produced greater quantities of better quality yarn with the same or less labour input. These advances were supplied by great leaps forward in man's levels of technological abilities, the main impact of which was to replace human skills and animal muscle power with machinery and inanimate power. The first breakthrough was a 'spinning frame', a machine that spun cotton fibres into many threads at once, but was operated by one pair of hands. Contrary to popular belief, it was not Sir Richard Arkwright (1732–92) who invented this method of spinning by rollers, but a John Wyatt of Birmingham and his business partner Lewis Paul. Paul took out a patent for a spinning machine in 1738, some 30 years before Arkwright.

Another development that predates Arkwright's water frame was the 'spinning jenny', invented by James Hargreaves (1720–78), a weaver from Standhill near Blackburn, sometime between 1764–67. The jenny, named after his daughter, was a significant advance for it spun eight threads at once, thus immediately increasing one spinner's output eightfold. Sadly, Hargreaves did not have the money to take

THE INDUSTRIAL REVOLUTION

The Industrial Revolution brought about a dramatic sequence of changes in Britain's social, economic and technological make-up. It was to establish the country as 'the workshop of the world' and give it dominion over the largest empire the world has ever known. The rapid technological developments were primarily concerned with the use of new materials (such as iron and steel), the replacement of traditional human and animal power with new energy sources (most significantly the steam engine), and the mechanization of processes that improved production levels without increasing labour requirements. Yet these could not be achieved without a significant human and cultural price.

The new place of work, the factory or mill, fuelled the social and socio-economic changes. Urbanization was essential, leading to rural depopulation and a gradual decline in traditional working practices. Agricultural techniques also had to improve in order to provide food for a larger non-agricultural population. The new factory worker had to change his or her perceptions as new skills were learned, and craftsmen and women became machine operators. And with improved transport and communication links, products could be transported more easily, allowing a boom in international trade.

The textile revolution of the 18th century was primarily a cotton one and it cannot be assessed only in terms of technological advances, for it came about for a number of reasons. Firstly, the raw materials were far cheaper than other textiles, such as linen, silk or wool, and also the mark-up achieved from converting raw material to cloth was much higher. As early as the 1720s it was realized how inefficient the processes of weaving and spinning (often it was women who spun, hence the word 'spinster') really were. Thoughts turned to improving every stage in the process that transformed cotton wool to fine cloth, sowing the seeds of industrialization much earlier in the 18th century. Prior to mechanization, for example, there was improvement in the hand tools of spinners and weavers. Further specialization was taking place with the building of workshops where manufactory — requiring attendance at a specific place of work — began to replace the traditional 'cottage industry' in which individual spinners and weavers worked from home.

Certainly industrialization dramatically increased the output of spun cotton. In 1765 the weight of spun cotton, all by hand, was 500,000 lb (226,800 kg). In 10 years this had risen to 2,000,000 lb (907,200 kg), a mixture of hand woven and machine, and by 1784 it had reached 16,000,000 lb (7,257,600 kg), all machine spun. The most obvious downside of mechanization was the enforced redeployment of skilled spinners and weavers to a sometimes appalling factory environment. The proliferation of 'dark Satanic mills' and the massive, rapid urbanization prompted by the changing technology also created unsanitary living conditions for the workers and a low life expectancy. The negative aspects of Britain's economic advance are vividly described in a detailed study by J. Phillips Kay, published in 1832. After describing the inadequate diet of the labourers, he examines their living and working locations, and the dehumanizing nature of their employment:

the population nourished on this aliment is crowded into one dense mass, in cottages separated by narrow, unpaved, and almost pestilential streets, in an atmosphere loaded with the smoke and exhalations of a large manufacturing city. The operatives are congregated in rooms and workshops during twelve hours in the day, in an enervating, heated atmosphere, which is frequently loaded with dust or filaments of cotton, or impure from constant respiration, or from other causes…

Among the most immoral features of the mills was their use of child labour; small bodies and nimble fingers were employed cleaning the machinery and watching the looms. One figure from the 1830s shows that of the 48,645 'hands' employed in the cotton manufacturing districts of Lancashire and Cheshire, 57 per cent were children, with those below 11 years old earning on average 2 shillings 4 pence a week. Urban living conditions did get better, however, with the introduction of gas lighting, piped water and underground sewage systems.

Life for the emerging middle classes substantially improved with the Industrial Revolution as they gained political influence and greater access to goods.

out a patent at the time, and simply used his invention at home for his own purposes. However, such a monumental invention could not avoid detection for long, and when discovered by local spinners, instead of offering their admiration and gratitude, they broke into Hargreaves's house and smashed the jenny. The subsequent persecution was so bad that Hargreaves was forced to flee the county. He moved to Nottingham, where he obtained a patent for his jenny in 1770.

Arkwright is perhaps the most famous of the inventors who helped mechanize the processes of manufacturing cotton cloth in Britain, indeed he was one of the first 'industrialists' to be knighted. Although a self-made man, he was not above stealing other peoples' ideas, appropriating the work of Wyatt and Paul and refining them so that his frame spun both the weft and the warp. He claimed he had invented a new machine, patented it, and set up a marketing campaign that brought him a fortune. Arkwright built his first mill in Nottingham in 1770 and until his death erected on average one mill a year. However, it was not all plain sailing; in 1779, a mob scoured the villages around Chorley in Lancashire, destroying all machinery associated with mechanical production, including Arkwright's mill. He also had problems selling his yarn as many Lancashire weavers refused to buy it, despite it being of better quality. This forced Arkwright to weave it himself, which he did very successfully, although he fell foul of a law intended to help the English cotton industry. Because his thread was so fine the resultant fabric was classed by the Excise as calico, subject to a higher duty than fustians, and illegal if sold already printed.

By 1775 technological advances had been made that had greatly improved the quality of spun thread, and the speed at which it could be produced. Yet there was still scope for improvement, in particular in the process of preparing the tangled cotton wool prior to spinning. Arkwright's second patent, taken out in December 1775, was for a series of machines that did exactly that – carding, drawing and roving. As we have already seen, Arkwright had a habit of attaching his name to existing ideas and this second patent was challenged in court in 1781 and again in 1785, when it was finally nullified. Despite this loss of income, Arkwright continued to make money from investments and his first patent, and died aged 59, a very wealthy man. And although some of Arkwright's business ethics were questionable, whatever he lacked in originality, he certainly made up for with his vigorous promotion of powered machinery and the transformation of the cotton spinning industry. As early as 1782 his own mills were employing upwards of 5,000 people and had required a capital investment of more than £200,000; and through his efforts (and those of others) cotton spinning was the first British industry to adopt large-scale factory production (although there were silk factories as early as 1719).

By the late 18th century, spinning technology had advanced in leaps and bounds. However, the development that caused the dam to burst, enabling huge

quantities of capital and labour to flood into cotton manufacture, was the invention of the 'mule'. Samuel Crompton (1753–1827) invented this machine in 1775, but, working in secret at night, it took him until the 1790s to perfect the technique of spinning the finest threads, which in turn enabled calicoes to be woven. Additional developments allowed the machine to be automated, so by the mid-1830s in a single room and with no hand to guide them several thousand perfect threads could be rapidly spun onto spindles. Crompton was too poor to patent the idea and sold the design for £60. The spinning mule transformed spinning, but Crompton lived in poverty, until in 1812 the Government awarded him £5,000 in grateful thanks for his contribution to British industry. A statistic which puts the impact of mechanization in perspective is that during the first half of the 18th century cotton wool imports little more than doubled, while within the 20-year period to 1833 they increased over eight-fold. In financial terms, this equates to a doubling of export values between 1700 and 1750, while between 1813 and 1833 the value of cotton exports rose 15-and-a-half-fold.

Such technological and mechanical advances made to 1790 would soon have reached a ceiling were it not for further progress, this time in developing a source of power more efficient than horses or water. The first author to describe using steam as mechanical power is thought to be the Renaissance engineer and garden designer, Salomon de Caus (or Caux) in 1615. But the first man to make wide-scale and effective use of steam power in industry was the Scot, James Watt (1736–1819). From a young age Watt was fascinated by engineering and his early work with steam involved improving the engines invented by Thomas Savery and Thomas Newcomen, which inefficiently pumped water from mines.

Watt obtained his patent for 'lessening the consumption of steam and fuel in fire engines' the same year as Arkwright gained his first patent (1769), but his process took some time to perfect. Watt's greatest improvement, the addition of a separate vessel to condense the steam, was recognized by Parliament, which, in an Act of 1775 granted him for 25 years 'the sole use and property of certain steam engines (or fire engines) of his invention, throughout His Majesty's dominions'. The first steam engine made for a cotton mill was installed in the works of Messrs Robinsons of Papplewick in Nottinghamshire in 1785, and many more followed as this new form of power enabled the spinning industry to increase its output still further. Watt became a national hero and a rich man, and had the honour of having an electrical unit of power named after him.

To match the ever-increasing production levels and quality of British yarn, the weaving sector of the industry also improved its loom technology. Water-powered looms had been invented as far back as the 17th century, but as the 19th century dawned the steam-driven 'power loom' revolutionized the weaving process. The first power loom was developed by the Rev. Dr Edmund Cartwright (1743–

OPPOSITE A trade union banner of the Amalgamated Society of Operative Cotton Spinners features pioneers of the industry, such as Richard Arkwright, developer of the spinning frame (right) and Samuel Crompton (left). The latter's 'Mule' of the late 18th century transformed the spinning process and the scale of industrial production. The trade union movement was to play a key role in improving conditions in factories and mills, though progress was slow.

ENSLAVEMENT ON TWO CONTINENTS

Mid-19th-century Britons might have been tempted to rest easy in the knowledge that their country had abolished slavery in all her territories by 1834. But any idea that the cotton that fashionably clothed British backs was freely produced was far from reality. In 1855, a book *Cotton is King* was published in Cincinnati, written 'By an American'. The anonymous author makes clear that although slavery may have been abolished in the West Indies, Britain was still profiting from American slavery:

> And what was England doing all this while? Having lost her supplies from the West Indies, she was quietly spinning away at American Slave-labor cotton; and, to ease the public conscience of the kingdom, was loudly talking of a Free-labor supply of the commodity from the banks of the Niger! But the expedition up that river failed, and 1845 found her manufacturing 626,496,000 lbs. [284,178,580 kg] of cotton, mostly the product of American slaves!

British imports of American cotton continued apace, reaching an unprecedented high of close on one billion pounds' weight (453,600,000 kg) by 1853. The author despaired of ever seeing slavery abolished in America:

> The year 1854, instead of finding Slavery perishing under the blows it had received, has witnessed the destruction of all the old barriers to its extension, and beholds it expanding widely enough for the profitable employment of the slave population, with all its natural increase, for 100 years to come!!

Enslavement to the cotton industry was also evident on British home territory. In 1813, *Tales of the Poor or Infant Sufferings* was printed for the Society for Bettering the Condition of the Poor in Sheffield and addressed to Her Royal Highness the Princess Charlotte of Wales. In the address, she was entreated thus: 'How much higher would it elevate a nation's hopes, should one of the first actions of your public life be to give MORE THAN LIFE, to thousands of unprotected infants...'. The volume contained a ballad, as a preface to which the authors quote a letter of 1810 sent by T.W. Gascoigne to the *Monthly Magazine*:

> Sir, I am a Freeman of the City of London, but, from unavoidable misfortunes, have been compelled, with my wife, to seek a refuge in St. Luke's Workhouse, where my wife lately lay in. During that time, the Parish Officers took away our only girl, little more than 11 years of age, and against our consent, bound her apprentice to a Cotton Manufactory, more than 200 miles from London.
>
> A respectable friend of mine made application to the Overseers, and offered to take her, but they would not let him have her, nor would they let me out of the gate, from the time they took her out and bound her, till after she had been sent into the country. My wife at the time had not lain in more than a week, and thus to lose her daughter nearly deprived her of her reason.
>
> I wish to be informed if such binding will stand good.

The anguished plea is followed by the ballad entitled 'Sally Brown, or the Orphan Cotton Spinner', its message clear from a few of its numerous stanzas:

> *The wretched Africans, when torn*
> *From home and kindred dear,*
> *And sold to toil from day to day,*
> *And weep from year to year,*
>
> *Are not more wretched or forlorn,*
> *More hopeless or more lost,*
> *Than these poor children thus on scenes*
> *Of sin and misery tost.*

The ballad, although poorly written, contained little exaggeration. Writing nearly 20 years later in *The Moral and Physical Conditions of the Working Classes Employed in the Cotton Manufacture in Manchester*, J. Phillips Kay observed no signs of improvement. He describes the deadening effect of repetitive factory labour among employees:

> They are drudges who ... assist the operations, of a mighty material force, which toils with an energy ever unconscious of fatigue.

1823) in 1785, but despite patenting this and other pieces of machinery, he never made money. He was only able to retire to Kent and spend his twilight years improving agricultural machinery thanks to an award from the Government of £10,000 in 1809 (although why he got twice the sum awarded to Crompton remains a mystery). The number of power looms in England and Scotland rose from 14,150 in 1820 to an estimated 100,000 in 1833, and not only did the speed of production rise, but the quality of the fabric also improved dramatically, so that British cotton textiles were now as fine as any imported from India.

TARIFFS AND TRADE

The expansion of overseas territories and determination to retain commercial rights already acquired offered many sectors of society the opportunity for trade. At the end of the 18th century the economy of the empire worked much as it had done since the Navigation Acts of the 17th century. That is to say, no foreign ships were permitted to enter colonial harbours and all trade between the colonies and Britain had to be conducted by British (or colony) owned and manned ships. British goods were also favoured with lower import taxes into the colonies. Thus in many ways the colonies were a regulated trading block, sending much of their

BELOW As Britain's demand for raw cotton escalated, its cultivation in the USA's Southern States soared in response. Steamships laden with cotton bales from St Louis and Natchez used the natural artery of the Mississippi to bring the crop to New Orleans. As this lithograph of 1884 shows, the levee was a hub of activity, handling almost half of all Europe's cotton exports.

produce to Britain and forced to import British goods in return. Despite the promotion of 'free trade' in the 19th century, many colonies continued to do most of their business with Britain. However, by the 1820s, Britain had seen that industrialization could massively increase production levels and now wanted a global market for its products. The home and colonial markets were opened up to foreign trade, and by the 1850s Britain had a free trading empire, with all preferential duties in Britain and the colonies gone, a state of affairs that lasted up until 1932 (with a hiatus during the First World War). Yet the empire remained a major marketplace, and between 1850 and 1870 it provided 20 per cent of Britain's imports, while it took 30 per cent of Britain's exports. The remaining 70 per cent were accounted for by 'free trade' with non-empire countries such as the USA, China, the Ottoman empire and former colonies of Spain and Portugal in South America. This raises the question: if the whole world traded with Britain, why did it maintain an expensive empire? The answer, at least in part, is economic: if trade sanctions and tariffs were imposed by other countries, the empire still provided an unrestricted marketplace for the vast quantities of manufactured goods coming out of British factories.

Lancashire had the highest concentration of cotton mills in the country, and a constant supply of raw cotton was required to keep the jennies turning. Manchester's coat of arms shows a ship bringing cotton from America and this emblem indicates one of the reasons why Lancashire's textile industry continued to develop, making it the heart of 'the workshop of the world'. In addition to easily accessible natural resources such as water and coal, and a relatively good transport network, it was close to the port of Liverpool. It was in 1784 that the first bale of American cotton arrived in Liverpool. Customs officials, thinking it impossible that cotton could have been produced in the United States, seized it, and since, under the terms of the Navigation Act, it was an illegal import, it was left to decay on the quayside. From this early misunderstanding, however, Liverpool rose to become the country's leading port for the import of cotton from the USA. Between 1802 and 1833 the percentage of the nation's cotton imports that passed through Liverpool bound for the Lancashire mills rose from 48 per cent to over 90 per cent.

COTTON IN AMERICA

No evidence exists of specialist cotton plantations in America before 1800, although by this point it was an established crop – America was supplying Britain with 189,316 lb (85,874 kg) of raw cotton per annum by 1791. The American growers quickly recognized the impact that new technology was having on the British textile industry and realized that a large supply of raw cotton would be needed. Cotton cultivation spread like wildfire. It was first cultivated in Tennessee in 1807 and by the 1820s huge monoculture plantations of up to 5,000 acres

(2,023 ha) were springing up in the New South (Georgia, Alabama, Louisiana and Mississippi). Indeed, so successful did the Americans become at cultivating cotton that 322,215,122 lb (146,156,779 kg) were exported to Britain in 1833, and the value of this export, some £8.5 million, was more than half the value of the total exports of the USA. Thus, by the 1830s there had developed interdependence between the plough in Mississippi and the bobbin in Manchester. The agricultural and industrial enterprises were inseparably linked, the fortunes of one dependent on the other. The impact of pests in the cotton fields, such as the dreaded cotton caterpillar, the boll-worm, the cotton louse and a form of blight, was correspondingly financially devastating.

Not only planters, but merchants and steamboatmen on the Mississippi were integrally linked to the cotton economy. The 'season' officially opened on the river on 1 September, and arrival of the 'fleecy staple' was anticipated with much excitement. Steamboats, 'loaded to the guards' with 4,000–7,000 bales, plied the Mississippi, often stopping at 40 or 50 landings between Memphis and New Orleans. Smaller boats, known as 'local traders', brought hundreds of bales from plantations on smaller rivers to Natchez for sale or transport to New Orleans. Cotton lay at the heart of the South's identity, and pride in it sustained towns after the Civil War; as an observer from the North remarked of Natchez in 1883: 'People in this part of Mississippi are clean crazy on cotton. The butter on the table comes from the North, the hams from the Northern prairies, the potatoes from the North, but cotton comes right out the soil and nothing else does. Given a man and a mule ... they will take to cotton as naturally as a gander and a goose to a pond.'

Slaves were to become an essential labour force for the American plantation owners in the Southern States, with cotton cultivation requiring approximately 20 slaves per 100 acres (41 ha). Even after the British abolished slavery in 1807 there remained a very profitable illegal slave trade. Indeed, between 1820 and 1870 the Royal Navy seized 1,600 ships and 150,000 slaves from illegal Atlantic slavers who were willing to take substantial risks to smuggle their human cargo through the West Indies, Mexico and Texas, and even from the shores of Africa itself. Another way that prohibition was avoided

BELOW The dramatic increase in American cotton exports was made possible by large plantations and the South's 'peculiar institution' of slavery. Painted in 1827, this chained and kneeling girl echoes the image of earlier abolitionist campaigns. However, freedom for the USA's approximately four million slaves was not achieved until after the Civil War.

LIFE ON A COTTON PLANTATION

The farming of cotton in 19th-century America paid nearly two-thirds of the national debt, employing capital of 2 billion dollars; landed property and implements accounted for about 200 million dollars, the balance being estimated as the value of the slaves.

THE PLANTER

Many eyewitness accounts of the life of a Southern planter and his family are recorded in women's diaries. These give scant detail about the methods of the plantations or the lives of the workers, but concentrate instead on the niceties of middle-class colonial life. An indolent lifestyle is recorded, one in which mint-juleps were drunk first thing in the morning, days were passed in visits, playing music, riding, hunting and the like and relaxation from such strenuous pursuits was found by lounging in hammocks or playing croquet.

In his book *The Rise and Fall of King Cotton* Anthony Burton quotes lawyer John Quitman's observations of life in Natchez in 1821: 'In the city proper, and the surrounding country, there is genteel and well-regulated society … The planters are the prominent feature … They live profusely: drink costly Port, Madeira, and sherry, after the English fashion, and are exceedingly hospitable.' Sunny days might pass without a thought for of the slaves – except, perhaps, when diseases that were rife in the slave community as a result of poor diet and sanitation failed to observe social distinctions and also affected the white community.

Contemporary colonialist perception of the production of cotton is found in the words of American cotton enthusiast W. J. Barbee, writing in 1866: 'We have mosquitoes, buffalo-gnats, and gad-flies, but they do not continue all the year. We have the boll-worm, the cotton louse, and the cotton caterpillar, which sometimes sadden the heart of the planter, but we always make something, and not unfrequently we make "a mighty big crop".'

THE SLAVE

If penetrating first-hand accounts of planters' lives are hard to find, direct testimony of the lives of slaves is, of course, rarer still. In 1976, the oral accounts of a number of ex-slaves were recorded in *Weevils in the Wheat: Interviews with Virginian Ex-slaves.*

Baily Cunningham was born in about 1838 and was interviewed about his early life in his 100th year in 1938. He describes his diet as a 19th-century slave thus: 'We ate twice a day, about sunup and at sundown. All the work hands ate in the cabins and all the children took their *cymblin* [squash] soup bowl to the big kitchen and got it full of cabbage soup, then we were allowed to go [to] the table where the white folks ate and get the crumbs from the table.'

An interview in 1937 with Charles Grandy, born in Norfolk, Virginia in 1842, describes how his working life started at the age of five: 'he was carried to the field to pull grass from the young cotton and other growing crops. This work was done by hand because he was still too young to use the farm implements. Now he went to his task daily; from early in the morning until late in the evening … Often he would fall asleep before reaching home, and spend a good portion of the night on the bare ground. Awakening, he would find it quite a problem to locate his home in the darkness.'

These were the contrasting lifestyles that supported this extraordinarily valuable industry. While one small child enjoyed a life of fine clothes, piano lessons and leisurely days, another was forced to pick cotton until he was close to collapse.

in the Old South was by 'breeding' slaves on plantations where the soil was too impoverished for cotton growing. This unpleasant activity became more profitable when prohibition forced the price of slaves in America up dramatically; as Hobhouse has noted, in 1800 a good 'field hand' could be expected to fetch around $50, but by 1850 this figure had risen to $800–$1,000 in real terms.

The other enormous 'advantage' that the Southern States enjoyed was land – some 500 million acres (202 million ha) of it suitable for cotton cultivation, and in 1850 only 2 per cent (10 million acres or 4 million ha) of this was used to produce 4 million bales of cotton and provide subsistence crops for the plantation owners and slaves. It is not surprising, therefore, that Thomas Jefferson declared, 'It is cheaper for Americans to buy new land than to manure the old.'

However, the major problem for plantation growers was low efficiency in processing the harvested cotton pods, a solution for which was provided by the American folk hero Eli Whitney (1765–1825). From a humble Yankee farm background he showed his mechanical talent at an early age before becoming a student at Yale University in 1788, where he studied 'Mathematicks and Natural Philosophy'. Whitney moved to Savannah, Georgia, where, talking to Southern farmers, he became aware of their difficulty in finding a cash crop that would make them money. Tobacco removed so many nutrients from the soil that it could only be planted for a year and the problem with cotton was that 'ginning' – separating the fibres from the seed – was very labour intensive, with a slave perhaps able to 'gin' a couple of pounds of cotton each day.

What was needed was a more efficient method of 'ginning', and according to the traditional story, Phineas Miller, a plantation manager, challenged Whitney to create a machine to solve the problem. Like many great inventions, the solution was reached through a mixture of research and inspiration. For a month Whitney meticulously observed the hand movements required to clean cotton, and then he saw a cat pounce on a chicken. The bird escaped, and the cat's claws were left clutching a few feathers. So was born Whitney's 'cotton gin' that mimicked the process of holding the seed in one hand and teasing out the lint with the other. This machine was so efficient that a single slave could now gin 50 lb (23 kg) of cotton a day. Sadly, the first machine was stolen and copies made before a patent was granted in March 1794. It was such a simple idea that it could be easily replicated and to add to Whitney's woes his factory burned down. With years spent in litigation for patent infringement, and only $100,000 voted to him by the Cotton States in recognition of his invention (except Georgia, where it was invented), Whitney became disillusioned. He had made viable an industry that had taken up 20 years of his life and brought him only a meagre return, while others became extremely rich on the back of his idea.

Cotton really was king in Dixie, which, within the 66 years between 1784 and 1850, went from supplying no cotton to Britain, to holding a massive 82 per cent market share, during a time when British imports rose a staggering 150-fold to 1,500 million lb (680 million kg). The $80 million value of this crop (a figure that rose almost two-and-a-half times by 1860) meant that for the first time the South had the income to service its debts, something earlier economic crops such as tobacco, indigo, rice, sugar and grain had not given it. Cotton was also a survival crop for the States because, with Britain now imposing a large import duty on tobacco, and war and tariffs causing problems with exports of grain and meat to the West Indies, it was the only crop with an assured market. It was also the catalyst that precipitated the American Civil War (1861–65), the chief cause of which was the slavery question, particularly on cotton plantations.

The American Civil War also caused much debate in Britain about the risk of 'having all your eggs in one basket' and the problems of relying on a single source for the majority of a raw material. In the 1860s pressure was put on the Government by, amongst others, the Manchester Chamber of Commerce and the Cotton Supply Association, to develop a cotton plantation industry in India. It seems one of the quirks of the story of cotton and the empire that an Indian cotton plantation industry had not been established earlier. For, in the case of almost all other economic crops, if Britain held territory where it could be cultivated, it would exploit that opportunity to the full. Admittedly, imports of raw cotton grown in India had been discovered to be of poor quality for mechanized production – the fibres were too short – and it was not well received in the Lancashire mills. It seems likely that in the early 19th century there was neither the will nor the desire to develop an Indian cotton plantation system, perhaps because the friendly relationships with the USA were so mutually beneficial. In *The Cotton Question*, published in New York in 1866, the author W.J. Barbee confidently predicted, 'The cry will be for years to come, aye for ages, "Give us more cotton – good cotton, American cotton – fine fibre".'

The American Civil War did give Indian cotton growing a boost in the short term – exports of raw cotton rose from £3.5 million to £36 million during the war years, dropping back to £8 million upon the return of peace. Across the century, however, whereas India had once supplied Britain with fine cotton calicoes, now Britain began exporting the cloth to India. In 1813, for example, Calcutta was exporting cotton goods to Britain with a value of £2 million; 17 years later the roles had reversed and Calcutta had become a captive market, forced to import the same £2 million of cotton products from Britain in the form of homespun cottons from Lancashire. A degree of industrialization in the subcontinent, aided by improved transport links, had created some immensely wealthy Indian cotton dynasties such as the Sarabhais, a Jain family of millionaire textile barons from Gujarat, and the Parsee Tatas in Bombay, yet the potential of the Indian cotton industry was deliberately restricted. This manipulation of cotton production through taxes and tariffs to benefit Britain's coffers formed the basis of Mahatma Gandhi's celebrated *Swadeshi* campaign against British imported cloth in the 1930s. Gandhi encouraged Indians to spin and weave as a daily demonstration of independence from foreign powers, denouncing tariffs as a corrupting instrument of political control 'no better than beef or liquor'.

CONSUMPTION AT HOME AND ABROAD

Throughout the 18th century certain sectors of the population across Europe possessed an increasing disposable income. At the same time, merchants — the economic pioneers of their age — criss-crossed the globe bringing back ever larger quantities of desirable products, amongst which plant products such as sugar, tobacco, cotton, tea, coffee and chocolate were eagerly consumed. One of the reasons for the success of Indian calicoes and other foreign products was that, even though they became 'everyday items', they came from faraway lands and so retained a touch of the exotic.

Fashionable dresses of the early 19th century were dominated by muslin, lawn and other finely woven linens and cottons. A softer and lighter material than the formal gowns of the previous century, cotton gave a flattering, flowing silhouette and allowed women greater freedom of movement. It was ideal for dancing in, as Elizabeth Ham recalled in her description of a ball in Ireland in the early 1800s: 'My gown was a very delicate sprigged India muslin over a bodice of blue satin. It sat beautifully around the waist.'

Indian cottons also became accessible to a wider public, as increased imports made them more affordable. For example, by the 1830s the retail price of printed muslin was between one and four shillings a yard, while ordinary print cotton was fourpence (4d) a yard. So, allowing seven yards for a dress, the total was an outlay of two shillings and fourpence (2s 4d), well within the range of a labouring man wishing to buy it for his wife. Put another way, by 1850 cotton cloth cost one per cent of its 1784 price and was of much better quality.

The impact of cotton on the advancement of Britain to a position of global dominance in the 19th century cannot be understated. In many ways, the need to improve the cotton spinning industry precipitated the Industrial Revolution and the ensuing mechanization was to give Britain the position of world leader in the production of cheap, high-quality cotton cloth. The technological advances and innovations that followed made Britain the world's most industrialized nation; they were also used to increase the country's military and naval (and consequently political) might as overseas trade and colonial acquisitions continued to increase.

As the cotton industry was developing, Britain was fighting the Napoleonic Wars (1799–1815). The British blockade of French ports and a heavy import duty served to stifle the French cotton industry, and the fighting prevented indigenous industries developing elsewhere in Europe. Britain took advantage of these handicaps and its technological advantages in order to exploit fully the continent's increasing demand for fine fabrics by exporting cotton yarn spun in

Lancashire's mills; by 1805 half to two-thirds of the total output of cotton yarn was exported. Between 1812 and 1820 the value of exported yarn rose from £794,465 to £2,022,253, while cotton goods rose 35 per cent from £16,517,690 to £22,289,645 in the three years to 1815. Taxation on this income contributed towards the cost of the war, around £1,650 million. By 1820, the total annual value of British cotton manufacture was running at an estimated £31,338,693 and employing 1,500,000 people with an average weekly wage of 10 s 6d (£36 per annum). So massive was the cotton industry by the 1830s that it employed about 9 per cent of the population, and accounted for half of

Britain's exports. Taxation derived from, and investments made with, the huge profits coming from the cotton industry assisted the Government with the vastly expensive task of running an empire that continued to grow (in part because of the increasing overseas trade in cotton and other products).

Without doubt, the most controversial aspects of the cotton industry were the use of child labour in its mills and factories (addressed by a series of reforms in the later part of the century) and the continuation of slavery in the USA. Emancipation for the latter was finally achieved when the 13th Amendment to the Constitution was passed by Congress in January 1865 and ratified by the states the following December. Demand from Britain for raw cotton in the mid-19th century was seen as an immense opportunity by the USA, anxious to repair the ravages of the Civil War on its economy and describing the crop in 1866 as 'a wonderful source of wealth, enriching the planter, the manufacturer, the cotton broker, the shipmaster and the merchant'. The enthusiastic W.J. Barbee also noted that cotton had effectively 'paid nearly two-thirds of the national debt of the United States for the last fifty years' and pithily assessed its political importance in the new regime: 'if "commerce is king", cotton is prime minister'. For those who had enjoyed the lifestyle of pre-Civil War cotton planters, characterized by elegant socializing and the magnificent plantation houses of Southern towns, the new economic climate must, however, have been hard to accommodate.

The British cotton industry continued to produce throughout the 19th century, but as other European nations became increasingly industrialized, its stranglehold on the manufacture of cotton cloth loosened. The death knell for the industry, as for other heavy industries, was the First World War. By the late 1920s Lancashire cotton mills were on a 32-hour week, although a century earlier they had been working almost non-stop. Many former labourers joined the long queues outside the Labour Exchange. Spinning had become uneconomic, since the return on the fabric was less than the costs of the raw material (80 per cent of which still came from the USA) and the processing. A combination of the economic Depression in the 1930s, the Second World War and the subsequent loss of its colonies (many beginning to grow cotton themselves) meant that the British cotton industry never recovered. It could only look back to the days when it was the plant product that began a revolution and financed an empire.

BUY
INDIAN
TEA

THE TEA TRANSFER

For almost two centuries, tea's popularity in Europe was matched by widespread ignorance of its origins and cultivation. The secrets of the plant and its processing were held by the Chinese, exclusive exporters of tea to the West in a trade dominated first by Portugal and Holland, and then by Britain's East India Company. Restrictive trading practices, including dealing only in silver bullion, prompted the Company to engage in botanical piracy – tea plants were smuggled from China and established in Indian plantations in Assam and Sikkim. Their success changed the subcontinent's physical and commercial map, as tea became a key crop in areas such as Assam, the Nilgiri Hills, Darjeeling and Ceylon. As supplies increased, tea became a popular rather than a luxury beverage, and novelties such as tea shops and dances contributed to Europe's new urban social fabric.

DISCOVERY AND EARLY USE

The origins of tea as a drink stretch back far into the province of legend. One day in 2737 BC the Emperor of China, Shennong, 'the Divine Healer', who had previously discovered the healing power of a number of herbs, and issued an edict requiring that all drinking water should be boiled as a hygienic precaution, was resting. He was awoken from his reverie by the enticing smell issuing from a nearby pot of boiling water. Investigating the pot, the emperor noticed that a number of leaves from a nearby bush had accidentally fallen into the bubbling water. Being a courageous man of science, the emperor tried the green infusion and declared that it gave the drinker 'vigour of body, contentment of mind and determination of purpose'. Just for the record, his predecessor, Fu Xi, the first emperor, is said to have given humanity knowledge of fire, cooking and music, while the third emperor also contributed to human happiness and knowledge by revealing the secrets of the grape and astronomy.

There is mention of tea being prepared by servants in a Chinese text of 50 BC, and by the 3rd century AD tea was being cultivated in the province of Sichuan. The first detailed description of tea-drinking is found in a dictionary dating from AD 350. Kuo Po noted that the fresh green leaves were picked, pressed into cakes and then roasted to a reddish hue. These were crumbled into water and boiled with the addition of onion, ginger and orange to create an herbal soup. Disgusting as this may sound, it was recommended as a cure for a host of ailments including stomach problems and poor eyesight. Given such a method of preparation, it is perhaps not surprising that it was a further 300 years before tea became China's national drink in the Tang Dynasty (AD 618–906). By this time the crumbled bricks of tea were boiled only with a little salt, and the word *cha* was used to describe tea. Furthermore, since tea bricks could be easily transported, tea began its migration from China to Tibet and Russia, and along the Silk Road to India and Turkey.

There is another legend, this time a Buddhist one, which states that the great Indian master Bodhidharma discovered tea in AD 519. During the fifth year of a seven-year sleepless contemplation of Buddha, Bodhidharma began to feel drowsy. To dispel his tiredness he either plucked a few leaves from a nearby bush and chewed them, or, according to another version, took a more drastic course of action. He ripped off his eyelids and cast them to the ground; where they fell, two tea trees sprang up with the miraculous power to keep him awake. There is an ancient Buddhist tradition of drinking tea before an image of Bodhidharma, and in order to keep alert during long religious ceremonies Buddhist priests drink tea. The spread of tea cultivation and culture throughout China is in fact largely accredited to the movement of Buddhist priests throughout the country.

The first book on tea, *Cha Jing*, was written in China by Li Yu in around AD 780. Possibly commissioned by tea merchants as 'promotional literature' to encourage increased consumption amongst the upper classes, the three beautifully illustrated volumes describe the cultivation, manufacture and drinking of tea, as well as offering a historical summary. The Japanese 'Father of Tea' was Yeisei, a Buddhist priest. Whilst travelling in China, Yeisei had seen the value of tea in enhancing religious mediation, and he took some tea seeds with him when he sailed for Japan. Tea was instantly popular in Japan, not least because of its religious connections and the fact that it found favour at the imperial court. Soon it was taken beyond its role as a pleasurable drink and elevated to an art form – the Japanese tea ceremony ('Cha-no-yu' or 'the hot water for tea'), possibly inspired by Li Yu's book, which became increasingly important throughout the Muromachi period (1338–1573). The journalist-historian Lafcadio Hearn, one of the few foreigners ever to be granted Japanese citizenship, wrote an interesting description of this complex art form in the 1890s:

> The tea ceremony requires years of training and practice to graduate in art … yet the whole of this art, as to its detail, signifies no more than the making and serving of a cup of tea. The supremely important matter is that the act be performed in the most perfect, most polite, most graceful, most charming manner possible.

The tea ceremony also gave birth to a range of associated art forms. Based on the simplicity of a forest cottage dwelling, a special style of architecture, *chaseki*, evolved for the design of the teahouses, while the geishas, the cultural/artistic hostesses, began to specialize in the presentation of the tea ceremony.

Through their trade links with the East and a geographical location midway between East and West, the Arabs acquired tea in around 850, and they are presumed to have brought it to Europe via Venice in around 1559. However, by this date the Portuguese had already opened up the sea routes to China, perhaps as early as 1515. The first European personally to encounter tea and write about it was the Portuguese Jesuit Father Jasper de Cruz, who, having spent the previous four years as a missionary at a commercial mission, penned his account in 1560. The Portuguese transported Chinese tea to Lisbon, where the Dutch, who were at that time allies of Portugal, made regular shipments of tea north, to ports in France, Holland and the Baltic coast. Yet for several centuries Europeans were to drink tea without ever having seen a tea plant, because their traders were not allowed to venture into China's interior.

DEVELOPMENT AND CHANGE

As the political map of Europe altered in the early 17th century, Portugal and the Netherlands became less close, and the Dutch, now with a strong navy of their own, began to develop trade links with the East. The first detailed study of tea

TEA PLANT PROFILE

BOTANICAL DETAILS

Tea is an infusion made from the dried leaves of a camellia, *Camellia sinensis*. This is a species of the genus more widely known as a garden plant grown for ornamental flowers, rather than a harvestable leaf. The two principal species cultivated for tea leaf is the small-leaved China plant (*C. sinensis sinensis*) and the large-leaved Assam plant (*C. sinensis assamica*). Hybrids of these two varieties are also grown. The most well-known constituent of tea is caffeine, which gives the beverage its stimulating

character but contributes only a little to colour, flavour and aroma. About 4 per cent of the solids in the fresh tea leaf are caffeine, and one teacup contains about 1 grain (60 to 90 mg) of caffeine. In terms of flavour, the most important chemicals in tea are the tannins, or polyphenols, which are colourless, bitter-tasting substances that give the drink its astringency. When acted upon by an enzyme called polyphenol oxidase, polyphenols acquire a reddish colour and form the flavouring compounds of the beverage. Certain volatile oils also contribute to the aroma and flavour of tea, while various sugars and amino acids add nuances to the brew.

ORIGINS AND HABITAT

Camellia sinensis is indigenous to China and parts of India, where it can reach 65 ft (20 m). Its favoured growing conditions are a deep, well-drained, acid soil, a warm, humid climate and an annual rainfall in excess of 39 in (100 cm). Given such conditions, tea will grow to an altitude of 6,900 ft (2,100m), and, just as with wine, aspect, soil, altitude and climate will affect the flavour and characteristics of the tea.

DESCRIPTION

An evergreen shrub with green, shiny, pointed leaves, and white, insignificant flowers in winter. Tea bushes are planted about 5 ft (1.5 m) apart, in rows 3 ft (1 m) apart. At higher altitudes the rows follow the natural contours to prevent soil erosion, alternatively the hillsides are terraced. The bushes take between three and five years to reach maturity, during which time they are trained into a fan shape, with a flat top, known as a 'plucking plateau', about 3 ft x 5 ft (1 m x 1.5 m) across. Before the first plucking, the bushes are severely pruned back by a method known as 'lung pruning'.

PROCESSING

Plucking is still by hand, carried out every 7–14 days, depending on altitude, when only the top two leaves and a bud are harvested from the sprigs on the plucking plateau. A skilled plucker can gather 66–77 lb (30–35 kg) a day, sufficient to produce about 16½ –20 lb (7.5–9 kg) of processed black tea. The fresh tips are taken to the factory for processing. Here, the plucked leaf is spread on vast trays or racks and 'withered' – left to dehydrate in air at 77–86°F (25–30°C), a process that lasts 10 to 16 hours, depending on the wetness of the leaf. Next, the withered leaf is mechanically crushed to release its natural enzymes, which oxidize on contact with the air. This is either done by the 'orthodox' process, whereby the leaf is rolled, producing large leaf particles known as grades, or by the 'unorthodox' method. In this case the tea is put through a CTC (cuts-tear-curl) machine that chops the leaf up into smaller particles, which are more suited to modern demands for tea bags and a quicker brewing tea. The broken leaf is then 'fermented' or left to oxidize – laid out in a cool, humid atmosphere for 3–4 hours, and gently turned until all the leaves become a golden russet colour. The broken, fermented leaf is then 'fired' or dried by passing slowly through hot air chambers in which all moisture is removed; the leaf turns a dark brown or black. The 'black tea' is finally passed through a series of wire mesh sieves to sort it into grades or leaf particle sizes, before being weighed and packed into chests or 'tea sacks'. Samples of the 'make' are then sent to selling brokers worldwide, who evaluate the tea for quality and price.

published in Europe came from the Dutchman, Dr Wilhelm ten Rhyne (1649–1700), who, in 1678 added an appendix to Jacob Breyn's *Exoticarum plantarum centuria prima* (First Century of Exotic Plants). Dr Wilhelm based his work on studies made while he was chief surgeon to the Dutch East India Company factory (trading station) on the tiny, artificial island of Deshima in Nagasaki harbour between 1674 and 1676. In 1690 the German physician Engelbert Kaempfer (1651–1715) took up the same post, returning in 1693, and in 1712 he published his account of Japanese tea to complement that of 'my much honoured friend' in his *Amoenitates Exoticae* (Exotic Pleasures). Kaempfer is justly famous for his pioneering study of Japanese flora, much of it done in secrecy, and his work was recognized by Linnaeus in the first edition of his epoch-making *Species Plantarum* (1753). In this work, at Kaempfer's suggestion, he classifies tea as *Thea sinensis*.

THE EAST INDIA COMPANY

Throughout the 17th century France and Holland led Europe in the use of this new beverage and the early beginnings of tea in Britain are obscure. During the early years of the 17th century the East India Company (see page 67) worked hard to establish a monopoly on the tea trade with the East. In 1637 the East India Company reached China, where the edicts of the declining Ming dynasty restricted trade to the port region of Canton, conducted under the auspices of an official from the imperial household. In 1644 the East India Company was given permission to establish a 'factory', or trading base, in the port of Amoy (Xiamen), but xenophobic attitudes remained a feature of the new Qing dynasty, limiting foreign trade until its enforced expansion under the Treaty of Nanjing after the First Opium War (see page 132).

Tea became a popular drink in the truest sense of the word between 1700 and 1710, presenting the East India Company with the perennial problem of obtaining a regular supply. The Company had already established a mass market in Europe for one imported product – calicoes – and achieved a similar success with tea, which replaced the cotton trade as imports began to decline from the mid-18th century onwards. In 1713 the East India Company made a breakthrough and secured an agreement with the Chinese allowing them to trade direct with Canton. In 1717 there began regular exchange of silver for Chinese goods, and the consolidation of the Company's monopoly on legal tea imports that was to last until 1834. The Company legally imported about 50 tons of tea in 1700, which had a wholesale value of £4,000 per ton (£2 per pound, or just over £4 per kilo); by 1800 this figure had reached over 15,000 tons, with the average for the century at about 4,000 tons per year. Considering that the Company was making £100 for each of the 375,000 tons of tea that was imported during the century, this was a very lucrative trade indeed. Neither were

ABOVE Energetic labourers pack the dried tea leaves into chests or 'tea sacks' ready for embarkation in this Chinese School painting of *c.*1790. Despite the presence of European traders and their agents, pure tea leaves were often supplemented to help cater for the vast export demand. Such additions might define a blend, but were often purely makeweights.

successive governments of the day slow to realize the potential tax revenue from tea, setting duty at an exorbitant 119 per cent.

In China, the activities of the East India Company were to become a catalyst for the expansion of British influence there. The indifference of China's rulers to trade in anything other than silver bullion was to create a serious problem for the East India Company, as domestic demand for tea and silks continued to grow and they struggled to obtain sufficient silver to meet it. The Company's consequent financing of the tea trade with illegal opium exports was to prove disastrous for China, creating appalling levels of drug addiction and, finally, the legacy of the Opium Wars: military defeat, costly reparations and enforced trading concessions.

TAXES AND TARIFFS

The short-sighted greed for tax revenue on the part of governments actually served as a catalyst to inspire another boom industry of the 18th century. As with luxuries such as brandy, tobacco, lace and wine, which were also subject to high taxes, an extensive and elaborate tea-smuggling industry developed. It has been calculated that tea smuggling became so widespread that, although the East India Company was importing huge quantities of tea legally, this made up only a quarter of the total amount of tea consumed in Britain. Small, fast boats would slip out of harbours around the coast to rendezvous with European ships – and with some East Indiamen. Each ship's captain was allowed a certain space in the hold to be filled with goods for personal trade. Many took advantage to bring back tea that, unbeknownst to the Company, was sold on to smugglers. The tea chests were brought ashore and hidden in secret cellars, behind false walls, in the local church and even in castles – on one day alone 2,000 lb (900 kg) of illegal tea was seized by the authorities from Herstmonceux Castle in Sussex. From these secret repositories a highly organized, illicit transport network would move the tea around the country.

The level of smuggling on the south and west coasts got so out of hand that an unofficial state of war existed between the 'army' of smugglers and customs officials. There were battles at sea and on land, and contraband tea that had been seized was often 'liberated' from the customs houses by gangs of smugglers. Fatalities were not uncommon, as revealed by this lament from the headstone of one smuggler, Robert Trotman:

> A little tea, one leaf I did not steal.
> For guiltless bloodshed I to God appeal.
> Put tea in one scale, human blood in t'other,
> And think what 'tis to slay a harmless brother.

Despite the vast quantities of tea that came into Britain 'tax free', smuggled tea was still relatively expensive, costing up to 10s 6d a pound in 1777, approximately a third of the average weekly wage. Finally, the Government woke up to the absurdity of the situation and in 1784 the First Lord of the Treasury, William Pitt the Younger, took the necessary step and introduced the Commutation Act. This slashed tea tax to a reasonable 12.5 per cent, a move that effectively put the smugglers out of business.

The Chairman of London Tea Dealers, Robert Twining, was a friend of William Pitt and instrumental in getting the tax rates reduced. Already the head of his grandfather's now famous firm, Twining emphasized the much greater levels of revenue that the Government could obtain through a moderate sales tax that would enable wider consumption of the beverage. A lampooning response to the Commutation Act points out how this in fact benefited rich traders far more than the ordinary dealer in tea. Assuming the form of a mocking letter to the Emperor of China, it pleads

> As the subject so much relates to the salutiferous and chat-inspiring plant,
> that vegitates in your sublime Empire, may it please you, Most Magnificent,
> by all your extensive and all powerful protection, to rescue it from oblivion
> and the devil of Leadenhall-street.

TEA AND THE AMERICAN REVOLUTION

Taxes on imported crops such as tea were also the catalyst to the rebellion of the American colonies, which were becoming increasingly resentful about Britain's protectionist policies on trade. In the tradition of the 16th and 17th centuries, the role of colonies was still perceived to be that of provider of raw materials for the mother country, which the latter was unable to grow herself, and in turn to offer a controllable market for manufactured exports. Colonial enterprises, such as the Virginia Company which founded the colony at Chesapeake in 1607 (see page 23), were undertaken on an economic basis, and any attempts by settlers to establish their own terms were not considered acceptable. In the case of America, the eastern seaboard in particular associated British government with restrictions on commerce and industry, and disliked the influence of British merchants and Caribbean sugar and tobacco planters in determining tariffs on their goods.

On 10 February 1763 the Treaty of Paris was signed to mark the end of the Seven Years' War, a worldwide series of conflicts fought for the control of Germany and for supremacy in colonial North America and India. It had involved most of the major powers of Europe, in particular Britain, Prussia and Hanover pitched against Austria, Saxony, France, Russia, Sweden and Spain. The North American theatre, known as the French and Indian War, involved Britain and its American colonies against the French and their Algonquian allies. Amongst the various terms of the peace Britain acquired almost the entire French empire in North America and took control of Florida from Spain. Rightly or wrongly, the British Government considered that it had fought the war at least in part for the benefit of the colonies, and thought it fair that the colonies pay for much of the cost of the war effort through tax increases on colonial imports of glass, red and white lead, paints, paper and tea.

The taxes were tremendously unpopular in America and began an inexorable decline in relationships between the colonies and Government. In 1773 the Prime Minister, Lord North, secured the Tea Act, which eliminated the customs duty on the East India Company's tea and permitted its direct export to America, thus bypassing the colonial agents. In doing so he wanted to assist the East India Company (which had incurred great military expenses in expanding British trade in India and in suppressing French interests in the area) and also to demonstrate parliamentary supremacy to the colonies. The Act in fact served to incite further resentment, compounded by the lack of American representation in the British Parliament, and gave rise to the famous slogan 'No taxation without representation'. North's show of force was counterproductive, and when in November 1773 three British ships arrived in Boston carrying 342 chests of tea, the citizenry would not permit the unloading. In response, the Royal Governor of Massachusetts, Thomas Hutchinson, refused to allow the tea ships to return to England until the duty had been paid. So on the evening of 16 December, a group of Bostonians, many of them disguised as Native Americans and led by one Samuel Adams, boarded the vessels and emptied the tea chests into the sea. This event, which became known as the Boston Tea Party, was followed in 1774 by further Acts and rhetoric from both sides before the situation descended into revolution and war in 1775.

Soon after America became an independent country, it began to import tea direct from China, Its newer, faster clippers (see page 107) sailed more efficiently than the slower, heavier British 'tea wagons' that had until then dominated the trade, forcing the British to update their fleet also. American tea barons included John Jacob Astor of New York, Stephen Girard of Philadelphia and T. H. Perkins of Boston, all of whom made their millions from the tea trade. Astor began his tea trading in 1800. He required a minimum profit on each venture of 50 per cent, but in fact he often made 100 per cent. Girard, known as the 'gentle tea merchant', made important loans to the young American Government that enabled re-arming for the 1812 war. Perkins, a member of one of Boston's oldest sailing families, was trusted implicitly by the Chinese and this enabled him to conduct major commercial transactions.

By the middle of the 19th century, however, the American Government, following the British initiative of transferring tea from China to India (see page 99) and establishing plantations on sovereign land, decided to create an American tea industry. Robert Fortune was charged by the Commissioner of Patents, the Hon. Charles Mason, to undertake a fourth trip to China between 1858 and 1859 to secure tea plants and seeds. As a result of his explorations 32,000 flourishing plants were grown, ready for transplanting, but unfortunately, the Civil War effectively scuppered the plan. The war also caused the failure of another of Fortune's schemes – a National Arboretum to be located in Washington DC. It took nearly a further three-quarters of a century before the idea came to fruition in 1927.

The United States saw the birth of two further tea innovations. In 1904 St Louis hosted the World Trade Fair. Among the merchants and traders who flocked from around the world to display their wares was a tea plantation owner, Richard Blechynden. His marketing ploy was to attract custom by dispensing free tea samples. However, a heat wave hit St Louis, and no-one was interested in hot drinks. Undeterred, this resourceful man simply added ice to the brewed tea and served the first 'iced tea'. Alongside the Egyptian fan dancer, Blechynden's iced tea was the talk of the Fair.

Four years later, another tea merchant, Thomas Sullivan of New York developed 'bagged tea'. His daily business involved wrapping samples of tea to offer to potential clients, and he immediately recognized the marketing opportunity when he discovered that one of his restaurant clients was brewing his samples still in the wraps to avoid the mess of tea leaves in the kitchen.

EXPANSION IN CHINA

Following the loss of the American colonies, Asia became the primary focus of Britain's colonial aspirations for much of the 19th century. The East India Company maintained a monopoly on the Chinese tea trade until 1834, a valuable property although tea consumption dropped a little between 1801 and 1810, with 24,000,000 lb (10,886,400 kg) imported. By the middle of the century, however, this figure had almost doubled and the average annual consumption stood at 1½ lb (680 g) per capita. Yet with 5 per cent of the nation's gross domestic product tied up in tea, still no European merchant or *fankwei*, 'foreign devil', (depending on your perspective) had penetrated beyond the tiny trading dock in Canton; there was widespread ignorance about the plant's cultivation or processing techniques. Such uncertainty was played upon by Chinese merchants, who were well aware of the huge demand for tea. Although the East India Company had agents in Canton to try the tea before it was purchased, the Chinese were not above adulterating the pure leaves — nor indeed were merchants in Britain, equally anxious to spin out this valuable resource. Henry Hobhouse has observed that as well as blending tea with citrus or other herbs (the scented bergamot that flavours Earl Grey tea is a familiar example), less palatable additions included bark, leaves from entirely different species, sawdust, iron filings, soot and the appealing 'smouch', a mix of ash leaf and sheep dung.

BELOW Painted on silk, this 19th-century Chinese illustration of a tea depot shows the final stages of tea purchase: weighing, tasting, negotiation, crating and transportation. Following China's defeat by Britain in the First Opium War of 1842, the ports of Amoy, Fuzhou, Shanghai and Ningbo, as well as Canton, were opened to European traders.

TRANSFER TO INDIA

In 1820 David Scott, the recently appointed Commissioner of Assam, sent leaves from a camellia plant to Dr Wallich at the Calcutta Botanic Garden, one of the many colonial Botanic Gardens which were linked to, and run by, the Royal Botanic Gardens at Kew (see page 149). The leaves were sent to London for identification, where it was declared that they came from a tea plant – the first time that tea had been acknowledged by the British to grow wild in India. It was quickly recognized that parts of Assam, a region nestling in the foothills of the Himalayas, had the perfect combination of climate, aspect and soil needed to cultivate tea successfully as a colonial plantation crop. A decade or so later the British began the first experimental tea plantation with a few seedlings that it had acquired from China. Unfortunately these died, and an attempt was subsequently made to cultivate the indigenous tea plants of Assam. This experiment also proved unsuccessful, and it was a further 13 years before a concerted effort was made to establish a tea industry in India. In the event, it was not native Indian tea plants that were cultivated, but plants and seed acquired from the great tea-growing areas of China.

In 1848, the East India Company decided to send a plant hunter to China 'for the purpose of obtaining the finest varieties of the Tea-plant, as well as native manufacturers and implements, for the Government plantations in the Himalayas'. The defeat of China in the First Opium War (see page 132) had served to open up trade with its coast and allow for limited access inland. However, the main tea growing areas were a considerable distance into the hinterland, and the East India Company therefore wisely decided to engage the services of a seasoned plant hunter, experienced at travelling through China incognito. The man they chose was Robert Fortune.

Born on 16 September 1812 at Kelloe in Berwickshire, Fortune spent his horticultural apprenticeship in the gardens of a nearby landowner before moving to Edinburgh Botanic Garden. From here he was appointed Superintendent of the Hothouse Department at the (Royal) Horticultural Society's garden at Chiswick in 1842. His big break came when he was chosen to undertake a plant-hunting expedition to China on behalf of the Society.

Fortune set off on 26 February 1843 bound for Hong Kong, where he arrived after a four-month journey on 6 July. The expedition was expected to only take a year, but in the event Fortune spent the next three years searching for a long list of plants set out in his contract, as well as new, unknown species; he experienced great hardship, undertaking journeys at considerable personal risk to acquire new plants and receiving a paltry £100 per annum. The Society even baulked initially at procuring him firearms for his personal protection – they were to save his life – and required that he should sell them before his return, retain the receipt and reimburse the money! Fortune's first book, *Three Years' Wanderings in the Northern*

Provinces of China (1847), provides a vivid account of his adventures: his most daring escape occurred when the boat upon which he was a passenger came under attack from a number of pirate vessels. Fortune, running a high fever, was twice forced to repel the pirate attacks single-handed, armed only with a 12-bore shotgun and pistols.

Despite his trials and tribulations, Fortune acquired an impressive collection of garden plants, and in total (he made four trips to China and one to Japan) he is credited with introducing over 120 ornamental species to Britain, many of which we take for granted today. Amongst his best-known introductions are *Mahonia japonica*, *Lonicera fragrantissima*, *Jasminum nudiflorum*, *Weigela florida* and *Anemone hupehensis* var. *japonica*.

Not dissuaded by his earlier (mis)adventures, Fortune returned to China in August 1848, with a 500 per cent pay rise. Tea was grown in the easily accessible area around Ning-po, but the product was not to Western taste, and although Fortune did gather seed and plants here, as well as in other tea-growing districts, his main targets were the tea regions further inland. Once again Fortune donned his familiar disguise and had his head shaved — by his guide, who used a razor so blunt it skinned his scalp and brought tears to his eyes — and set off into the unknown. He travelled by boat, foot or sedan-chair and stayed at rudimentary

OPPOSITE Men laden with huge packs of tea rest briefly in the Chinese province of Sichuan in the Himalayas in 1908. Bound into bricks, the tea's weight was extraordinary: each man might carry up to 317 lb (143 kg) for up to 6 miles (10 km) over difficult terrain.

TEA TYPES AND BLENDS

In the West 'black tea' (in contrast to 'green' and 'oolong' tea, which are processed in slightly different ways) is the most widely drunk (comprising over 90 per cent of tea consumed in Britain and the US). It produces a strong, amber brew that can contain up to 35 different teas, made to recipes that are closely guarded trade secrets. Since the earliest export of tea, blends, some official and others less so, have determined the character of individual teas, such as English Breakfast (the prototype blended tea developed in Edinburgh by one Drysdale, a Scottish Tea Master), Earl Grey and Darjeeling. Earl Grey, a blend of black teas and bergamot oil, is named after an actual Earl Grey (1764–1845) who allegedly received the recipe from a Chinese Mandarin seeking to influence trade relations. Darjeeling comes from India (see page 104), is reserved for afternoon tea, and is traditionally served without milk.

It is the job of the tea blender — a tea taster of many years' experience — to ensure that his company's blend maintains its consistency. During the course of a day, a blender can taste between 200 and 1,000 teas, adjusting his recipe to ensure that the blend tastes just right. Traditionally, tasting of each consignment was performed on the docks before the tea was loaded onto the ships, to ensure that the flavour was consistent and the tea not adulterated, although this was a common practice and often unperceived. The Assam Directory and Tea Areas handbook, published in Calcutta in 1943, lists an official glossary of tasting terms for the use of planters and brokers, and includes some intriguing descriptions: 'bakey', for example, means a stewed taste through being fired at too high a temperature or left too long in the dryer, whereas 'malty', although a consequence of high firing, is also a characteristic of the leaf. 'Weathery' is, unsurprisingly, a consequence of climate, found in mid-season rains teas that have not sufficiently withered; 'pungent' is a term of praise for a tea astringent but not bitter, whilst the damning 'dull', 'thin', 'coarse' and 'stalky' are clearly self-explanatory.

Chinese inns or in Buddhist temples on the 200-mile (320-km) journey inland to the unvisited Hwuy-chow district. Fortune relates the story of his expedition in his second book *A Journey to the Tea Countries* (1852). He did not experience such scalp-tingling adventures as on his earlier trip, but there was the odd moment of tension, and the occasional incident. For example, on his first night in disguise he had to forgo dinner lest his ineptitude with chopsticks — he had not used them for three years — give away his true identity. Fortune's descriptions of the countryside, the flora and the people are enchanting, such as this evocation of the Hwuy-chow district in November 1848:

> This part of the country was exceedingly beautiful and full of interest. Many of the less fertile hills were clothed with junipers and pines, whilst on others, the patches of ripening corn afforded a striking contrast to the dark-green leaves of the tea-bushes with which they were dotted. I had now the pleasure of seeing many groups of the beautiful 'funeral cypress'; it was growing on the sides of the hills, generally near villages or amongst the graves. Everywhere it was beautiful, and produced a striking effect in the appearance of the landscape.

Indeed, Fortune indulged in a bit of 'freelancing' and continued to collect ornamental species. And on this trip, as well as discovering the funeral cypress (*Cupressus funerbis*) and *Mahonia japonica*, he found and reintroduced the Chusan Palm (*Trachycarpus fortuneii*), first brought to the West in 1830. Fortune also recorded that the hills of Sung-lo or Sung-lo-shan in the province of Kiang-nan and district of Hien-ning (old place names) are famous in China because it was here that the green tea shrub was first discovered and green tea first made. He quotes the book *Hieu-ning-hien chy*, published in 1693, that states:

> The hill or mountain where tea is produced is Sung-lo Mountain. A bonze (priest) of the sect of Fo taught a Kiang-nan man, named Ko Ty, the art of making tea, and thus it was called Sung-lo tea. The tea got speedily into great repute, so that the bonze became rich and abandoned the profession of priest. The man is gone and only the name remains. Ye men of learning and travellers who seek Sung-lo tea may now search in vain, that which is sold in the markets is a mere counterfeit.

It was from these mountains that Fortune collected seed and tea plants before returning to Canton, and dispatching a batch of seed to the East India Company in India in the autumn of 1848. In early 1849 he set off on another collecting trip, this time to the town of Hokow and the Woo-e-shan mountains, where he enjoyed the local white wine and acquired tea seedlings from the local Buddhist priests. He also heard the traditional story that in the areas where the tea shrubs were inaccessible, stones were thrown at the monkeys, who, angered, responded by throwing down branches – of tea. Fortune, with a magnificent display of even-handed Victorian scepticism, states, 'I should not like to assert that no tea is gathered by … monkeys, but I think that it may be safely affirmed that the quantities produced in such ways are exceedingly small.'

Another mystery that Fortune was able to solve as a result of his tea gathering expeditions was that of the difference between green and black tea. The secrecy that the Chinese maintained around tea cultivation and tea making meant that for centuries Western botanists had been left to speculate about the plant. It seems that their conclusions were drawn from the product arriving in the West, for, as John Hill declared in his *Treatise on Tea* (1753), green tea and black tea came from different plants. This perceived wisdom, namely that the two types of tea were made from different plants, was first challenged by Fortune in his book *Three Years' Wanderings*. He agreed with the (incorrect) Linnaean classification that there were, indeed, two types of tea plant – that the Cantonese tea plant *Thea bohea* was different from the more northerly *Thea viridis* – but realized that both green and black tea could be made from each plant. The difference between green and black tea, Fortune maintained, was in the manufacturing process, not the plant itself. This announcement was greeted with derision in Britain, and it took the explanation presented in his second book, *Yeddo and Peking* (1863), and demonstrations by the tea experts whom he had himself imported into India before Fortune won the argument.

Fortune returned to Canton and dispatched another batch of seed to India in 1849. The first batch had not succeeded because tea seed has a very short period of vitality and the long sea journey had rendered it infertile. This time, however, he sowed the seeds in Wardian cases (a sealed system in which the plants were protected from the outside atmosphere) in which the juvenile plants were also to be transported. This technique proved successful and was employed again when, after spending the year 1850 gathering more plants and information about tea cultivation and manufacture, Fortune left China bound for India on 16 February 1851. He arrived in Calcutta on 15 March.

Fortune's exploits on behalf of the East India Company had been a complete success. He had brought to India 23,892 young plants and approximately 17,000 germinated seedlings. Equally important as the plants were the practical collection of machinery used for tea production, and the group of eight expert Chinese tea growers and makers who were able to pass on their knowledge and expertise to the new plantation managers.

At exactly the same time as Fortune was being greeted by Dr Falconer, Superintendent of the Calcutta Botanic Gardens, another famous plant hunter and future Director of Kew, (Sir) Joseph Dalton Hooker, was relaxing aboard a boat taking him home after spending three years exploring Sikkim. Hooker had been the first Westerner ever to enter this mountain kingdom in the northeast Himalayas, in which he discovered the stunningly beautiful Himalayan rhododendrons which, when bred to create the Hardy Hybrids, caused rhododendromania amongst British gardeners – a passion that continues to this day. During his second trip in 1849, however, Hooker and his travelling companion, Archibald Campbell, had been illegally arrested and imprisoned by the Sikkimese authorities, providing Britain with the perfect excuse to annex the southern part of Sikkim around Darjeeling. It seems a convenient coincidence that just as Fortune was acquiring tea plants for the East India Company to establish tea plantations, the British authorities (in effect the Company, as India's government) were acquiring the only fertile part of Sikkim, land that was perfect for the cultivation of tea.

Tea plantations were duly established in Sikkim and Assam, and the first Assam was auctioned in London in 1839. It made a relatively slow impact (only 3 per cent of tea sold came from India in 1857), but this was to change, and by 1890 it formed 90 per cent of the domestic market). Tea became one of north India's principal exports during the second half of the 19th century, and the value of its imports into Britain rose a staggering 837 per cent in 75 years between 1854 and 1929 (£24, 000 to £20, 087,000). Tea continues to provide India with a sizeable amount of foreign income; it exports some 200, 000 metric tonnes of tea each year, primarily India Tea, Assam, Darjeeling and Nilgiri.

LIVING ON A TEA PLANTATION

The pattern of life on a tea plantation in India has been meticulously recorded by W. Kenneth Warren, who lived in Assam for many years from the beginning of the 20th century until Indian independence in 1948. Initially, the young man was somewhat disappointed at finding such 'civilized' conditions, rather than an isolated bungalow in the perilous jungle, but he consoled himself with the social and sporting opportunities open to the colonial families. 'Altogether life was easy and pleasant, with polo twice a week and tennis both at the club and in private bungalows, [plus] excellent fishing and shooting when one was fortunate enough to get a few days' leave.' Despite the problems of the Rains, when all forms of meat or chicken had to be eaten immediately or would decay, and the reliance on unpredictable punkah-wallahs instead of electric fans, he clearly found the living on a tea garden to be 'extremely pleasant', characterized by a paternalistic concern for the welfare of indentured native labour, 'a valuable and costly asset [which] therefore required specially considerate and tactful handling'. It was a lifestyle of stability and confidence in the structures of the empire that two World Wars and the growing movement for independence in India were to change beyond all recognition.

CLIPPER RACES

Despite new plantations in India, the tea industry centred on China throughout much of the second half of the 19th century. The atmosphere of free trade meant that the East India Company had lost its monopoly on the importing of tea in 1834, and new competition prompted replacement of the traditional East Indiamen ships with sleek, fast tea clippers. The heyday of the clippers was during the 1850s when they raced against one another to bring back to London the first new-season tea — often arriving literally minutes apart, the race continuing right up the River Thames. The first arrival of tea commanded a premium price, although this was largely a reflection of prestige value rather than any significant difference in the quality. Nevertheless, the races, an endurance test for the clipper crews lasting over several months, generated considerable public excitement.

The *Cutty Sark* was the fastest clipper of her day, and enjoyed a famous rivalry with the *Thermopylae*. In the race of 1872, both vessels sailed from Shanghai within an hour of one another in mid-June and raced each other home around the tip of India and Africa, past St Helena and ultimately back to Britain, encountering monsoon gales, 'unfriendly waterspouts', 'heavy head gales' and the odd problematic calm. The *Thermopylae* finally won, but the *Cutty Sark* had the moral victory, having been defeated only by a broken rudder which occasioned 11 days' delay and put her a week behind, arriving on 18 October. The strain of three months' constant pressure and little sleep was immense, particularly on the captains, and in his reminiscences of 1914, Basil Lubbock, an ex-sailor, claimed, 'A born racing skipper has always been as rare as a born cavalry leader ... it required dash and steadiness, daring and prudence ... not attributes of character often found in conjunction.' Nevertheless, the standard of crew on the clippers was high, and their pride in the magnificent ships went far beyond their commercial role.

The clipper races finally ended when steam power superseded sail and the Suez Canal became an established part of the homeward route. However, the races and the ever-increasing quantities of tea imported, now supplemented by the Indian plantations, show that tea continued to be an extraordinarily popular drink throughout the 19th century, enjoyed by both sexes and all sectors of society.

CONSUMPTION AT HOME

The beginnings of tea drinking in Britain are uncertain, but it seems likely that it first reached England between 1652 and 1654. Initially, tea was a luxury item and its consumption restricted to those who could afford it, which would explain why it was sold from an apothecary's shop, alongside costly and rare spices. Because it was so expensive, tea was kept in a locked caddy, over which the lady of the house maintained strict control and took personal charge of the key to prevent servants stealing the valuable contents.

OPPOSITE Women workers on a tea garden in Ceylon (Sri Lanka), photographed *c*.1935. Plucking has traditionally been a female task due to the manual dexterity it requires. The warm and moist climate of Ceylon prompted the transfer of two key crops by British authorities, tea and rubber, both of which are still grown on plantations.

The first great merchant to sell tea was Thomas Galway, who offered the leaf in both dry and liquid form at his coffee house in London in 1657. In 1660 he was retailing tea at between £6 and £10 per pound (£13 and £22 per kilo). As with so many other new plant products, there raged a scholarly but heated debate about the pros and cons of tea consumption. Galway must have been aware of this dialogue because he was anxious to emphasize the health benefits of the drink to his customers – the following extract from an advertising broadsheet that he issued extols tea as:

> wholesome, preserving perfect health until extreme old age, good for clearing the sight [able to cure] gripping of the guts, cold, dropsies, scurveys [and claiming that] it could make the body active and lusty.

As tea imports increased and prices became more affordable consumption spread amongst the general population. Peter Stuyvesant took tea across the Atlantic and introduced it to the settlement of New Amsterdam (later re-named New York by the English). The settlers became confirmed tea drinkers, and when the British acquired the colony, they discovered that the inhabitants consumed more tea at that time than all of England put together. And in 1680 the social critic, the

BELOW Holland was one of the first European countries to import Chinese tea in the late 16th century. Throughout the next century, it was more successful than Britain in trading with China, and imported vast quantities of tea, silk and porcelain. The prosperity of Dutch merchants at that time is reflected in the traditional costumes and furnishings of this 20th-century photograph.

Marquise de Seven, Marie de Rabutin-Chantal, made the first mention of milk being added to tea.

The year 1660 was an auspicious one for the tea trade for it also saw the Restoration of Charles II, a monarch who had become very partial to tea during his exile in France as a guest of Louis XIV at Versailles. Charles's wife was the Portuguese Catherine de Braganza, also a confirmed tea drinker. Tea was brought back from Asia as a gift to the royal family in the 1660s and rapidly became the fashionable drink among the upper classes, to the delight of the East India Company, its sole importer. As demand increased, imports rose, from 40,000 lb (18,144 kg) in 1699 to an annual average of 240,000 lb (108,864 kg) by 1708 and over 1,000,000 lb (453,600 kg) by the mid-1720s. Significantly, it did not remain an élite product for long; if in 1680 tea drinking was an aristocratic pastime, a century later it had become the established drink of ordinary people throughout the country. Provision of tea and sugar even became part of some servants' terms of employment.

Even though good tea remained relatively expensive (and smuggled tea was often of better quality than that available legally), by 1780 tea was as much a part of the diet of the working classes as the refined gentry, although the calibre of the tea they drank was poles apart. The rich could afford the best leaves, which were used only once, while the poorer members of society had to do with the dregs.

ABOVE An early European version of the teapot, this elegant silver kettle was produced in The Hague in 1770. It reflects the traditional Chinese method of brewing tea, but includes an elaborate stand and lamp to keep the mixture hot.

These were, in fact, often the used tea leaves of the wealthy, sold by the kitchen servants to dealers who then recoloured and resold them. Even these recycled leaves were often re-used. Another method used by crooked dealers and black marketeers to maximize their profits was adulteration, prevalent both in Britain and even before the tea left its country of origin (see page 98). The 8th-century Chinese writer Li Yu perhaps explains the secret of its continuing popularity when he acknowedges 'its goodness is a decision for the mouth to make'.

One significant aspect of mass tea drinking was the increased demand for sugar (see page 60), the annual consumption of which rose from 4 lb (1.8 kg) per capita in 1700 to 10 lb (4.5 kg) in 1748 and 20 lb (9 kg) in 1800. One of the reasons why sugar was put in tea was for its calorific value, giving the drinker an instant lift, much as ale had done for centuries, but without the alcohol. Indeed, it was because tea, although a mild stimulant, did not lead to the kind of behaviour depicted so famously in Hogarth's *Gin Lane* that, while it did not receive active approbation from religious writers, neither was it damned. Yet tea did receive strong criticism from certain quarters. By the middle of the 18th century, tea was seen by some as an unwholesome drink that sapped the strength of workers. In 1757, Jonas Hanway, pioneer of the umbrella and prison reformer, called tea drinking an 'epidemical disease', adding:

> You may see labourers who are mending the road drinking their tea … it is ever so … sold out of cups to haymakers … were they sons of tea-sippers who won the fields of Crecy and Agincourt or dyed the Danube's shores with Gallic blood?

This position would have met with the approval of Dr Johnson (himself a confessed tea addict) who believed that 'tea is a liquor not proper for the lower classes of people, as it supplies no strength to labour, or relief to disease, but gratifies the taste without nourishing the body'.

COFFEE AND CHOCOLATE

As coffee was introduced into one European country after another, consumption increased and the Dutch began importing from their colonial plantations. In 1714 the French managed to smuggle a single cutting to the island of Martinique in the West Indies. This was the lone parent plant from which all of Latin America's great coffee plantations were to grow.

Coffee arrived in Britain in 1650 and quickly became popular as a beverage of the professional classes and intelligentsia who gathered in the many Coffee Houses to relax, debate and drink. The first recorded Coffee House was in Oxford, and was open by 1650; the first in London, was the Sign of Pasqua Rosee, open by 1652, and by 1683 there were reported to be over 2,000 such establishments countrywide. In many ways these were the taverns of the middle classes. Unlike tea, however, coffee did not cross the social divide and become a drink of the masses, perhaps because there was not the seemingly endless supply of coffee that promised a large profit to merchants in the way tea did.

Another drink that was introduced at this time, and also failed to reach the same level of popularity as tea was chocolate. Columbus brought cocoa beans to Spain on his fourth voyage in 1502, and the Spanish *conquistadors*, who arrived in Mexico in 1519, maintained a monopoly on chocolate, only allowing import of the beans to Spain. In 1634, however, the Dutch settled Curacao and from this base smuggled out beans from Venezuela. The Dutch subsequently planted cocoa plantations in Ceylon (Sri Lanka) and throughout their Indonesian colonies.

Drinking chocolate made from the processed cocoa beans became a luxury item in Europe; chocolate reached Italy in 1606 and became popular in France with the marriage of the Spanish princess Maria Theresa to Louis XIV in 1660. The first record of chocolate becoming available in Britain is 1657, when a Frenchman opened a shop in London, selling solid chocolate to be made into the beverage. Chocolate houses, soon appeared across Europe and by 1765 chocolate manufacture began in the American colonies at Dorchester, in Massachusetts, using cocoa beans from the West Indies. In 1828 the Dutchman C.J. van Houten patented a process for obtaining 'chocolate powder' by pressing most of the cocoa butter from ground and roasted cocoa beans. The next evolutionary phase in chocolate's history was the combination of cocoa butter with chocolate liquor and sugar to produce eating chocolate. This was done by the British firm of Fry and Sons in 1847, and in 1876 Daniel Peter of Switzerland added dried milk to the mix to create milk chocolate.

Others took a more positive approach. The 18th-century historical writer Agnes Strickland extolled the virtues of a drink that was a 'counter-charm to the habits of intoxication'. The debate about the positive and negative effects of tea drinking was to rage well into the 19th century, with one commentator, William Cobbett, writing in *Cottage Economy* that:

> I view tea drinking as a destroyer of health, an enfeebler of the frame, an engenderer of effeminacy and laziness, a debaucher of youth and a maker of misery in old age.

Cobbett also famously observed that a family of pigs could be raised on the nourishing waste from domestic beer production, while the only thing ever successfully raised on tea was sleepless nights.

Throughout the 18th and 19th centuries the consumption of tea became an intrinsic part of many social activities indulged in by various sectors of society. The tea garden enabled members of both sexes to associate freely, in contrast to the male preserve of coffee houses, and, taking its inspiration from the Dutch 'tavern garden teas', it became a very popular form of entertainment. On Saturdays and Sundays, men and women all over the country would dress up, pay an entrance fee and take tea out of doors while listening to an orchestra play, admiring the manicured gardens full of hidden arbours, enjoying flowery walks, playing bowls, and, in the evenings gambling or watching fireworks. Perhaps the most famous tea gardens were Vauxhall Gardens in London, which opened in 1732. It was at one such gathering that Lord Nelson met the love of his life, Emma, later Lady Hamilton. Tea gardens were also responsible for another habit that continues to this day, albeit in a different form. On the tables at which the guests sat to be served tea were small, locked wooden boxes inscribed with the letters 'TIPS'. Upon sitting down it was the custom to drop a coin into the box 'To Insure Prompt Service' from the waiters.

A social custom that has survived longer than the tea garden is afternoon tea. The concept, which came from the Continent, was adopted and adapted by Anna, 7th Duchess of Bedford (1788–1861) at Belvoir Castle in the early 1800s. At that time the meals of the day were only two – a large hearty breakfast and an even larger dinner served late in the evening. In order to stave off her afternoon hunger pangs, the duchess invited a group of lady friends to join her for an additional meal at five o'clock in her rooms. Here, the group was served small cakes, examples of a recent invention by the Earl of Sandwich, assorted sweets and, of course, tea. This practice, which began in the summer when the duchess was 'in the country', proved so popular that she continued it when she returned to London, sending cards to her friends asking them to join her for 'tea and a walk in the fields'. Leading social hostesses quickly picked up the practice of inviting friends to afternoon tea, and the etiquette of the British tea ceremony soon developed. The emphasis was on conversation and presentation. A pot of tea was brought from the kitchen to the lady of the house and her waiting guests. The hostess would then dispense tea from the fine porcelain teapot into equally elegant cups. The pot was then recharged from another pot, usually of silver, that contained water kept heated over a small flame. Tea cuisine quickly expanded to include wafer-thin crustless sandwiches with shrimp or fish pastes, toasted breads with jams, and regional specialities such as scones and crumpets. Afternoon tea or 'low tea' was distinguished in social terms from 'high tea' or 'meat tea', the latter becoming the chief meal of the day for the middle and working classes. It was more substantial than the light afternoon snack accompanied by a genteel cuppa, and consisted of meat, vegetables, bread and butter all, of course, washed down with big mugs of tea.

Initially, the fine porcelain used by socially correct hostesses also came from China. Tea, and another important Chinese export, silk, are very light and during transportation needed to be kept constantly dry in order to prevent deterioration. Therefore these valuable products were stored in the centre of the ship, away from water in the bilges and the risk of seepage through the decks. (As a point of interest, if tea is stored correctly it has a very long 'shelf life'.)

Ships, such as the East Indiamen and tea clippers that raced one another to bring home the new crop of tea, however, required the correct 'trim' to sail well, and this demanded ballast. Clearly the tea and silk did not provide this, but it was soon realized that Chinese porcelain – 'china' as it became known in Britain – was ideal for the job. Henry Hobhouse has outlined the intriguing consequences of this discovery. So much ballast was required, for example, that the 'supercargo' traders who arranged this aspect of the ship's voyage could strike very hard bargains with the Chinese porcelain manufacturers. As 'china' flooded the British marketplace, fine porcelain became ridiculously cheap. In 1712, for example, a 216-piece dinner service cost a mere £5 10s. And because there was so much of it, it soon made its way down the social ladder as chipped, damaged and discarded pieces were recycled by the less well off. This aesthetic 'trickle-down' effect continued until the end of the 18th century, when the East India Company ceased to use porcelain as ballast in its ships.

However, its legacy also served to stimulate the British pottery industry. Pioneers such as Josiah Wedgwood soon began to improve their techniques and produce pottery that was adapted to the British way of consuming tea. In China, tea was brewed in the kettle and drunk only a few degrees above blood temperature when it is at its most flavoursome, removing the need for a cup with a handle. The British liked their tea hot however, and preferred to brew it in a teapot (the design of which had evolved from Chinese wine flasks, but with an added handle). The shape of such items precluded easy packing and thus required

RIGHT The British institution of after- noon tea became a habit imitated across much of fashionable Europe. This illustration from *La Vie Parisienne* in 1923 emphasizes the interval of peace and serenity it offers the sophisticated lady about town. Her elegant sensuality is enhanced by the provocative cigarette.

them to be made in Britain. Wedgwood became the most successful British pottery manufacturer, catering for the rich by producing exclusive items, which subsequently became the staples of the popular mass market. By the time of his death in 1795 he was exporting across Europe, to the USA and the colonies. His remarkable success fuelled the rapid growth of the English pottery and porcelain industry, with the area in the Midlands in which production was focused becoming known as 'The Potteries'.

The pottery industry was not the only business to be affected by China and tea. Europe had been collectively fascinated by the exotic East since the early trading days of the 16th century (Albrecht Dürer notably collected examples of blue and white Ming porcelain), and many imitations of Chinese and Japanese motifs began to appear in the West. The later years of the 18th century saw the fashion for *Chinoiserie* – a fictitous, idealized admiration for all things Chinese – influence the design of contemporary furniture, textiles, decoration, ceramics and even gardens. The incorrect but seductive perception of Chinese society and beliefs survived the eyewitness accounts of trade missions to manifest itself in whole rooms of porcelain, wallpaper and lacquered panels throughout Europe's châteaux and stately homes. Fashionable gardens began to feature pagodas and pavilions, and to reflect a concern for scenery within new styles of asymmetrical design. The Prince Regent's creation of the extraordinary Brighton Pavilion in 1821 revived the trend for *Chinoiserie* in the 19th century, encouraging British craftsmen and industrialists to develop their own interpretations which could benefit from new techniques of mass production. As with all ideas that came from abroad, however, things Chinese were heavily anglicized.

Throughout the 19th century tea continued to be a phenomenally popular drink, enjoyed by both sexes and all sectors of society. Those who could would pause from their labours and take a 'tea break', a tradition beginning back in the 18th century when the working day commenced at around five or six in the morning. However, between 1741 and 1820 industrialists, landowners and clerics attempted to end the tea break, maintaining that the imbibing of this beverage made working people slothful. Indeed, it is interesting to consider to what extent the criticisms levelled at tea were simply a reflection of the fact that people of necessity stopped to drink it. In any case the workers stood firm, with tea cup in hand, and the tea break remains with us to this day.

During the 19th century it continued to be fashionable to invite friends to call and take afternoon tea – known as *tiffin* in the colonies – and in the second half of the century a new environment developed in which ladies could take tea. In 1864 the manageress of an Aerated Bread Company shop persuaded her employers to allow her to serve food and liquid refreshments to customers in the shop. Thus her regular customers were soon enjoying a rest and a chat over a cup of tea and cakes. Word quickly spread and the shop was besieged with new customers wanting the same thing. So was born the tea shop, a concept that gained almost overnight approbation and spread rapidly across Britain. More than just profitable businesses, tea shops also helped the slow process of women's emancipation. Running a tea shop was perceived as a genteel employment, suitable for a lady to engage in – primarily a female domain (in contrast to the Coffee Houses of the previous century) where an unchaperoned lady could meet with other female friends. Today, 140 years after their inception, tea shops remain incredibly popular. So ingrained in the national psyche has the ritual of visiting a tea shop become that taking tea and cakes has become more important that the tea drink itself. Furthermore, the British tea shop is now a national institution that has achieved the elevated status of an international tourist attraction.

The tea shop, it could be argued, inspired another social experience that centred on being seen to consume tea in public. Beginning in the late 1880s, élite hotels in England and the USA began to build specially decorated rooms given over to the service of afternoon tea. Served in the late afternoon, Victorian ladies and their gentlemen friends could meet in elegant surroundings, sit at a table amongst the palm trees, take tea and converse while listening to the string quartet. So popular did this pastime become, that the elegance of many hotels was judged on its tea services, for example, the Ritz in London and the Plaza in New York. By 1910 many hotels had changed with the times and, in response to the dance crazes, had begun to host afternoon tea dances. Considered a waste of time by older people, tea dances offered an opportunity for the newly independent young career girl to meet friends. Indeed, the editor of *Vogue* once fired a large number of female secretarial workers for 'wasting their time at tea dances'.

Tea remains irrefutably Briton's favourite drink, although other culinary habits have fortunately moved on from George Orwell's sardonic observation in 1944 that 'the English ... regard such things as garlic and olive oil with disgust, life is unliveable to them unless they have tea and puddings'. In 1996, the average daily consumption for persons over the age of 10 was 8.39 cups per person per day — a massive 42 per cent of everything the British nation drinks. If some of the recent research indicating the benefits of tea in reducing the risk of cardiovascular disease and cancer are correct, the world should be grateful for the errant leaves that fell into Emperor Shennong's pot of water nearly 5,000 years ago.

THE FUME OF POPPIES

THE ILLICIT OPIUM TRADE of the 18th and 19th centuries offers a singularly inglorious example of economic forces in action. As Western supplies of silver bullion began to prove inadequate to export demands for Chinese tea and silk, the lucrative fields of Bengal were tapped to provide an alternative — albeit illegal — means of exchange. The East India Company remained officially unaccountable for the trade over which they exerted monopolistic control, as the drug's impact permeated all levels of Chinese society. Defeat in the eventual Opium Wars was to prove disastrous for China, revealing to European powers the weakness of its empire in a predatory age. Subsequent indemnities and the enforced opening of China's ports to foreign trade did nothing to restrict the flow of opium; by the end of the 19th century mass addiction had become a symptom of the nation's decline.

Discovery and Early Use

It is not known when the properties of the opium poppy were first discovered, but archaeological records reveal that it was cultivated in the Near and Middle East at least as far back as the 4th millennium BC. In Mesopotamia the Sumerians were clearly aware of its euphoric qualities, for they named the poppy Hul Gil, or the 'plant of joy', and its use as a mind-altering substance and, more importantly, as a medicine spread throughout Asia Minor to Egypt and the Phoenician, Minoan and Cypriot trade routes around the Mediterranean.

One of the earliest references to it in literature is in Homer's Odyssey. At a symposium in Sparta, Odysseus's son Telemachus and Menelaus, the king of Sparta, grew maudlin at the thought of the missing Greek hero and the companions they had lost on the plains of Troy. To lighten the mood of the party, Helen poured a drug called nepenthes into the wine. The drug brought 'forgetfulness of evil' and 'those who had drunk of this mixture did not shed a tear the whole day long, even though their mother or father were dead, even though a brother or a beloved son had been killed before their eyes'. Hippocrates also noted opium's medical effectiveness in the 5th century BC, and in Roman times the Greek physician Galen thought it an almost universal panacea. The Romans enjoyed taking opium recreationally and could purchase their supplies from local shops and peripatetic quacks.

Arabian physicians continued to recognize the medicinal virtues of the plant which, due to the Islamic prohibition of alcohol, also became popular as a social drug. The Arabs recorded their findings in medical texts that were to have a profound influence on European physicians in the period leading up to the Renaissance. The expansion of the Arabic world brought them into contact with Persia, India and China, and opium first entered China along these trade routes during the 8th century AD. It soon became established as an important item in Chinese medicine cabinets and remained primarily a remedy rather than a recreational drug for nearly 1,000 years. In Persia and India opium began to be used socially in the 15th century and from there it swiftly became a popular indulgence. Opium grew well in India and became a major source of revenue for the Mogul empire in north India.

As with sugar, when the Muslim Arabs expanded west throughout the Mediterranean and North Africa, they took opium with them. As with spices and silks, the Crusaders became some of the first Europeans to spread the knowledge of the new plant product from the East, and Western Europe began trading in opium as early as the 11th century. In the Middle Ages, British apothecaries were primarily interested in the soporific properties of opium. In the 14th century, John Arderne prescribed mixtures of the drug to induce sleep and as an emollient. The connection between opium and drowsiness was to continue into Elizabethan times, when Shakespeare wrote in *Othello*:

Opium Plant Profile

Botanical Details

Classified in 1753 by Linnaeus as *Papaver somniferum* – 'sleep inducing' – the opium poppy is a herbaceous annual plant. The active principles of opium reside in its alkaloids, such as morphine, codeine and thebaine, which produce two remarkable effects: they relieve pain and induce euphoria. Before it is processed into purer morphine or heroin, the opium naturally contains between 7 to 15 per cent morphine, the primary active ingredient. It takes about 18,000 capsules grown in the space of 1 acre (0.4 ha) to produce just 20 lb (9 kg) of opium (although this yield can vary slightly according to temperature, light and time of harvest).

Origins

Native to Greece, southeastern Europe and western Asia, the plant has become established in many countries and is often viewed as a weed due to its habit of appearing among other crops. In the Mogul empire, two regions of India specialized in poppy cultivation. 'Bengal Opium' was grown along the Hooghly Valley to the north and west of Calcutta and on the western side of India 'Malwa Opium' was produced from the countryside near Bombay. Grown commercially in countries such as China, Pakistan, Iran, Turkey, Afghanistan, India and Central and South America, the cultivation of the opium poppy, both licit and illicit, is now carried on chiefly across Asia, from Turkey to Laos.

Description

Reaching a height of 4 ft (1.2 m), the poppy produces fragile flowers of red, white, purple or violet with a span of about 8 in (20 cm). Opium is collected during the days between the fall of the petals and the maturing of the egg-shaped seed capsules. The source of the opium is the skin of the seed pod rather than the poppy seeds which, because they develop after the opium, are harmless.

Habitat

The poppy requires a temperate climate of approximately 45–73°F (7–23°C), and consequently when grown in tropical locations it is planted in the mountains at an elevation of 3,000 ft (900 m) above sea level. It grows best in a nutrient-rich, moist soil with a moderate annual rainfall of about 3 ft (1 m). As a result of the work-intensive nature of harvesting the poppy, and because the fields must be weeded often, opium can only be cultivated profitably where land and labour are cheap, as in Asia.

Processing

Toward evening cuts are made into, but not through, the skin of the unripe seed pod with a multi-clawed knife. During the night a milky-white liquid oozes out of the pod, coagulates and oxidizes into a brown gum. This gum is then carefully scraped from the pod, moulded into small balls and then allowed to dry in the sun in shallow trays. Raw opium is sold as lumps, cakes or bricks and can be eaten, mixed into a drink or smoked.

The other cash crop derived from the opium poppy is poppy seeds, which have a mild, nutty taste and are popular in curries, breads, pastries and baked goods, and are crushed down to make a cooking oil. It takes 1 acre (0.4 ha) of opium poppies to produce about 200 lb (90 kg) of the tiny greyish to dark blue seeds.

Not poppy, nor mandragora,
Nor all the drowsy syrups of the world,
Shall ever medicine thee to that sweet sleep
Which thou owed'st yesterday.

By the 16th century opium had become a popular remedy and was being enthusiastically endorsed by the likes of the German maverick, Paracelsus. Aureolus Theophrastus Bombastus von Hohenheim, to give him his full name, denounced the ancient works of Hippocrates, Galen and Avicenna and administered opium to his patients with abandon. He was clearly successful in his prescription of opium, which he dubbed 'the stone of immortality', and built up a popular following. Paracelsus developed a painkiller in the shape of a black pill called laudanum (not to be confused with the later variety). It contained opium, thebaicum, citrus juice and a trace of gold.

DEVELOPMENT AND CHANGE

Direct East-West trade can be traced back to the epoch-making voyage of Vasco da Gama around the Cape of Good Hope and on to India. In the following centuries intrepid Europeans streamed toward the alluring East. They were inspired either by religious fervour, the lust for adventure or, most commonly, the desire to make a handsome profit.

The Portuguese and Spanish led the first expeditions (they held a virtual monopoly of trade with China in the 16th century) and were quick to realize the potential of opium as a commodity. In 1513 Affonso de Albuquerque wrote to his monarch from India: 'If your Highness would believe me I would order

RIGHT Dried opium cakes, shaped into balls, are tested and weighed by Chinese dealers prior to sale. Although consuming and trading in opium were made illegal in 1729, the constant demand from addicts encouraged smugglers to risk their lives for substantial profits.

poppies ... to be sown in all the fields of Portugal and command afyam [opium] to be made ... and the labourers would gain much also, and people of India are lost without it, if they do not eat it.' Many early travellers to the Middle East and India remarked on the fact that opium was used by the natives as a stimulant and an appetite suppresser rather than the European use as a relaxant.

Portugal was the first European nation to establish trading posts on the Chinese coast, and in 1557 Portugal was allowed to lease the small peninsula of Macao on the southwest side of the Canton estuary (the British East India Company was also allowed to set up business here soon afterwards, see page 93. However, the Chinese were prepared to allow only a limited amount of freedom and Macao remained a European trading base rather than a colony). While Britain and Europe were enamoured of the luxurious goods of the Orient, and imported great quantities of tea, silk and porcelain, China was self-sufficient and was not interested in what the West had to offer. Indeed, the ruling philosophy, Confucianism, looked down upon traders and the Chinese viewed the Western 'barbarians' with contempt.

The Portuguese were the first foreign traders to be faced with the conundrum of how to barter with a country that was not interested in their produce. As a portent of future health problems, the Portuguese merchants imported tobacco from their Brazilian colony. It is interesting to note that on two occasions Europeans have resorted to selling addictive substances when normal goods and chattels were unwanted. Although the Chinese quickly began to grow their own tobacco in order to stifle the profiteering Portuguese, they fatefully developed a passion for smoking a mixture of Indian opium and tobacco in a pipe (pipe smoking had been introduced by the Spanish, who superseded their neighbours in the Orient a century later).

OPIUM AND THE EAST INDIA COMPANY

The inglorious story of British opium exports to China is one of human suffering and economic success. It showed the skill and ruthlessness of British merchants in perceiving and exploiting a niche – one that ensured a captive market whose needs would increase rather than fall away. However, the East India Company were not the only Europeans engaged in this trade – not only the Portuguese, who had begun competing in the opium trade with Indian and Arab merchants, but also the Dutch were active in this area.

After winning monopoly rights to the opium trade in Java (from which they supplied Chinese markets), the Dutch East India Company began making impressive profits (a 400 per cent profit on shipments was not unusual in the 1670s). The success of the Dutch, who purchased cheap Indian opium and sold it with a considerable mark-up in the closed market of Java and to Asian merchants for distribution throughout the Far East, was a particular inspiration for British traders. It demonstrated that opium was an ideal cargo — easily transported, with no risk of deterioration between harvesting location and market, with a low weight and high retail cost. There are similarities with the spice trade, but the crucial difference is the damage this physically and mentally addictive substance causes to the user. On a national scale, this addiction became a disastrous symptom of Chinese decline; by the early 20th century 27 per cent of China's adult male population were addicted to opium, consuming 39,000 tons of the drug in 1906. It is a level of mass addiction that has never been encountered before or since.

Even by the early 18th century opium smoking was spreading across China, prompting the first imperial attempt to suppress the habit. In 1729 the Qing emperor issued an edict banning the smoking of opium and the importation of the drug except under licence for medical reasons. Punishment for breaking the law was severe and anyone found to be an opium shopkeeper was to be strangled. His actions came too late, however, for there was now a sufficient number of Chinese addicts to encourage smugglers to ignore the imperial orders.

The British were latecomers to the opium trade, but they quickly made up for lost time as the East India Company's expansion in India (see page 70) served to strengthen its political dominance in the region. At the battle of Plassey in 1757, the brilliant commander Robert Clive (who himself later became addicted to opium) defeated the 50,000-strong Mogul forces with an army of just 3,000, and at the cost of just 73 empire soldiers killed and wounded. Plassey proved to be a decisive victory over the French, who also sought economic influence on the east coast of India. One of the most significant outcomes of the battle was that Britain now controlled the rich opium fields of Bengal and within 15 years 75 tons of opium were being exported to China each year.

THE START OF CHINA'S DECLINE

Following the collapse of the Ming dynasty, China was ruled between 1644 and 1911 by the foreign Qing dynasty. Hailing from the southeast of Manchuria the new leaders, the Manchus, went through a period of acculturation and consolidated their power base by establishing a healthy working relationship with the Chinese government officials. The Manchus maintained their control on the military and successfully put down a number of rebellions in the 18th century. Through the astute leadership of a succession of Manchu emperors, China enjoyed a period of prosperity and growth.

During the 17th century China could rightly claim to be superior in many ways to her contemporaries in the West, but while the Qing dynasty continued to expand in the 18th century, problems began to appear. During the Ming dynasty and the early part of the Qing era China's population had been prevented from expanding too quickly by a series of epidemics and uprisings. However, with the

THE FUME OF POPPIES

stability of Manchu rule came a sharp rise in the population figure from 100 million in 1650 to 300 million by the turn of the 19th century. It would continue to increase during the century and by 1850 the figure stood at 420 million people. This growth put a great strain on the land, which was already being intensively farmed, and inevitably it led to impoverishment and hardship.

By now European powers were on the ascendancy and were making great technological advances. While the Chinese Government became increasingly bureaucratic, corrupt and inefficient, Western countries were well organized and looking to expand their economies through increased trade. Rather than face up to the reality of the situation, China preferred to retain her haughty indifference to outsiders and cling on to her belief in her innate superiority. The closed-door policy toward Western merchants was in reality more a defensive tactic than a hostile one, for China felt she had everything to lose and nothing to gain through contact with the West.

In 1715 the British built a permanent factory outside the city walls of Canton (Guangzhou) in order to facilitate better trading conditions. Canton lies about 80 miles (200 km) northwest of the Macao peninsula and, with a suitable harbour at Whampoa (Huangpu) just 12 miles (30 km) away, was the preferred entrepôt in the early days of exchange. By 1757 Peking (Beijing) had become concerned by the increase in commerce with the West and designated Canton as the only port where foreigners were permitted to trade.

The barely concealed enmity towards the 'barbarians' and the claustrophobic atmosphere (the city gates remained shut to foreigners, while the factories had to squeeze into a narrow strip of land by the river) did not deter the European merchants and a global trade network flourished. East India carriers of 800 to 1,000 tons set sail from London in the early spring and, after rounding the Cape of Good Hope, would arrive in the South China Sea before the monsoon season (between the months of May and September). Because of the vagaries of the weather, the time a voyage took could vary considerably. In general, a round trip from London to Hong Kong and back would take a total of between 9 and 12 months' sailing time. The Company ships would offload their goods of tin, lead, woollens and cotton from India at Whampoa and reload with the precious cargoes of silk, delicate chinaware and, most importantly, tea. As China's need for raw materials from Europe was questionable at the best of times, the West was forced to pay for the Eastern luxuries in silver. This trade imbalance became increasingly unbearable for the European parties, and was eventually to lead to the Opium Wars of the mid-19th century.

BELOW A bronze market weight in the shape of a bird, used for measuring opium for illegal sale by Chinese shopkeepers. It dates from the mid-19th century, when imports of Indian opium were soaring following China's defeat in the Opium Wars. Commissioner Lin observed before the confrontation, 'the vice has spread far and wide and the poison penetrated deeper and deeper'.

ABOVE This painting of *c.*1810 shows a row of Hongs, or trading bases, on the wharf-side at Canton. Flags identify each factory's nationality, as France, Holland, Denmark, Sweden and the USA followed the British lead of 1715 and set up offices. The stringent restrictions of the so-called 'Canton System', in which an imperial household official supervised all transactions, were much reduced after the Opium Wars.

THE MISSION OF LORD MACARTNEY

The exclusion of the outside world, as noted by Arthur Cotterell in his *History of China*, was in part a protective measure adopted by the Manchu to maintain their own supremacy. When the British Ambassador Lord Macartney visited the great Manchu Emperor Qianlong in 1793, he was received not in the grand Summer Palace but rather in the more appropriate setting of a horsehair yurt or tent. Qianlong was distinctly unimpressed by the British delegation and their gifts, and in a letter to George III he wrote: 'Our ways have no resemblance to yours, and even were your envoy competent to acquire some rudiments of them, he could not transplant them to your barbarous land. Strange and costly objects do not interest me. As your Ambassador can see for himself, we possess all things. I set no value on strange objects and ingenious, and have no use for your country's manufactures.' His lack of enthusiasm was reciprocated by Lord Macartney, who acutely perceived the dangers in China's resistance to foreign developments and predicted 'a nation that does not advance must retrograde and finally fall back to barbarism and misery'. At the time of his mission, few provinces could meet their taxation targets, and the extravagances and corruption of the court were increasing pressure on the empire's social and economic structures.

A broad lack of understanding of the Chinese people, their culture, customs, sense of justice and etiquette was to have an extremely damaging effect. During Lord Macartney's diplomatic visit he had refused to 'kowtow' to the emperor, that is, to prostrate himself three times in front of the emperor as a way of showing deference to a superior. In order to retain face, the court officials falsified the records and reported that Macartney had shown proper obeisance. When Lord Amherst embarked on a similarly futile mission in 1816, he too was prepared to bow appropriately, but refused to kowtow. Sensing a repeat of the Macartney débâcle, the mandarins hatched a plan to deprive Amherst of sleep and then give him a quick shove in the back when he was bowing to the emperor. Despite his tiredness Amherst avoided the clumsy attempt to make him appear to kowtow and maintained his dignity. Sadly, these petty disputes over protocol prevented any serious discussions from taking place, and yet another emissary, Lord Napier, had no greater success. Blame should be apportioned equally, for China's intransigence was matched by Britain's failure to comprehend or reconcile the cultural differences. When the East India Company's charter ended in 1834, only a handful of people involved in the foreign trade structures could converse with the Chinese in their own language.

OPIUM SMUGGLING

The policy of encouraging China to buy opium was instigated because of the vast trade deficit between the two countries. Whilst China's export of tea and silk continued to expand, the East India Company could not obtain sufficient silver to trade in return, particularly with the disruption to international trade patterns caused by the Napoleonic Wars in Europe. The source of the flood of opium that was to engulf China in the 19th century can be traced back to 1772 when Warren Hastings, the British Governor-General of India, recognized the economic potential of the opium industry the Company had acquired thanks to Robert Clive's victory at Plassey (see page 122). He established a colonial monopoly, which gave the Company the exclusive right to purchase opium from Bengal's farmers and sell it to private merchants for export. As the opium trade was officially illegal in China, the Company could not risk exporting the opium itself, for it did not want to damage its trade monopoly in Canton. Instead, private traders who were licensed and controlled by the Company smuggled the opium to Macao on what were known as 'country ships'. The island of Lintin later became the centre for organized smuggling, in which huge quantities of opium were transferred from Western ships to fast, flat-bottomed Chinese vessels known locally as 'fast crabs'. These boats were manned by up to 40 oarsmen who could easily evade the lackadaisical customs officers (an added incentive to row harder when pursued by customs was the knowledge that the death penalty awaited those who were captured). Although the official, and highly disingenuous, policy of the East India Company was to refuse to acknowledge the trade, there was in effect, as Henry Hobhouse has powerfully described, a triangular trade established to parallel that of the Caribbean, Africa and Europe. In this version, opium was bought from the East India Company in auctions at Calcutta and traded for silver

ABOVE A Mogul-style portrait of Warren Hastings, who became India's first governor-general in 1774. He strengthened the political authority of the Bengal colony and founded a Board of Revenue in Calcutta to control income from the province. Officially unrecognized by the East India Company, the illicit opium trade made a significant contribution to the region's riches.

coin with Chinese merchants; this was then brought back to Calcutta and sold via banker's drafts to the East India Company, whose agents used it to buy tea in Canton. Any immediate connection with opium was consequently avoided, and the Company's responsibility for the traffic could officially be denied.

Another futile attempt at ridding China of opium was made in 1799 when the emperor decreed a total ban on the drug. Trade duly increased and smuggled opium found its way into the imperial court at Peking. The emperor was horrified to discover that some of his bodyguards and eunuchs were addicts. Initially it had been young men from rich families who had developed a taste for opium, but soon drug taking was to be found in all walks of life. It affected business and weakened the government infrastructure, which was already in a state of decline. Bribery was endemic, and one of the ways the Company managed to justify its actions was to point out that if the Chinese wanted to stop the import of opium they only had to enforce their own laws. Of course, this was not as straightforward in practice as it might sound. One of the demands China made for allowing trade in Canton was that a select number of businessmen, supervised by an Imperial Commissioner of Customs (known as the Hoppo to the British) was given a strict monopoly on trade. This was known as 'The Canton System' and it allowed the guild of businessmen, called the Hong merchants, to fix prices and the volume of trade as they saw fit. There was no recourse to people higher up in the chain of command, such as the mandarins of Canton or the governor of the province. Naturally this system was open to abuse and bribery became the acceptable way of conducting business. Indeed, much of China's administration seemed to be oiled with extravagant fees, backhanders and presents. When a rather officious new governor arrived from Peking and arrested and tortured some local men for their involvement in the opium trade, the Company's response was that business would only be delayed for a short time. All they had to do was work out new bribery rates with officials to take into account the increased risk.

On the whole, this system of conducting business succeeded — ironically, in fact, it proved to be too successful. For the first quarter of the 19th century Britain had deliberately restricted the production of Indian opium exports to 4,000 chests, each containing 40 balls and weighing 140 lb (63.5 kg). This was a purely commercial decision, made in order to maintain a high price for the opium, rather than any expression of concern over the number of Chinese becoming addicts (the Company's directors supported the restriction as long as it resulted in good profits, otherwise: 'the expediency of proportionately increasing the annual provision will naturally engage your attention'). It is no coincidence that the amount of revenue raised by the opium trade managed to cover the cost of purchasing of China's tea crop without reducing value through oversupply of a commodity in such escalating demand. The illicit trade was well balanced and the Company, keen to retain this equilibrium, was reluctant to increase opium production. However, with potentially vast profits to be made (the price per chest of opium went from 415 rupees in 1799 to 2,428 rupees in 1814) and an apparently insatiable demand for opium in China, it was inevitable that foreign competitors would try to undercut the British. India, after all, was not the only supplier of the drug. Opium from Turkey, for example, was transported all the way round the Cape to China by American entrepreneurs who were forbidden to bid at the opium markets in Calcutta. This elongated trade route remained in operation until Americans were finally allowed access to Indian opium following

BELOW A photograph of an opium den, c.1900. Consumption of the drug in China spanned all social classes, from peasants to the Dowager Empress, Ci Xi. As the empire fragmented into corruption and territorial leases to foreign powers, opium became a symbol of national decline.

the end of the Company's monopoly in 1834. A more serious and prolonged threat, however, emerged from the native states in western India, where the princes were encouraging their people to grow the popular Malwa opium. Like its Bengal rival, Malwa opium was of a high quality and sold for twice as much as its inferiors. By 1811 Malwa opium had captured 40 per cent of the Chinese market, and a little over a decade later Britain abandoned its self-imposed production restrictions, lowered its opium prices and encouraged new areas to grow poppies (by the 1840s cultivation had doubled to 176,000 acres or 71,200 ha). Through a policy of coercion and co-operation introduced in 1827, the Indian Princes were persuaded to sell all their opium through the Company at Bombay or Calcutta. Britain's stranglehold over India was so complete that the Princes knew that any dissenters invariably lost control of their thrones and sometimes even forfeited their lives.

The illicit drug trade continued to flourish and the introduction of fast, armed boats known as opium clippers ensured that even when the Chinese made a show of law enforcement, the authorities could easily be evaded. By 1820 'country' ships were so confident of not being intercepted that they were sailing up the Canton River to the port of Whampoa. Between 1820 and the outbreak of the First Opium War just under 20 years later China's opium imports increased nearly 10 fold from 270 tons to 2,558 tons. This naturally had a profoundly deleterious effect on the health of China's population and it is estimated that by the 1830s there were 3,000,000 addicts. Meanwhile, profits from the trade were immense; in 1830, Hobhouse has estimated that the British exported nearly 1,500 tons of opium per year, generating nearly £2 million in contemporary currency (the equivalent of almost £1 billion today).

THE IMPACT OF OPIUM

Through the publication of works such as Thomas De Quincey's *Confessions of an English Opium-eater* (1821), the British public were becoming more conversant with opium and the dangers of addiction. Concern over the Government's involvement in the iniquitous business of drug smuggling presented Lord Palmerston with the opportunity to send a Government official to attempt to persuade the Chinese into opening up their ports to foreigners and to legalize the opium trade. Palmerston claimed that this course of action would help to stem the flow of opium and would therefore be beneficial to China; however, there were other reasons for wanting improved trade relations. The East India Company's monopoly had been abolished by the British Parliament in 1833 and the trade was subsequently open to any individual. Free traders flocked to Macao and business flourished – between 1830 and 1836 the number of chests of imported Indian opium rose from 18,956 to 30,302. Led by the partnership of James Matheson and William Jardine, merchants were now illegally selling opium along the coast of China. To fill the administrative role of the Company's old Select Committee in Canton the British Government appointed Lord Napier of Meristoun as Chief Superintendent of Trade and dispatched him to Canton in 1834. Napier was a retired naval officer with no background in business or knowledge of China. It appears that he was selected by Palmerston because it was felt that he would be able to withstand the pressure of the posting and to present Britain's case forcefully. Unfortunately Napier was also a tactless man, who lacked the cunning necessary to outwit the Chinese. He upset the Viceroy of Canton by his demands and failure to play the protocol game, and a partial trade ban was imposed followed by an order for the British to leave Canton. In response Napier called two naval frigates up the Canton River to provide a show of strength, but the Chinese simply blocked their way back. Now suffering from fever, Napier was advised by his doctor (and to everyone's relief) to return to Macao for the good of his health. The final ignominy for the Chief Superintendent of Trade was having to accept the offer of a berth on a Chinese boat on his journey to the coast. The 80 mile (130 km) voyage took five days to complete and the boat was assiduously escorted by Chinese guards the whole way. Napier's fever worsened and he died a few days after reaching Macao.

One of the greatest obstacles to Sino-Anglo relationships, exemplified by the failure of three successive diplomatic and trade missions, was a complete lack of understanding of one another. British references to the inscrutable and unpredictable Oriental are legion, while China failed to grasp the importance of global events and life beyond her own borders. The first indication China had that she could not be disconnected from the outside world was a minor incident in 1808 when a squadron of British soldiers was landed at Macao. Napoleon had shown his intent to bring Spain and Portugal into his empire and the British Government, aware of how this might destabilize Macao, were resolved to protect their property. The imperial court took exception to British warships in the Canton estuary and demanded that they withdraw. The British duly complied and the Chinese were placated, but, as historians such as J.M. Roberts acknowledge, the event should have indicated to the Chinese how occurrences on the other side of the world could have ramifications for their own country. Britain was an aggressively acquisitive and confident nation, whose empire-building programme was powered by industrialization and implemented by soldiers and merchants. In contrast China viewed such people with scorn and held no ambition to conquer lands thousands of miles away.

Opium was now undermining China's social and economic life. A paper placarded in the streets of Canton highlighted the physical horrors of opium smoking in an attempt to control addiction levels: 'the constitution gives way, the interior gradually decays, thousands of worms and maggots gnaw the intestines, their faces become discoloured … their necks sink in, and their whole frame is hateful as that of a ghost or devil'. Drug abuse provided a graphic metaphor for the corruption at the heart of the body politic, as acknowledged by a Chinese Minister of State in 1842: 'multitudes of our Chinese subjects consume it, wasting their property and destroying their lives; and the calamities arising therefrom are unutterable.' It was rampant among Chinese soldiers and the civil service leading to widespread corruption and low morale. China's social structure laid emphasis on moral obligation and responsibility to the family, community and ultimately the emperor himself, the acknowledged mediator between nature and human society. In this role the emperor was more akin to a spiritual leader than simply a head of state, and his perceived inability to combat the destruction wrought by opium addiction could be seen as a threat to the status of the Qing themselves. Something had to be seen to be done.

There were calls from some Chinese officials for the legalization of opium with the payment of duty. They pointed out that prohibition had completely failed to suppress the trade and argued that the ban had in fact added to the problem as smuggling had created a network of illegal activities. Harsh punishments had not succeeded because the importer was not going to be punished himself, rather he would just have to raise the level of bribery. Besides, if a smuggler knew that capture meant the death penalty he would risk everything, including his life, not to be caught – what more did he have to lose? The Emperor Dao Guang had personal experience of the devastation wrought by the poppy, for three of his sons had died of opium addiction. He considered the legalization option, but was won over by its opponents, who argued that as it was the opium traders who were the cause of the spread of the drug, the logical course of action was to target them. Consequently the emperor entrusted the task of eradicating the opium trade to a keen prohibitionist, Commissioner Li Zexu. Li was dispatched to Canton in 1839 and soon after arriving he drafted a letter to Queen Victoria in which he forcibly expressed his feelings:

there is a class of evil foreigner that makes opium and brings it for sale, tempting fools to destroy themselves, merely in order to reap profit. Formerly the number of opium smokers was small; but now the vice has spread far and wide and the poison penetrated deeper and deeper. If there are some foolish people who yield to this craving to their own detriment, it is they who have brought upon themselves their own ruin, and in a country so populous and flourishing, we can well do without them. But our great, unified Manchu Empire regards itself as responsible for the habits and morals of its subjects and cannot rest content to see any of them become victims to a deadly poison. For this reason we have decided to inflict very severe penalties on opium dealers and opium smokers, in order to put a stop for ever to the propagation of this vice. It appears that this poisonous article is

OPINIONS ON THE OPIUM TRADE

In 1856, Major-General Alexander of the Madras Army addressed a series of letters to the Earl of Shaftesbury — reformer, philanthropist and Member of Parliament — about the effects of British opium smuggling on India, China and the commerce of Great Britain. He quotes figures suggesting that in 1856, Britain had received from China produce to the value of just over £9 million; £2.3 million of this was paid for with legal merchandise, whereas £6.7 million was paid for in opium or in silver — the proceeds of selling contraband opium to China.

The effects of this, he says, are threefold. Firstly, 'the consumption of this destructive drug is just so much capital destroyed, besides involving thousands of Chinese families annually in ruin, causing the death of many more, and spreading poverty and crime over the land.' Secondly, within China, 'the whole machinery of commerce is impeded and contracted within the narrowest dimensions'. And thirdly, 'The injurious influence on the legal foreign trade is plain. Our own prosperity as a commercial nation is wrapt up with the prosperity of the nations with which we deal. As China becomes less and less able to bear the drain of silver, she is gradually paying for the opium with her produce, thus supplanting the foreign legal merchandise.'

Alexander also quotes a number of Chinese commentators who echo his words, such as Kinshan, one of the 'literati' of Nanjing, writing in 1836:

Opium is a poisonous drug, brought from foreign countries. At first the smokers of it merely strive to follow the fashion of the day, but in the sequel the poison takes effect, and the habit becomes fixed. The sleeping smokers are like corpses, — lean and haggard as demons; such are the injuries it does to life; it throws whole families into ruin, dissipates every kind of property, and destroys man himself.

By 1883, the then Governor of Hong Kong, Sir John Pope Hennessy, was reporting that:

In the little colony under my government one million sterling changes hands every month in the article of opium. But, with commercial activity and profits, there comes an increase of crime from opium, from its consumption, and from its smuggling. Hong Kong wages a chronic opium war on a small scale with China. A desperate class of men, the opium smugglers make the colony the base of their operations...'.

Meanwhile, an executive from the firm of Jardine, Matheson, & Co. and Chairman of the Hong Kong Chamber of Commerce writes in 1882 to the President of the London Chamber of Commerce of Hennessy's account: 'The picture thus sensationally drawn is one which, from its great exaggerations, gives an untrue representation of the state of things prevailing in these waters...'. His letter, reflecting the views of several in officialdom, is attached as an appendix to William H. Bereton's questionable little book, *The Truth About Opium: Being a Refutation of the Fallacies of the Anti-Opium Society and a Defence of the Indo-China Opium Trade*.

Perhaps more honest, although it is nonetheless shocking, is the attitude of R.C. Hurley, writing from the India Office in Hong Kong in 1909. He extols the virtues of opium in controlling the 'natural, inherent restlessness' of the Chinese people. He observes that 'in the course of a most natural evolution Opium has been called upon to play a part not unimportant, both as a controlling sedative as well as a developing agent and useful medium'. (Opium's position as a 'useful medium', as Hurley describes it, refers to the amount of revenue accruing to the British government.)

These 'defences' of the opium trade make wholly unconvincing reading. The last word should perhaps go to a Chinese paper written to dissuade men from opium-smoking, which was posted up for general public edification in the streets of Canton:

In every item, in every respect, the evil is becoming more grave daily, more deeply-rooted than before; so much so, that its baneful influence seems to threaten, little by little, to degrade the whole population of the Celestial Empire to a level with reptiles, wild beasts, dogs and swine.

manufactured by certain devilish persons in places subject to your rule. It is not, of course, either made or sold at your bidding, nor do all the countries you rule produce it, but only certain of them. I am told that in your own country opium smoking is forbidden under severe penalties. This means that you are aware of how harmful it is. But better than to forbid the smoking of it would be to forbid the sale of it and, better still, to forbid the production of it, which is the only way of cleansing the contamination at its source. So long as you do not take it yourselves, but continue to make it and tempt the people of China to buy it, you will be showing yourselves careful of your own lives, but careless of the lives of other people, indifferent in your greed for gain to the harm you do to others; such conduct is repugnant to human feeling and at variance with the Way of Heaven.

THE FIRST OPIUM WAR

Li's first action was to demand that the British merchants hand over their illegal stocks of opium. Over the years the merchants had had to put up with several zealous officials who had attempted to assert the law and they assumed that Li was another such figure. To appease him, and protect their tea export business, the British offered to hand over 1,000 chests of opium. Li was not to be fobbed off quite so easily, however, for he knew that the trade was much more extensive than the traders were claiming. A ban on all trade and movement of British ships along the Canton River was imposed at Li's behest and the Chief Superintendent of Trade, Captain Charles Elliot, rushed to Canton to try and placate Li. Elliot realized that Li was determined to carry out the emperor's edict, and advised the opium merchants to hand over all the remaining opium, which came to a total of 20,000 chests. The opium was mixed with salt and lime before being flushed into the sea. Li noted with amusement the interest the locals showed in watching the process, although he records that they were only allowed to observe from behind fences to prevent any pilfering.

This was to be Li's first and last successful operation against the opium dealers, for Elliot demanded that the British leave Canton and return to the coast. Here smuggling became such an enormous enterprise that Li was powerless to stop it. His crackdown on customs officers was also doomed to failure for there were just too many corrupt individuals to deal with the organization as a whole. The vital tea industry was maintained by using American go-betweens, who bought the tea at Canton and then exchanged it with the British in Hong Kong.

On 21 June 1840 the British expeditionary force under the command of Sir James Gordon Bremer arrived at Macao, heralding the start of the First Opium War. During the next two years the naval flotilla consisting of five ships of war, three steamers and 21 transports were to take on and defeat a nation with a population of over 300 million, generating considerable contemporary shock.

This remarkable achievement was due to a combination of superior technology and tactics being used against a undisciplined, demoralized force. Despite the early warning signals of Britain's global ambitions, China had not taken any precautions and had slipped behind militarily and technologically. The country had no navy as such, but rather there were a number of smaller forces under the control of local governors-general. Communications were a shambles as officers in charge sent back highly inaccurate accounts of engagements. Wishing to get recognized and rewarded, the officers falsified the records by claiming to have inflicted far greater damage and suffered far fewer losses than they had. The emperor was consequently unaware of the true status of the conflict with the British. In skirmish after skirmish the Chinese were surprised by the advanced weaponry and skill displayed by the enemy. When the British landed at Amoy in September 1841 they suffered no losses while at least 100 Chinese fell beneath the deadly fusillade of musket fire. The scenario was repeated as the British laid siege to fort after fort, or occupied cities that they then ransomed back to the Chinese. In one battle the British prevailed despite being outnumbered 40-to-1.

At the start of the conflict operations were confined to the Canton River environs, but after the capture of the strategic island of Hong Kong Bremer turned the fleet northward. His intention was to intimidate the emperor into submission through a dramatic display of British firepower. Wusong, Shanghai and Zhenjiang were shelled and captured by landing forces during June and July 1842. The British suffered severe losses during the campaign from sunstroke, malaria, dysentery and cholera. Of the 34 men who died during the capture of Zhenjiang, 16 perished from heat exhaustion. The emperor relieved Commissioner Li of his post and sent him into exile.

Li's downfall was precipitated by his mistaken belief that seizure of opium and the threat to end legitimate trade would force the British into submission. With a trade so steeped in the art of smuggling and avoidance of official edicts it was no surprise that Western merchants were able to circumnavigate the new regulations and keep the contraband flowing into China's opium dens and shops. China had been severely shaken by its ineffectual defences and the clear superiority of Western war machinery. For a country effectively to be held ransom by a small naval fleet was deeply humiliating, and served to highlight the weakness of the empire to predatory Western powers. It was only some neat chicanery by the Chinese authorities that delayed the inevitable capitulation until the summer of 1842. Signed at the end of the war, the Treaty of Nanjing forced the Chinese Government to cede the island of Hong Kong, pay a hefty fine and open the ports of Amoy, Fuzhou, Shanghai and Ningbo. This was the first time the Chinese had ceded sovereign land to a foreign power and allowed its citizens to live under foreign rule; it contrasted deeply to the previous century when all foreign trade was conducted by the *yang guizi* in semi-official limbo at Canton.

ABOVE The dramatic destruction of Chinese war junks in the First Opium War of 1841 is portrayed in this 19th-century engraving. The limitations of the Chinese naval power were starkly exposed by the superior fire-power of the British and Indian force, only 4,000 strong. The Qing dynasty's weakness was noted by several predatory European countries.

The financial burden of the treaty put an onerous strain on the depleted resources of the Qing dynasty and left it vulnerable to attack at a time when European forces, sustained by their worldwide empires and industrial technology, were at their most confident. The treaty also fixed the customs duties on imports at such a low level that China was unable to protect her inchoate industries from cheap imports. In the long term, however, it was the opening of the ports that was to have the most harmful effect. Britain assumed the mantle of imperial potentate, much to the annoyance of the other Western powers – led by the USA and France – who successfully negotiated their own treaties with the enervated Chinese Government. However, China still refused to legalize opium.

Everyday life in China after 1842 was hard as the economy suffered under the severe impositions of the Nanjing Treaty. Although the Manchu leaders had been accepted many years earlier, there remained a residual dislike of being ruled by 'foreigners'. Rebellion was fomented by angry citizens who chaffed at the incompetent authorities and the influence of the 'foreign devils'. Matters came to a head in 1850 when the scholar Hong Xiuquan led a countryside rebellion against the Qing dynasty. Believing himself to be the brother of Jesus Christ, Hong wanted to impose authoritarian Christian rule. The Taiping rebellion lasted 14 years; it was eventually put down with the help of Western powers at the staggering cost of 30 million lives. Further concessions to foreign regimes – the Treaty of Tianjin (1858) and Convention of Peking (1860) – were the result.

The 10 years following the First Opium War saw the import of Indian opium double and by 1858 it had reached 4,810 tons per year. Distracted by the Taiping rebellion and unwilling to risk a further confrontation with the West, the Chinese authorities watched helplessly as ever-increasing amounts of opium were smuggled onto the mainland. When the smugglers realized that the Canton authorities were not risking the wrath of the British by searching their ships they registered their vessels as British and sailed around the Canton estuary with impunity. The Western countries were still unhappy with the outcome of the Nanjing Treaty, however, for the opium trade was still technically illegal and communication with the Chinese authorities continued at a local level with the imperial court remaining detached and isolated in Peking. In 1854 the British and French requested that their treaties be revised, but their demands were rejected. The emperor had also determined to instigate a new initiative to stop the nefarious drug trade. He sent Yeh Ming-Chen, a supporter of Commissioner Li, to Canton to cultivate anti-British sentiment among the local Chinese merchants. This he proceeded to do with considerable success and soon the British began looking for an excuse for a show of arms to emphasize their superiority. Yeh duly provided one when in October 1856 the crew of a smuggling boat, the *Arrow*, were arrested near Canton. The boat had been flying the Union Jack at the time, for it had been registered in Hong Kong (although later it was discovered that the licence had expired by the time of her capture) and the British reacted with righteous indignation. The navy was summoned and when the Chinese refused to capitulate Canton was bombarded (Yeh's official residence was given special attention).

The Second Opium War, which lasted from 1856 to 1860, was similar in nature to the First. Initially fighting was concentrated in the south, with Canton being captured in 1858. When the Chinese resistance continued the British forces, aided by the French, targeted Peking. The city was looted and the Summer Palace was symbolically destroyed. The emperor was left under no illusion that peace negotiations were to be on British terms and there was to be no reneging on the deal. The petty excuse of the *Arrow* incident had served its purpose and the importation of opium was legalized. Not everyone was convinced the war could be morally justified and the leader of the armed forces, Lord Elgin, was so repulsed by the effect opium was having on China that he declined to give it a prominent part in the ensuing treaty.

Of course, the war had been fought for commercial reasons rather than injured national pride and in the aftermath China was once again forced to pay another forfeit. Ten more ports were opened to foreigners and imports of Indian opium rose from 4,800 tons in 1859 to 6,700 tons 20 years later and addiction spread throughout China. Even the Dowager Empress Ci Xi, who disastrously encouraged the nationalistic forces in the Boxer rebellion to assault the Legation quarter of Peking and incur the wrath of foreign powers, was known to indulge the habit. To countermand the British monopoly on the trade Chinese officials cut their losses and began to encourage local opium production. Poppy cultivation in the southwestern provinces of Sichuan and Yunnan spread rapidly after 1880 and began to challenge the higher quality Indian imports. A quarter of a century later the first official statistics show that the two regions were producing 19,100 tons of opium, just over half the national total. As the Indian trade declined the level of addiction did not decrease, rather the availability of Chinese homegrown opium encouraged drug taking. By 1906 China had 13.5 million addicts consuming about 39,000 tons of opium per year, and it was becoming increasingly prevalent in European countries, requiring some action from their governments. In the same year the Chinese and British governments finally introduced a treaty restricting the Indian opium trade, which was followed four years later by an agreement to dismantle the Indo-Chinese opium trade.

CONSUMPTION AT HOME

A great variety of opium preparations with different beneficial claims kept appearing right up to the 20th century. The most famous was created by Dr Thomas Sydenham in the 1660s when he combined 2 ounces of strained opium,

CHASING THE DRAGON

In 1850 an American medical doctor, Nathan Allen, wrote an *Essay on the Opium Trade* in which he describes in fascinating detail the preparation of opium in China and the manner in which it was smoked. To preface the account, he describes a first-hand experience of the purchase of the opium:

> We went on board this ship and saw the process of preparing the inspissated juice of the Opium for test, previous to purchase. On opening the chests, and clearing away a number of dry poppy leaves, an oblong dry cake, of a brown color, was taken out, weighing four or five pounds. In the boxes made up by the East India Company, greater care is taken ... A piece of Opium is taken as a sample from three separate balls, and prepared in three separate pots for smoking, to test its freedom from adulteration ... Shropps, Opium dealers, interpreters, and native accountants, were closely

standing together on different parts of the deck, which wore a busy and painfully animated appearance.

Later, he quotes from the writings of Mr S.W. Williams, who closely observes the actions of an opium smoker:

> The Opium smoker always lies down ... he holds the pipe ... so near to the lamp that the bowl can be brought up to it without stirring himself. A little Opium of the size of a pea, being taken on the end of a spoon-headed needle, is put upon the hole of the bowl, and set on fire at the lamp, and inhaled at one whiff, so that none of the smoke shall be lost ... When the pipe has burned out, the smoker lies listless for a moment while the fumes are dissipating, and then repeats the process until he has spent all his purchase ...

I ounce of saffron, a dram of cinnamon and of cloves in a pint of sherry wine to create a tincture he called 'Sydenhams's Laudanum'. Sydenham proselytized the cause of opium to an even greater extent than Paracelsus and was unstinting in his admiration:

> here I cannot but break out in praise of the great God, the giver of all good things, who hath granted to the human race, as comfort in their afflictions, no medicine of the value of opium, either in regard to the number of diseases it can control, or its efficiency in extirpating them … Medicine would be a cripple without it; and whosoever understands it well, will do more with it alone than he could well hope to do from any single medicine.

ABOVE An elegant case for storing opium, dating from the late 19th century. The box itself was produced in Lisbon, showing how prevalent use of the drug was to become in Europe. The 'Chinese' scenes on its panels reflect a contemporary fascination with the mysterious Orient.

Laudanum became a popular painkiller, but the other, self-destructive side of opium became increasingly obvious. Addiction to opium was recognized but quietly ignored during the 17th and 18th centuries. The physical and mental cravings were noted by such people as George Young, Dr Samuel Crumpe and Dr John Jones, but the prevailing belief of the time was that the dangers posed by opium were nominal. In his work *Mysteries of Opium Reveal'd* Dr Jones was one of the first to tackle the problems of addiction and withdrawal, but along with his contemporaries Jones passed no moral judgement on opium taking and felt that taken in moderation opium was harmless. Addiction was rare, and public attention was focused on the more evident damage of cheap spirits such as gin.

In 1806 a young German scientist called Frederich Sertuerner published the results of his successful experiments to find the primary active ingredient in opium. By diluting opium in acid and then neutralizing it with ammonia Sertuerner had managed to isolate the alkaloid morphine, which was 10 times stronger than normal opium. Named after Morpheus, the Greek god of sleep and dreams, morphine became such an integral part of surgery in the early 19th century that in 1831 Sertuerner was honoured by the French Government for his achievement. It was praised as 'God's own medicine' for its reliability and sustained effectiveness. The importance of morphine as a pain reliever was greatly increased in 1853 when the hypodermic syringe was perfected by Dr Alexander Wood. It was found that injected morphine acted much more quickly than when it was taken orally. The discovery had an immediate impact, for soldiers injured in battle could be given instantaneous pain relief. As with all 'wonder cures', however, there was a downside to the development. In the second half of the 19th century many soldiers were returning from conflicts addicted to this new opiate, which later became known as 'the soldiers' disease' or 'the army disease'.

BELOW An engraving of an opium den in London's East End, published in *The Graphic* in 1880. The accompanying article notes that 'sixpence worth, about a thimble full and half as much again' was the normal allowance. As the price of opium in Britain fell, many working-class smokers turned to it as a cheaper source of intoxication than alcohol.

By 1830 recreational and medicinal consumption of opium in Britain was still on the increase and 22,000 lb (10,000 kg) per year were being imported from Turkey and India. It was not until 1868 and the introduction of the first Pharmacy Act that an attempt to restrict opium consumption was made. Just six years later the most potent opium derivative was discovered by C.R. Wright when he boiled morphine over a stove. The result was heroin. Although it was tried and tested by a number of scientific bodies, heroin was marketed to the public in 1898 as a non-addicting substitute for codeine. In 1900 it passed a review board, which decided that the likelihood of addiction was acceptably low.

In some ways the havoc that heroin addiction has brought to the West in the last century could be viewed as poetic justice for its economic and political exploitation of a decaying Chinese empire. By the turn of the 19th century, China had already endured over 100 years of opium dependency and become a nation debilitated by the drug. Despite the modern British Government's enthusiasm for drug prohibition, it should not be forgotten that the biggest drugs cartel the world has seen once resided in the House of Commons, Westminster.

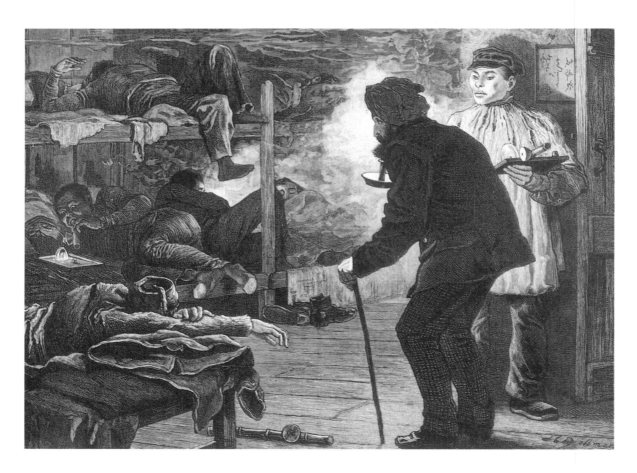

OPIUM AND THE ROMANTICS

Middle-class consumption of opium – often in the form of a tincture, the liquid laudanum – in 19th-century Britain was probably widespread, but the best-documented cases are, unsurprisingly, those of famous contemporaneous writers. Where opium eating was a significant part of the writers' daily lives, so it often became significant to the characters appearing in their works of fiction.

The two writers of fiction most famously addicted to opium are Samuel Taylor Coleridge, who wrote 'Kubla Khan' in 1797 while taking opium, and Wilkie Collins. Commentators and critics debate fiercely the extent to which the writings of these and others of the so-called 'Romantics' are influenced by opium: some believe that much imagery is a result of the authors' addiction, while others argue that alternative creative influences are more significant to the work.

It is also arguable to what extent these writers – who also include Dickens, Byron, Shelley, Keats and Elizabeth Barrett Browning – took opium for what we would now describe as recreational use. It seems clear that the initial use of the drug was often for medical reasons, for the relief of physical pain. The relief of stress, or severe mental pain, was another catalyst. As addiction progressed, the use of opium was essential for sleep, work and day-to-day functioning, and the writers cannot have been unaware of its stimulant and hallucinogenic effects.

There is strong evidence, for example, that Wilkie Collins lived in almost constant pain as a result of a serious rheumatic condition and that laudanum offered him the relief, particularly of sleep, that he needed in order to function. Opium is central to the plot of his great novel *The Moonstone*, in which the addiction of the semi-autobiographical character Ezra Jennings is described in detail – his terrible opium-induced dreams, his relief from pain and the stupefying effects of the drug. Wilkie Collins wrote the novel when his own consumption of the drug was at its height – it is said that the huge dose of laudanum that he took nightly, about a tablespoonful, was sufficient to kill someone who was less addicted.

Thomas De Quincey first took opium in 1804 for the relief of chronic stomach problems, his self-medication mutating in time to become equally a relief for anxiety and an indulgence of the pleasurable effects of the drug. In 1821 he published *Confessions of an English Opium-eater* in the *London Magazine*. The book describes his encounter with opium and the pleasure it afforded him, his subsequent addiction to the drug and the terrible mental pain that it caused. Thus opium became the entire inspiration for the literary work, whose complexity lies in the author's struggle to untangle the realities of his own life and the deceptions induced by the drug.

In the latter part of the book, De Quincey describes at length the pain of his opium-induced dreams; here he is in ancient Egypt, for example:

> I was buried, for a thousand years, in stone coffins, with mummies and sphinxes, in narrow chambers at the heart of eternal pyramids. I was kissed, with cancerous kisses, by crocodiles; and laid, confounded with all unutterable slimy things, amongst reeds and Nilotic mud.
>
> I thus give the reader some slight abstraction of my Oriental dreams, which always filled me with such amazement at the monstrous scenery, that horror seemed absorbed, for a while, in sheer astonishment. Sooner or late, came a reflux of feeling that swallowed up the astonishment, and left me, not so much in terror, as in hatred and abomination of what I saw. Over every form, and threat, and punishment, and dim sightless incarceration, brooded a sense of eternity and infinity that drove me into an oppression as of madness.

Contemporary reactions to De Quincey's *Confessions* were strikingly understated. Although there was condemnation of the book's subject matter, this first detailed description of English opium consumption was also the source of calm interest and appreciation of some masterly writing. Opium eating, after all, was not an unusual habit; by the middle of the 19th century, the British were consuming around 60,000 lb ((27,200 kg) of the drug annually. For many readers, De Quincey was eloquently describing a common experience.

THE QUEST FOR QUININE

LEFT This botanical drawing of a cinchona plant includes cross-sections of its bark. Skilful techniques of 'mossing', developed in the 1870s in India, helped to preserve the tree when parts of its bark were harvested.

ABOVE A hardwood carving of a district officer, believed to be a Mr B.J.A. Matthews, from Yoruba, Nigeria – a region notorious for its deadly malaria.

THE IMPACT OF CINCHONA – the tree species from which quinine is manufactured – on colonial expansion is indirect but important. The febrifugal properties of its bark were known to the Native Americans of Peru, and quinine was recognized in Europe as a cure for malaria by the mid-17th century. As foreign exploration and overseas trading bases increased, the need for cinchona grew in proportion and serious inroads were made into the natural stocks of Peru. Only through an effective plant transfer, from the Andes to the Nilgiri Hills of southern India, was cinchona established in plantations – an exercise conceived of, and supported by, the British empire's network of botanical gardens radiating from Kew Gardens. Greater availability of quinine opened up previously inaccessible regions of Africa and Asia to European acquisition.

DISCOVERY AND EARLY USE

It is supremely ironic that the continent from which the natural treatment for malaria first came was not afflicted with the disease until European settlers introduced it. The Native Americans already used 'quinquina' (the 'bark of barks) as a herbal remedy to treat fevers, and it seems very likely that it was they who discovered that the febrifugal properties of bark from certain species of *Cinchona* tree also provided some relief for the symptoms of malaria. Certainly the knowledge of plants' medical properties among the Peruvian Indians was considerable; they used an infusion of leaves for skin diseases, young branches for dental treatments, diluted resin as a laxative, dry resin for intestinal problems and an infusion of bark to combat swelling in the legs. The extraordinary skill of these born naturalists greatly impressed the Europeans with whom they came into contact. Documents from soldiers, merchants or missionaries bear witness to their remarkable knowledge of the plants, and significantly the Peruvian forces of Pizarro much preferred to have their wounds treated by the Native Americans than the European doctors.

It is widely believed that the Peruvian Indians told the Jesuit missionaries of their cinchona discovery around 1630. As early as 1633, Calancha, an Augustinian monk living in Peru, described how cinchona bark was ground into a fine powder and used to treat fever. It is possible that the missionaries may have come upon the bark independently, however, for one of their methods of discovering new medicines was to chew the bark of different trees. Cinchona bark is bitter and was therefore considered to have medicinal qualities.

In Europe, little progress was made in the understanding of what caused malaria until the late 19th century, although the disease was much more widespread on the Continent than it is today. The word 'malaria' is a derivation of the Italian *mala aria* or bad air, as it was thought that the disease was caused by miasma emanating from swamps. This was a logical deduction in the absence of modern scientific knowledge, for boggy areas and swamps were the breeding grounds for the malaria-transmitting mosquito. Prior to the introduction of quinine, treatments for the disease known from antiquity ranged from the reasonable to the ridiculous. Some physicians mixed all sorts of herbs to try and affect a cure, others bled patients to achieve a balance of blood and bile. One physician took the latter course of action to extremes and, determining the blood was bad, tied off the arteries of a patient, while another, realizing the hopelessness of finding a cure, prescribed reading Homer's *Iliad*. Yet in some areas, centuries before it was understood that malaria is a mosquito-born disease, people took precautions to prevent insects from biting. For example, Herodotus (485–25 BC) noted that in the swampy region of Egypt, some people slept in tower-like structures out of the reach of the mosquitoes, and others slept under fishing nets, the smell deterring the mosquitoes. It is interesting to note that there

are no references to malaria in the Mayan or Aztec civilizations, although the *Anopheles* mosquito is indigenous to the New World.

From the mid-17th century ground cinchona bark mixed with wine was held to be the most effective, albeit a very expensive, treatment for malaria. One traditional remedy was one half cup of bark decoction, one to three times daily. Just as with other new 'wonder drugs', there were those who opposed it. Particularly vehement condemnation of cinchona came from the 17th-century medical establishment. At this time, the profession was still in the thrall of Galen's dictum laid down in the 2nd century AD, which strongly promoted bleeding as a way to expel corrupt humours. Even when the efficacy of the Jesuits'

ABOVE Mass production of quinine opened up Africa and Southeast Asia to commercial interests and travellers. This photograph, dating from 1900, shows a tourist group at the Schwedagon pagoda in Burma.

CINCHONA PLANT PROFILE

BOTANICAL DETAILS

The genus *Cinchona* contains about 40 species of evergreen tree, all of which are indigenous to the Andean highlands of South America. It is a member of the madder family or *Rubiaceae*, which contains over 10,000 species in about 630 genera distributed worldwide, most of which occur in tropical and subtropical regions. Other notable members of the family are the genus *Coffea* (coffee, see page 110) and *Gardenia*,

ornamental garden plants primarily grown for their wonderful smelling flowers.

The importance of these trees lies in their bark, which naturally produces four alkaloid chemicals: cinchonine, quinidine, cinchonidine and quinine. Quinine is a febrifuge, and although not a cure for malaria (because it does not kill the parasite in all stages of its life cycle), it suppresses and reduces the recurring attacks of fever that characterize the disease. Quinine is a white crystalline alkaloid with the formula $C_{20}H_{24}N_2O_2$. It has a bitter taste, which is what gives tonic water its distinctive flavour (tonic waters usually contain around 100 to 300 parts per million quinine). It is almost insoluble in water, but dissolves readily in alcohol and other organic solvents.

ORIGINS

The three most important species and cultivars of the *Cinchona* genus are *Cinchona officinalis* and *C.o* 'Ledgeriana', which naturally occur in Bolivia, Ecuador and southeastern Peru, and *C. pubescens* 'Succirubra', which is native to Peru and Ecuador.

DESCRIPTION

Reaching a mature height of 50–65 ft (15–20 m), all three have laurel-like leaves, and take 3 to 4 years to reach flowering size. The blooms, which look similar to those of lilac, are small, fragrant, and yellow, white or pink in colour and borne in clusters at the end of branches. The fruits are ½–1 in (1–3 cm) oblong capsules with numerous small, flat, winged seeds.

HABITAT

All grow at an elevation of between 4,900 and 9,800 ft (1,500 and 3,000 m), in areas with an average annual rainfall of 590 in (1,500 cm).

PROCESSING

The way the trees are grown and the harvesting technique used today are very similar to those of 150 years ago when the first plantations were established in India (prior to this the bark had been harvested from the wild). Seedling or grafted trees are planted in their cropping positions when 9 in (23 cm) tall and require 10 years' growth before the bark yields its highest quinine content. Strips of bark about 1½ in (4 cm) wide are removed from the trunk by beating the trees with sticks to loosen it, before the strips are peeled away with a knife, rolled, rapidly dried and dispatched to the processing plant, where the quinine is extracted. The stripped parts of the trunk are then 'mossed', a technique developed by William G. McIvor in the 1870s in which layers of damp moss are wrapped around the bare areas. The moss has an antibacterial action that helps prevent infection, while protecting the regenerating bark from dehydration and damage by sunlight. Areas of the trunk are cropped in rotation with the new bark often yielding a higher level of quinine. Bark from pruned branches is also harvested, and hard pruning the older tree helps to promote new growth and increase the yield of each tree. Today it is estimated that the annual world harvest of bark is 5,000 to 10,000 metric tons, converted into 300 to 500 metric tons of quinine for a yield of 5–6 per cent.

Nearly half of the natural quinine produced enters the food industry. A further 30 per cent is converted to Quinidine, a prescription cardiac drug. Although superseded by synthetic antimalarial drugs, natural quinine is making a comeback in areas where strains of the malarial parasite *Plasmodium falciparum* have developed a resistance to manmade drugs. It also remains a herbal remedy, used in Brazil, for example, to treat fevers, anaemia, dyspepsia, debility and gastrointestinal disorders, as well as malaria.

powder was demonstrated, the medical profession shunned it, using the excuse of its religious connections. A more likely reason for its rejection was that bleeding was more profitable. For instead of a short course of efficacious bark infusions, several expensive bleedings would have been administered, and since this was no cure the fevers would return, requiring further, costly treatment.

It was deception that finally saw cinchona accepted as a valuable medicine. In 1678, Robert Talbor was named physician to Charles II in recognition of his curing the king of malaria using a secret formula. A year later, Louis XIV of France purchased the secret to save his son. So grateful was Louis that he gave Talbor a pension, a title and 2,000 *louis d'or*. Perhaps neither king would have been quite so generous had they known Talbor's secret was simply Jesuits' bark. However, Talbor's medical 'triumphs' did ensure that cinchona became accepted as a legitimate treatment for malaria, rather than a Popish plot to poison all Protestants, and *Cortex Peruanus* entered the official London pharmacopoeia. Throughout the 18th century the use of Jesuits' bark became the accepted form of treating malaria, but, although its use became more widespread, it remained a very expensive product. In the 1780s bark retailed at about £1 a pound, and considering 2 lb (4.4 kg) was required to treat a case of malaria, with a subsequent intake of one pound a week as a prophylaxis, only the rich could afford protection from malaria. This remained the case as Europe continued to expand its political dominance over other parts of the world.

The legend of how cinchona bark reached Europe concerns the Countess of Chinchón, wife of the Spanish viceroy of Peru, who in 1638 was very ill with fever in Lima. Nothing the court physician, Dr Juan de Vega, did seemed to help, and in desperation the viceroy agreed with the doctor that a native remedy, quinquina, obtained from Loxa far away to the north in what is now Ecuador, be tried. Cinchona bark was prepared as an infusion of powdered bark mixed with wine. To the great relief of the viceroy, the doctor and no doubt the lady herself, the countess made a full recovery and is alleged to have returned to Spain in 1640 with a considerable quantity of the bark. This she used to help cure fevers on her husband's estates, some 25 miles (40 km) southeast of Madrid. Although these claims are often disputed, Linnaeus named the genus *Cinchona* in her honour, although he mis-spelt the word, an error the 1866 International Botanical Congress decided not to change.

Once the Jesuits realized just how profitable cinchona bark could be if sold in malaria-ridden Europe, it became a thriving export business. They made use of their close connections with many Native Americans to organize the harvest and powdering of the bark in South America and its subsequent sale across Europe, although the Order reaped the economic benefit. 'Jesuits' bark' or 'Jesuits' powder', as cinchona became known in the 1650s, was treated by Protestants with the same grave suspicion that they reserved for the Jesuits. Henry Hobhouse has noted that one celebrated Protestant who gave up his life rather than take 'the powder of the devil' was Oliver Cromwell, who succumbed to malaria in 1658, the same year in which James Thompson first advertised the cinchona bark for sale in England.

The Jesuits maintained their monopoly over supplying cinchona to Spain, Portugal and Italy; it was also readily available in France and, despite Protestant animosity, Germany and the Netherlands. Its widespread use demonstrates just how prevalent malaria was across huge swathes of 17th-century Europe, a problem that persisted right up until the 20th century. Horace Walpole observed that Rome was infected in 1750, and the British occupation of Cypress in 1878–79 cost many lives, not through bloodshed, but because quinine was not issued to the troops. What wiped out malaria in Europe was the draining of low-lying, swampy land. This removed the mosquito's breeding grounds, clearing the insects from the area and so breaking the cycle of infection.

DEVELOPMENT AND CHANGE

As the West colonized North America, it took with it malaria. In the British settlements in Virginia, malaria killed far more colonists than the Native Americans did, and many Native Americans also died from introduced malaria. Indeed, the USA was infected with malaria as late as the 1940s. In another twist of fate, it is often forgotten that many of the West Africans who were enslaved and used as labour in area of America where malaria was endemic, also suffered from sickle-cell anaemia, a natural condition that provides partial immunity to malaria. Although the condition was unknown at the time, it meant that the mortality rate amongst slaves was lower that it otherwise would have been. One of the first military purchases by the Continental Congress at the outbreak of the War of Independence was $300-worth of quinine to protect General Washington's troops. Among the worst outbreaks of malaria or 'swamp fever' was in the summer of 1828 in the settlement of Bytown (Ottawa) and along the construction route of the Rideau Canal. It lasted until the autumn, when the weather became too cold for the mosquito. During the American Civil War (1861–65) malaria hit the Union Army hard, with over 50 per cent of the white troops and 80 per cent of the black soldiers infected annually. Even in the 20th century malaria was a major source of ill-health, with an estimated more than 600,000 cases in 1914; it also saw malaria used somewhat bizarrely as a cure for syphilis. Indeed, J. Wagner von Jauregg was awarded the 1927 Nobel Prize for Medicine for deliberately infecting syphilis sufferers with malaria, which in 3–4 fever cycles literally 'burned to death' the temperature-sensitive bacteria. The patient was then treated with quinine to cure the malaria. This form of malaria therapy continued until the mid-1950s when antibiotics replaced it.

As Britain continued to acquire more territories in which malaria was endemic, so the demand for the cinchona bark grew. As early as 1795 concerns began to be aired that too many trees were being cut down for their bark — one report put the number of trees felled per annum at over 25,000. The potential loss of cinchona supplies, on which Britain's further expansion was clearly going to depend, moved the unofficial director of the recently founded Royal Gardens at Kew, Sir Joseph Banks, to call on the Government to establish cinchona plantations in the colonies.

THE SPOKES AND THE HUB

Such a notion also keyed in to one of Banks's personal projects, which he hoped to use his role at Kew to achieve — namely, the organization of a scientific study to collect, identify and record the entire flora of Britain's colonies. This proposal had two main ramifications — it would be necessary to send plant hunters to the colonies to acquire plant material for study, and a suitable location would be needed to grow, study and store the newly introduced specimens. He sought to establish Kew as a clearing house for the import and subsequent re-export of economically important crops (as well as garden treasures). Banks was also commercially astute and quickly realized the enormous economic benefit to Britain if key crops from one colony could be transferred and successfully grown in another. Another of his pet projects was the colonization of Australia (at one stage it was proposed to call it Banksia, but in the end he had to make do with a genus named after him, rather than an entire country).

Banks's educated botanists were sent to remote, unexplored parts of the empire and beyond, with specific instructions to find and bring back new plants. Francis Masson was Kew's first official plant hunter, and he sailed with Captain Cook on his second circumnavigation in 1772, as far as South Africa, which he explored for three years. David Nelson collected in Tasmania and the Pacific islands, including Hawaii, before joining the infamous *Bounty* voyage, and dying of fever in Timor in 1789. In 1780 William Brass was sent to botanize in West Africa and in April 1791 Archibald Menzies set sail with Captain Vancouver bound for the Pacific northwest of America, returning south along the Chilean coast. It was in Valparaiso that Menzies acquired the seed of his most famous introduction, the monkey puzzle tree (*Araucaria aucana*). Robert Brown was sent to Australia in July 1801 in the place of Mungo Park (the famous explorer of Africa). Brown met the loyal, but undisciplined and argumentative George Caley, a collector Banks had sent out in 1800 and about whom he had made the observation that 'had he been born a gentleman he would long ago have been shot in a duel'. Banks also managed to get William Kerr into China in 1804, where he collected from the East India Company's trading post in Canton. In 1814 — the year that Kerr died

ABOVE A portrait of Sir Joseph Banks (1743–1820) in 1809. The first unofficial director of Kew Gardens and the architect of its enduring scientific credentials, Banks's eagerness to record the flora of Britain's colonial heritage was mixed with a desire to preserve the ecosystems in which they flourished. The widespread felling of cinchona trees for their valuable bark was a particular concern.

– James Bowie and Allan Cunningham were sent to botanize Brazil; two years later Bowie sailed for Cape Town to continue Masson's work, and Cunningham sailed for Australia. The last notable explorer commissioned by Banks was David Lockhart, who joined the ill-fated Congo expedition of 1816. Of the 56 men involved, 21 died, mostly of malaria, and it may have been this tragedy that prompted Banks to call for the acquisition of cinchona seeds and the establishment of plantations in the colonies.

As early as 1816, the surgeon George Govan recommended cinchona as a desirable crop to be grown in the proposed botanical garden at Saharanpur in India. Later, and inspired by the success of Robert Fortune (see page 99) in establishing tea plants in India, John Forbes Royle's *Illustrations of the Botany of Himalayan Mountains* recommended that a similar strategy should be adopted for cinchona, assuring the relevant authorities 'that after Chinese teas, more important plants could be introduced into India'. Despite a lack of support from the East India Company, Royle did indeed give six young cinchonas to Robert Fortune, of which five reached Calcutta alive. Unfortunately, in the vagaries of plant transfers, two of the plants died there and three others expired in a Darjeeling garden.

It is often reiterated that it was primarily concern over the possible extinction of the trees in the wild that led Western colonial powers to acquire seed and seedlings, and develop their own plantations. However, such an explanation overlooks (as did perhaps the scientists of the day) the fact that if a cinchona tree is cut to the ground, it will naturally regenerate and send up shoots. This technique of coppicing, used by the Native Americans, was the subject of a doctoral thesis by William Dawson Hooker, son of Sir William Jackson Hooker (see page 149), who sadly died young. It was a technique adopted and improved by McIvor, the Scots gardener who was put in charge of the British cinchona plantations in India in 1860. It also explains how, when the tree was considered to be on the verge of extinction, the Andean Republics managed to export 2,000,000 lb (907,200 kg) of bark in 1860, rising to 19,840,000 lb (9,000,000 kg) in 1881. The export figures plummeted to 4,410,000 lb (2,000,000 kg) in 1884, by which time the British and Dutch plantations had grown into maturity.

It was the first two directors of Kew – Sir William Jackson Hooker and his son, Sir Joseph Dalton Hooker – who established the famous 'hub and spoke' arrangement in which Kew provided the hub and the spokes were the colonial botanic gardens. As well as cinchona and rubber (see pages 162–83), important economic plant transfers included tea to Jamaica, mahogany raised from seed at Kew and cork oak to India, an improved strain of tobacco to Natal in South Africa, and Liberian coffee, also grown at Kew, to the West and East Indies.

In reality, it was more than just concerns about the long-term ability of the South American republics to supply cinchona that decided the British

KEW AND BOTANICAL IMPERIALISM

'Well-ripened seeds of rarities will always be acceptable. Simply address Hooker at Kew …'. This quote from the Director's Annual Report to Parliament, 1851, sums up the collectivist policy of Kew from 1842 onwards. The history of the gardens at Kew as a location for plant collections and horticultural knowledge can be traced back to the 1660s when Sir Henry Capel gathered his botanical rarities and exotics around Kew House. In 1730 Kew House was leased by Frederick, Prince of Wales, who commissioned William Kent, the most fashionable landscape designer of the time, to create him a new garden. Following Frederick's death in 1751, Augusta, the Dowager Princess of Wales, and the controversial Earl of Bute engaged William Aiton to create a Physic Garden, enhancing Kew's role as a place of scientific plant study. The following year, George III built his mother one of the biggest stove (hot) houses in the country, adding a large collection of trees to the garden; he was later to employ 'Capability' Brown to lay out the grounds.

In 1771 the young Joseph Banks, just back from voyaging with Captain Cook on his epic circumnavigation (1768–71) during which he discovered and claimed Australia, made his first trip to Kew. He replaced Bute as the unofficial director of the Royal Garden the following year. The king and Banks shared a passion for plants, and Banks had a vision, startling in its simplicity but breathtaking in its dimension, that was to set Kew on the road to becoming the world's most famous Botanic garden. He wished to undertake a programme of scientific research and record that would encompass the entire flora of Britain's colonies. Banks diplomatically suggested to George III that the king of an ever-increasing powerful nation with a burgeoning empire should perhaps have a garden to reflect his status — possibly featuring many of the plants from the colonies over which he ruled? This notion met with royal approval, and Banks was given funds to formulate a policy for Kew's development.

Banks died in 1820, and in 1838 a Treasury Commission was established to examine Kew's future. The Committee's Report advised that it should become a governmental institution, a National Botanic Garden to oversee and co-ordinate the work of the many colonial gardens. Following Banks's lead, it further recommended that a particular emphasis be placed on economic crops — gathering information and specimens of 'everything that is useful in the vegetable kingdom'. The report notes that 'Medicine, commerce, agriculture, horticulture, and many valuable branches of manufacture would benefit from the adoption of such a system.'

The first official Director, appointed in 1842, was Sir William Jackson Hooker, previously Professor of Botany at Edinburgh University and father of William Dawson Hooker, author of a doctoral thesis on cinchona, and Joseph Dalton Hooker, who plant hunted in the Himalayas and succeeded his father at Kew. Sir William revivified the gardens and expanded Kew's extent from 15 to over 250 acres (6 to over 101 hectares) within five years. In 1848 both the Museum of Economic Botany and the Palm House, designed by Decimus Burton, were opened; the Library was inaugurated and Sir William's huge private collection of dried plant specimens became the nucleus for what is now the world's largest Herbarium. Hooker reinstated Banks's policies of establishing botanic gardens in the colonies and dispatching plant hunters. The latter practice ended when commercial nursery companies began using their own collectors, who shared their bounty with Kew in exchange for advice on where to collect, letters of introduction, and naming and publishing their discoveries.

In 1865 Sir Joseph Dalton Hooker became Director. He was particularly interested in the fields of taxonomy, economic botany and education. In 1876 he established the Jodrell Laboratory for research into plant physiology and anatomy, and by the turn of the century 700 Kew-trained botanists and gardeners were working around the world. Joseph further improved Kew's efficient infrastructure for the gathering, processing and redistribution of plant material and knowledge that proved essential in the development of many plantations in the colonies.

The Hookers nurtured a 'hub and spoke' relationship between Kew and the colonial botanic gardens. All new plant discoveries and botanical knowledge, gathered either by Kew's plant hunters or staff at the satellite gardens, were first sent to Kew. Information and dried specimens were stored, and new plants studied, cultivated and improved, prior to redistribution to appropriate colonies.

Government to establish its own cinchona plantations. Firstly, there was little quality control exerted on the bark produced in South America. Much of it was of a poor standard and adulterated with bark of other, non-quinine producing species of *Cinchona*, and hence useless. Secondly, purchasing the drug from South America was expensive – since the 1820s the East India Company had been spending in the region of £100,000 annually importing quinine. And thirdly, there was the Indian Mutiny, which had swept across the subcontinent in 1857. The uprising had taken time to quell and, as well as shocking the British back home, it had demonstrated the weaknesses and fallibilities in the Company's administration and military capabilities. The sense of alarm and outrage resulted in sweeping changes in 1858. The Crown, in the form of the India Office, replaced the Company as overall ruler of India, and the subsequent boom in civil servants sent to India to work with the new administration was matched by an increase in numbers of British soldiers – troops whose loyalty to the Crown was held to be beyond question. To keep the military and bureaucratic wheels turning, an even larger supply of quinine of a known quality was needed, which it was decided should be met by 'home grown' cinchona trees. In 1858 an agreement was reached between the India Office and Kew to send an expedition to gather eight species of cinchona tree from four areas of the Andes. The India Office footed the bill – £500 per area – while Hooker organized the plant hunting. He engaged Clements R. Markham to sail to South America and contacted Richard Spruce, who was already there, and had been collecting plants since 1849. With each man he sent a Kew-trained assistant: Weir with Markham and Cross with Spruce.

THE SEARCH FOR CINCHONA

Clements R. Markham was born in 1830, son of a canon of Windsor, who, aged 14, had joined the navy, rising to the position of lieutenant by the age of 21. He retired to become an amateur geographer and explorer, and made a trip to the Andes between 1852 and 1854. Immediately upon his return from the cinchona expedition, Markham published a book of his exploits. Reading it gives the strong impression that the whole cinchona transfer was his idea, and that he was the hero of the expedition – his co-conspirators hardly warrant a mention. However, his account is far from the whole truth. Markham and his assistant collected the 'Yellow bark' (*C. officinalis*) in southern Peru and the Caravaya region of Bolivia, where he also hired an Englishman living in Peru called Pritchett to collect in northern Peru. Markham was not well practised in either botany or diplomacy, for not only did he mis-time his collecting trips so that the seed he gathered from the trees was unripe, but also his way of acquiring live plants involved bribery and 'strong persuasion', and led to local resentment. As nearly all his seedlings died of heat during shipment through the Red Sea, his contribution to the cinchona transfer was not in fact the success his book claimed.

The other key member of the campaign, Richard Spruce (1817–92) was much more experienced and tactful. In fact, during the previous 10 years that he had spent collecting in South America, he had become well acquainted with the cinchona tree. Knowing that certain British colonies matched its preferred growing conditions, he had already offered to collect seed and plants on behalf of the British Government. Strangely, his suggestion, made through a Government agent, was not taken up, although why he did not make it direct to Hooker at Kew is a mystery. However, in 1859, Spruce, who was botanizing in Ecuador, having come up the Solimões and Pastaza Rivers from the Amazon basin, got his chance.

Spruce was a Yorkshireman, who had given up his post as a schoolmaster to become a plant hunter for Kew – an extremely curious decision for an apparent hypochondriac, as plant hunting was renowned for its hardships and frequent illnesses. Perhaps in some perverse way this is what attracted him, and certainly his correspondence is littered with complains about his many ailments. (He did in fact suffer many real illnesses and eventually lost the use of his legs, although he survived to the age of 75.)

Spruce, a self-taught botanist with a passion for mosses and liverworts, had had communication with Hooker and had pleaded with him for a position that offered 'less confinement and more exertion of the lungs than his late engagement and affording botanical pursuits'. His wish to work alone, away from 'active life', and to collect plants was realized in June 1849, when it was decided he should go to South America, specifically the Andes and the Amazon forest. Yet, even now, with his wish granted, he had another anxiety attack. He soldiered on, however, and for the next 15 years Spruce explored and collected, sending regular dispatches back to Kew. South America at this time was particularly lawless, and while the jungles provided their own form of natural danger, the greatest threats to Spruce's life came from people. In Venezuela in 1853 he was in San Carlos del Negro when it was rumoured that a massacre by local tribesmen was to occur on the feast day of St John. Most of the people fled, but Spruce remained, barricading himself inside a house. The night before the feast was a very rowdy one with the tribesmen getting drunk on alcohol looted from the deserted houses. However, despite the armed guard mounted by Spruce and the two Portuguese who had also remained, there was no violence. The feast day passed quietly, the tribesmen possibly sleeping off the worst excesses of the night before. The most exciting event was a strange-looking figure, emerging from a house on to the street brandishing a pair of pistols to prove to his companions that there really was no danger. This display of 'Victorian Englishman abroad' bravado became a habit of Spruce's, and seems at odds with his earlier, somewhat pathetic letters to Hooker.

Spruce succumbed to a very bad fever, possibly malaria, in mid-1854. For 38 days he lay on a bed in San Carlos, his life hanging by a thread. But it seems that contrary to his private worries about his health, he was made of sterner stuff than he himself believed. For, in spite of the malpractice by the nurse hired to tend him, who mocked him pitilessly, attempted to poison him (Spruce overheard the conversation) and locked him in his house in an attempt to hasten his demise and get her hands on his money, Spruce made a recovery. In November that year, Spruce's knowledge of local languages once again proved to be his saviour. This time, lying one night in his hammock in the jungle, he overheard his hired team, an old man and three sons, plotting to kill him, dump his body in the river and make off with his money. As he noted in his Journal, 'they discussed the disposal of the body, and themselves, after committing the crime, with a degree of skill and forethought which would have done credit to the most practised assassins', which they may well have been. Spruce got out of his hammock on the pretence of going into the bushes to commune with nature, but once out of sight he made for the canoe, where he barricaded himself in the tiny cabin, armed with a sword and shotgun. He spent a sleepless night listening to the men, drunk on *burech*, the local hooch, crashing through the jungle looking for him. The next morning the mystified men, who did not know Spruce spoke their language, were greeted by Spruce and his gun, and for the rest of the journey he had no more trouble.

Spruce seems to have had a knack for employing the 'wrong sort', however, for the following year he employed Charles Nelson to accompany him to Peru. Nelson, an Englishman, claimed that he was a simple prospector who had been drawn to the Upper Maraore in search of gold. While this part of his story was true, what Nelson neglected to tell Spruce was that he was a convicted murderer and a paranoid psychopath, who was deaf and thought anyone he saw laughing

BELOW A sharp tool is used to scrape bark from the cinchona tree in this mid-20th century photograph from Java (part of the Dutch East Indies until 1949). Areas of peeled bark are cropped in rotation, allowing the tree to recover between each treatment. Javanese plantations were to produce almost twice the yield of the British ones, although the species of seed used had first been offered to, and rejected by, British officials.

was laughing at his disability. His response to laughter was extreme violence, and after their departure Spruce quickly saw his hard-working, ideal companion disappear as the true nature of the man appeared. After an exhibition of Nelson's capacity for violence — in Yurimaguas he severely beat an elderly Native American and attacked a Portuguese man — Spruce became convinced that Nelson was just waiting for an opportunity to murder and rob him. He therefore paid him off with three months' wages and a passage to Barra. And while Spruce reached his destination, Nelson did not — he was murdered by his boatman.

Spruce and Cross were directed by Hooker to focus their search for cinchona on a large area of the Quintonian Andes. For Spruce this involved a long journey from where he had received Hooker's message, and it proved to be the hardest one undertaken in all his years spent in South America. Much of the journey was by canoe, and heavy rains had made the swollen river very dangerous. There was the constant danger of shipwreck on the rocks, and on one occasion Spruce was almost drowned when his canoe was sucked into a whirlpool. Sadly the experience was too much for his beloved dog, Sultan, whom he had raised from a puppy. The dog pined away for days and became so aggressive that Spruce was forced to shoot him. Things did not improve when Spruce took to the forest. The supposed trail they were to follow no longer existed, and Spruce and his team were forced to cut every foot of their way through the wild jungle and scramble over slippery rock-faces. The physically exhausting journey was made worse by the atrocious weather. As Spruce wrote:

> The rains set in with greater severity than ever – the dripping forest through which I had to push my way, soaking my garments so that towards evening my arms and shoulders were quite benumbed – and the mud, which even on the tops of the hills was often over the knees – made our progress very slow and painful.

Spruce's health began to fail and, to add to his miseries, he ran out of food, was nearly drowned a second time while crossing the flooded River Topo, and became caught up in yet another revolution, this time in Ambato in Ecuador. The relief Spruce must have felt when he reached the Quintonian Andes and set up his collecting base in an abandoned sugar cane factory must have been enormous. Misfortune was never far behind, however, and while directing operations from a hammock, his health having still not returned, Spruce heard that the company in Guayaquil, in which he had invested all his life savings – £700 that had been very hard earned by collecting, pressing and sending dried plant specimens back to collectors in Britain – had gone bankrupt.

Spruce was more tactful in his approach to gathering cinchona than Markham, and secured collecting rights to a large area of land by paying the lessee of the land $400 in local currency. The land, which was soon found to contain large tracts of *C. pubescens* 'Succirubra' or 'Red bark', was owned by two strange bedfellows, the Roman Catholic Church and a former President of Ecuador, General Flores. (Flores had been ousted 15 years previously and was now an active counter revolutionary.) For a three-month period beginning in June 1860, Spruce's team collected ripe seed and improvised a mini-nursery. In September the seed and approximately 1,000 seedlings were transported across the mountains and by raft to Guayaquil, a naturally hazardous journey, made worse by the ever-present threat of bandit attack. The expedition was a success, however, and on 31 December 1860, 637 seedlings and almost 100,000 seeds were loaded aboard a ship, addressed to Hooker at Kew.

It would appear that, as certain authors have claimed, the Peruvian operations to gather cinchona seed and plants were, at best, of questionable legality, while transferring plants from Bolivia was clearly against local law. In Ecuador, Spruce and Cross got their collection out months before a law was passed in May 1861 that made such removals illegal, yet Cross deliberately set out to break the law when he returned that autumn and smuggled out more seed. Such examples of underhand collecting, repeated in the case of the rubber transfer (see pages 162–83), open up Kew, and therefore the British Government, to accusations of 'botanical piratism' and lawbreaking. And although this is not the forum to hold such a legal debate, the destruction of native economies through the ruthless exploitation of another country's economic flora is an aspect of botanical imperialism that the West should not be proud of.

Spruce did not return with his bounty, but spent a further three years in South America, becoming more and more despondent and depressed. His request for a minor official position was rejected and he finally returned to England in 1864. His achievements were amazing: not only had he secured the cinchona seedling, which were now thriving in India, but he had also sent back over 7,000 plant specimens, made studies of local languages, mapped 10,000 miles (25,400 km) of river and made notes on rubber and its production. This last piece of work was to prove invaluable when Henry A. Wickham was dispatched to collect (or steal) seed (see page 171). Yet poor Spruce received no approbation, and the only reward for so much hard work and genuine loss of health was a miserly Government pension of £100 per annum. This was just sufficient to allow him to retire to Coneythorpe and return to the study of his favourite plants, however, and in 1885 his *magnum opus*, *Hepaticae Amazonicae et Andinea*, was published, in which he describes over 700 species of liverwort, of which he collected over 500.

Sowing the Seeds

The cinchona plants and seed that arrived at Kew in 1861 were cared for in a specially prepared forcing house, before being dispatched by Wardian case to their new home in the Indian Nilgiri Hills, where the growing conditions were very similar to those naturally occurring in the Andes. Upon their arrival they were cared for by the very capable William McIvor, the specially appointed Superintendent of the Government Garden in Ootacamund. McIvor had already spent a considerable time selecting the best place for the new Government plantations, and once planted out the cinchona trees began to thrive. By 1867 India cinchona trees covered 1,200 acres (500 ha), with plantations added in Sri Lanka and British Sikkim, land also used for tea cultivation, which had been annexed as a result of the arrest of Sir Joseph Hooker.

Unfortunately for the British, though, the trees grown from Spruce's seed were 'Red barks' (*Cinchona. pubescens* 'Succirubra') and naturally yielded less quinine than

Markham's 'Yellow bark' (*C. officinalis*), which had died while in shipment. And neither species yielded the high levels of quinine achieved by the trees grown by the Dutch in Java. Ironically, after an abortive attempt in 1853–54 to collect cinchona by Justus Charles Hasskarl, the Superintendent of the Buitenzorg Botanic Garden in Java, the seeds that the Dutch acquired were 'British rejects'. A British alpaca trader named Charles Ledger, whose Aymara servant had smuggled out a pound of seed from the Caravaya region of Bolivia in 1865, offered it to the British, who declined, so instead he sold it to the Dutch for £24 (his servant's reward was to be imprisoned for treason). From these seeds grew the 12,000 trees that were the foundation of the Java plantations, which were in full production by 1874; the species was named *C. ledgeriana* in his honour. Although the trees required elaborate protection from pests and diseases, the quinine yields of this species were very high – up to 13.5 per cent as compared with the British trees' yield of about 6.5 per cent.

The Dutchman in charge of the Java plantations, DeVrij, experimented with hybridizing and grafting, creating the high-yielding Ledger strains. DeVrij and McIvor exchanged notes and results, an unusual example of scientific co-operation in a commercial world, and concluded that the highest yield came from the 'Crown barks', a hybrid between *C. officinalis* and *C. pitayenis*. The hybrids did not grow as well in India as Java, however, and the Dutch, as they previously had done with spices, developed a virtual monopoly on quinine, supplying 97 per cent of the world market until the Second World War. The industry was run by an

RIGHT An engraving of the Governor of Madras planting the first cinchona tree in a new plantation in the Nilgiri Hills, Tamil Nadu, India. Great hopes were invested in this plantation, founded in 1862. Indian quinine was not sold commercially, but distributed at cost to Government Medical Departments.

Amsterdam-based combine called Kina, which undercut any competition, and huge profits were reaped, but both Bolivia and Peru, from where the resource originated, saw only the ruination of their native industry. Indeed today, Indonesia and India still cultivate cinchonas, but Zaire has become the top supplier in the world market in which other African countries – Burundi, Cameroon and Kenya – are main players. Much lower on the list of producers are the South American countries of Peru, Bolivia and Ecuador.

CONSUMPTION IN INDIA AND AFRICA

The role of quinine in European expansion is complicated and relatively localized. The emphasis was upon cultivating a crop for use among its own colonial administrators, rather than upon producing an economic crop to compete with the Dutch in a global market place. In India, for example, the quinine manufactured in the Nilgiri Hills processing plant was not put on the open market, but sold at cost to the Government Medical Departments of Madras, Colombo and Bombay. The transfer of cinchona was an example of imperial botany, undertaken in a climate of competitive acquisition of new territories by European powers. From here it was distributed to Government employees to ensure that India, a crucial hub of the British empire and its overseas trade, functioned effectively.

Private plantation owners were also given quinine for the mass treatment of their indigenous labourers. This was not philanthropy, but hard-nosed business practice; the plantation owners recognized that a fevered worker was not one working at capacity. Even as late as 1929 it was estimated that malaria cost the empire between £52 million and £62 million each year due to sickness; a plenteous supply of quinine was therefore essential for economic reasons. Quinine was also vital to national security since troops stationed in malaria-infected regions needed to be kept fighting fit. This model for India was applied to other colonies in which malaria was a problem, and so the greater part of British cinchona production went to keep British colonies functioning and protected.

The social impact of quinine on India is also worthy of note. In the years after the Sepoy Rebellion of 1857, many of the Britons who moved to India were only persuaded to do so by the availability of quinine. Not only did this protect their

BELOW Cinchona bark is dried on special racks set out in the hot Javanese sun. The productivity of Dutch plantations enabled them to dominate sales in Europe, while Britain cultivated the bark for use in the colonies where it grew. Despite information being exchanged between McIvor in India and one De Vrij in Java, the hybrid varieties preferred by the latter did not translate well to India.

own health, but for the first time it meant that it was also safe for wives and children to accompany them. Their influence upon the British Raj was significant, engendering a culture of Victorian respectability in which any relationship between Britain and Indian, other than that of master and servant, was at the least questionable and subject to scrutiny. Whereas previously it had been acceptable, if not the norm, for bachelor men to associate with, even to marry, local girls, the *memsahibs* of the British compounds, segregated from the local towns, were suspicious and contemptuous of such familiarity. This attitude did nothing to

MALARIA

Malaria is a potentially fatal infectious parasitic disease of the tropics transmitted by mosquitoes and marked by symptoms that include regular fevers and an enlarged spleen. When a female mosquito of the *Anopheles* genus bites a human who has malaria, it takes in, with the human blood, protozoa of the genus *Plasmodium*. There are four strains of human malaria of which *Plasmodium falciparum* is the most common and deadly form. The parasites develop in the gut of the mosquito and are transferred to other human hosts in the saliva of an infective mosquito each time the mosquito bites a new victim. Once in a human, the parasites are carried in the victim's bloodstream to the liver, where they invade the cells and multiply. After 9–16 days they return to the blood and penetrate the red cells, where they multiply again, progressively breaking down the red cells. This induces bouts of fever and anaemia in the infected individual. In the case of cerebral malaria, the infected red cells obstruct the blood vessels in the brain. Other vital organs can also be damaged, often leading to death.

The actual process of malaria transmission was only unravelled in 1880 when Charles-Louis-Alphonse Laveran, a French army physician working in Algeria, discovered the malaria parasite while viewing human blood slides under a microscope. Although he was later awarded the 1907 Nobel Prize for Medicine, the medical community of the time rejected Laveran's claim. It was not until 1886 that his discovery was accepted, four years after the hypothesis of mosquito transmission had first been made. Further evidence for establishing this link was put forward by Dr Ronald Ross, who, in the *British Medical Journal* for 18 December 1897, reported that he had discovered malaria cysts in the stomach wall of

anopheline mosquitoes, which had previously fed on the blood of a malaria sufferer. Seven months later the Italian scientist Giovanni Batista Grassi established the mosquito transmission route of infection.

If the number of fatal cases of malaria down the centuries is approximated and totalled, malaria tops the list as the world's most deadly disease. Records of fatal fevers with symptoms matching those of malaria have been recorded since writing began some 8,000 years ago. References can be found in Vedic writings from India dating back to 1600 BC, Hippocrates mentions it some 2,500 years ago, and it killed Alexander the Great in 323 BC. Rome was so badly hit by malaria that the Catholic Church fled the Vatican for Avignon, France, for 68 years from 1309.

Today malaria remains one of the planet's deadliest diseases and one of the leading causes of sickness and death in the developing world. About 40 per cent of the world's population – about two billion people – are at risk in 103 countries, and according to the World Health Organization (WHO) there are 300 to 500 million clinical cases of malaria each year. Malaria is one of the greatest threats in sub-Saharan Africa, where 90 per cent of the world's infected population live and 80 per cent to 90 per cent of global malaria deaths occur. And according to material from Third World Network Features, the direct and indirect costs of malaria in Africa alone amounted to US $800 million in 1987. The cost is not simply a financial one. Children aged one to four are the most vulnerable to infection and death, and malaria is responsible for as many as half the deaths of African children under the age of five, killing more than one million children per annum or, put another way, 2,800 per day.

improve relations between the two countries, indeed, it only served to reinforce the prejudices that had arisen on both sides as a result of the Indian Mutiny. However, the greatest losers of this institutionalized racism were those of Anglo-Indian blood, who fell between two stools. For years they had been accepted into British society on equal terms, but now their Indian blood made them offensive to the British *memsahibs*, for they acted as a permanent reminder of past national 'indiscretions'. From the other side, their previous place in British society and their English blood meant they were also outcasts from their Indian culture.

The Government was also aware of the problem of malaria amongst the indigenous Indians – in the Madras district alone there were 222,843 deaths in 1872, rising to 469,241 in 1877, and countless more sufferers. Despite the 'hype' of its worthy humanitarian ideal, to produce sufficient quinine that 'a dose of quinine can be purchased at any Indian post office', the reality was very different. In 1879, the head of the Medical Board, Madras Presidency, Surgeon-Major Bidie wrote that because of the expense, 'not one individual out of every hundred who suffers from fever is fortunate enough to secure the necessary supply of the healing bark'. Added to which, if you lived outside Bengal, the post offices were unlikely to stock quinine. Furthermore, as the 19th century drew to a close, the pressure of market forces ensured that any surplus Indian cinchona was processed into the more profitable sulphate of quinine, rather than totaquine or 'poor man's quinine'. This mix of alkaloids was less effective than sulphate of quinine, but also considerably less expensive, and for a minimal cost the British authorities, had they had the inclination to make a commitment to the Indian people, could have greatly improved the lives of many indigenous malaria sufferers. Even as recently as 1939, millions of Indians were falling victim, sometimes fatally, to the disease, following the decline of cinchona plantations in India – 97 per cent of the world's supplies were by then concentrated in Java, with Bengal and Madras supplying only 2.5 per cent. Unrelieved by Government assistance, commercial pressures (excessive cinchona production had brought the price down) and the relative difficulty of raising the trees had convinced the majority of Indian planters that this was not an economically viable crop. As a result, reliable protection from malaria continued to be unavailable for the vast majority of the subcontinent's inhabitants.

The use of quinine in India had clearly defined (but restricted) public health advantages, and soon cinchona plantations were established in all colonies where the trees would grow – Burma, Fiji, Mauritius, St Helena, Tanganyika, the Cameroons, Jamaica, Trinidad and Tobago. However, it was not just in existing colonies that cinchona had a large impact. Quinine has been described by Lucile H. Brockway in her recent assessment of its role in colonial expansion as 'the essential arm of mature British imperialism'. Certainly the drug was a major enabling factor in British penetration of Africa, and subsequent colonial acquisition in the late 19th and early 20th centuries. By the mid-1890s Britain no longer had her commanding lead as the world's most industrialized nation, and was facing severe competition from the USA and countries across Europe, notably France and Germany. British industry seemed unwilling to abandon its now ageing technology and modernize, however, and the Government was correspondingly unable to abandon its mantra-like policies on free trade. Fettered with these two out-of-date attitudes, the only course of action was, as had become traditional, to acquire previously unexploited areas of the world and exploit them. Africa was full of tropical raw materials that could be processed and exported to both the USA and Europe, thus helping Britain to balance her books. The continent was also referred to as 'the white man's grave', however, as it was riddled with malaria.

Evidence has shown that in early 19th-century Africa malaria was so endemic that it killed between 350 and 800 per 1,000 Europeans who ventured there — including a large number of slave traders on the Western coast. Cinchona cultivation therefore played an important role in allowing further exploration of the continent towards the end of the century. It seems unlikely that colonies such as Nigeria, for example, which were established in the short space of 50 years, could have been secured had not quinine been available. The cost in lives lost would have been simply too high, a fact amply demonstrated by early expeditions up the Niger River in 1830, 1832, and 1841, all of which were ravaged by fever and death. It is interesting to note that it was during a similar trip of 1854 that the prophylactic properties of quinine were established — all the expedition members, who had been taking the drug as a precaution rather than only once they had contracted the disease, survived.

RIGHT A painting of Cape Town and Table Bay in Cape Colony (later South Africa), dating from 1820. Despite the strategic importance of the continent, much of Africa's interior and some of its west coast were too dangerous for permanent European settlement before quinine became available in the 1880s.

Throughout most of the 19th century Britain had expanded with limited competition, but this was no longer the case. Its pace of territorial gain in Africa, although speedy, was tempered by competition from Belgium, Germany, Portugal and France, all of whom were also trying to profit from Africa's natural resources. The race really began after the Berlin Conference of 1884–85, at which the European powers cynically divided up their spheres of influence with the condition that a claimed territory had to be actually occupied. This led to another bout of gunboat diplomacy, both in establishing territorial claims and dissuading competing European powers. Colonial acquisition was seen as a form of patriotism, and a fascination developed with the heroic explorers of the newly accessible 'Dark Continent'.

The acquisition of parts of Africa enabled the British empire to survive for a few more decades into the 20th century, but whereas the empires of Europe's colonial powers have collapsed, the problem of malaria still persists.

FURTHER REFINING CINCHONA

At the same time as some scientists were working on the transmission pattern of malaria, others had been working on its cure. In 1820 the French chemists J.B. Caventou and P.J. Pelletier isolated the active ingredient, quinine, and until the discovery of synthetic drugs in the 20th century, sulphate of quinine extracted from cinchona bark was the standard antimalarial drug. Throughout the last century, however, there was a search for a synthetic form of the drug, a search that inadvertently yielded many important dye stuffs such as quinoline and mauveline, discovered in 1834 by W.H. Perkin.

In 1934 a German pharmaceutical company developed the first synthetic antimalarial drug, resochin, a member of a class of compounds known as 4-amino quinolines. It underwent a slight modification to create sontochin, which in 1943 was acquired by the Americans when Tunis was liberated from the Germans; its composition slightly changed, it was renamed chloroquine. At this stage in the war the acquisition was a great boon: since 1942, when Java was captured by the Japanese, there had been a shortage of natural quinine, essential to protect over 25 million troops. A year later, and partly as a result of the huge scientific programme instigated by the Java crisis, the first synthetic quinine was manufactured from coal tar by the American chemists Robert B. Woodward and William E. Doering. The 1950s saw the WHO initiate strategies for the global eradication of malaria, including spraying the pesticide DDT to kill *Anopheles* mosquitoes, and the widespread use of synthetic antimalarial drugs. However, all that was achieved was to create populations of mosquito resistance to pesticides and chloroquine-resistant strains of *Plasmodium falciparum*. So whereas in the early 1960s only 10 per cent of the world's population was at risk of contracting malaria, by the early 1970s the figure had risen to 40 per cent.

Malaria continues to be a huge challenge to medical science, and quinine as a treatment is making a comeback. It is interesting to speculate whether greater investment would be made in antimalarial research were it still a Western disease. Precedents have been set – the acquisition of cinchona plants when increased amounts of quinine were required to keep India operating efficiently in the 19th century, and the push to develop synthetic antimalarial drugs when supplies of quinine were cut off by the Japanese army during the Second World War. Had this research not been successful, troops would have been at risk in the Mediterranean and Pacific theatres of war.

Quinine has now been completely synthesized. Its synthetic analogue is called mefloquine, and research continues worldwide into finding a prevention and cure for malaria. At present great hopes are pinned on a 'new' antimalarial drug called qinghaosu (artemisinin). Another natural plant extract, qinghaosu is produced from a type of wormwood (*Artemisia annua*). Used as an infusion called *qinghao* by the Chinese for more than 2,000 years, the drug has not been widely available outside the country. So far it has proven successful in treating the most deadly forms of falciparum malaria and chloroquine-resistant strains of *Plasmodium falciparum*. In 1987 a Colombian biochemist, Dr Manuel Elkin Patarroyo, announced he had developed the first synthetic vaccine against *Plasmodium falciparum*, which he donated to the WHO for further research in 1992. Whatever future role cinchona may have in malaria prevention, it is certain that, without its historic transfer from South America to India, the shape of the British empire would not have changed as it did between 1860 and 1914.

RICHES FROM RUBBER

OPPOSITE A 19th-
century illustration
of hunters in the
Brazilian rainforest,
published in an
account of his travels
by Carl Friedrich von
Martius. The region's
unique flora was a
great attraction for
European artists and
naturalists.

ABOVE A botanical
drawing of a young
rubber plant.

AN INTEGRAL, if often unrecognized, feature of modern life, rubber is essential for tyres, fan belts, rubber bands, erasers and a multitude of everyday items. The tapping of rubber from trees of the Amazon delta in Brazil was a traditional Native American practice, but European explorers and botanists were quick to realize that such limited production methods could not fulfil rubber's commercial potential. Assisted by Kew Gardens and the India Office, wild rubber collection was replaced in the 1880s by colonial plantations in Malaya and Ceylon. Initial scepticism about rubber's economic viability was overcome by the energy of the Singapore Botanic Garden's director, plus the rapid development of motor transport with which rubber was closely associated. The transfer's success was ultimately beneficial for Malaya, but damaging for Brazil's financial and ecological welfare.

DISCOVERY AND EARLY USE

The plants that produce rubber are spread right across the globe and grow in many different habitats. It is therefore safe to assume that humankind has known about rubber for thousands of years. Yet, unlike other economic crops of importance, rubber led a relatively anonymous life until the last 150 years or so. The Indians of South America appear to be the only people to have understood the properties of rubber, and the Aztecs of what is now Mexico are the first to be recorded using the substance. A wall painting dating to the 6th century AD depicts a scene of a tributary offering of crude rubber. With the arrival of Columbus in the New World, and the resulting Spanish influx, further evidence starts to appear concerning the Native American usage of rubber. Antonio de Herrera Tordesillas describes a ritual game played with a rubber ball at the court of the Aztec Emperor Montezuma II, and the Mayans and Toltec people are known to have taken part in similar activities. Rubber was also used to make raincoats, shoes, jars, torches and musical instruments, all of which must have been made from the indigenous *Castilla elastica* – the Para tree now favoured for rubber cultivation does not grow in the Mexican region.

The first description of latex extraction is made by Juan de Torquemada, who noted that if a receptacle was not at hand the Native Americans would place the latex on their bodies and allow it to solidify. However, no real interest in rubber was shown by any European until Charles de la Condamine, a French mathematician, published an account of his journey to South America in 1735. It was undertaken on behalf of the Paris Academy of Sciences to measure an arc of the meridian line on the equator, but the journey home was to turn out to be more significant than the true purpose of the trip. Condamine explored Brazil and Peru and described how the local people used coagulated latex 'to make boots of it of one single piece which are impervious to water, and which when smoked look like real leather.' In 1747 the first description of the rubber tree and latex tapping was made by a military engineer and amateur botanist, François Fresneau, who was posted to French Guiana. The publications of Fresneau and Condamine created considerable excitement among French scientists, and an attempt was made to discover a solvent that could turn the crude rubber into a substance for commercial exploitation.

In 1818 a British medical student named James Syme used rubber to waterproof cloth and the first raincoats. Another early use of the substance was as an eraser of pencil marks, hence the name 'rubber', complemented by balloons, rubber bands, braces, boots for the army and other ideas that met with varying degrees of success. In 1820 Thomas Hancock, an English manufacturer of rubber goods such as driving belts, industrial rollers and rubber hoses, invented a machine he called the 'pickle', which chewed up waste strips for reuse. It was discovered that the masticated rubber was more malleable, while maintaining

ABOVE An engraving of 1874 shows the traditional method of making rubber on the banks of the Madeira, a tributary of the Amazon. Latex from the tree is poured on to a rubber ball at the end of a stick, which is then heated in a damp, oily fire. More and more latex was added, until the rubber ball was large enough to be sold.

much of its elasticity. In Scotland at the same time Charles Macintosh had discovered a way of using rubber as a waterproofing material by dissolving it in coal tar naphth, a process he patented in 1823. Hancock and Macintosh joined forces in 1834, and three years later Hancock invented a machine for spreading rubber onto material. (Hancock was in fact to have another, less apparent, link to the rubber industry boom, for it was he who, in 1855, suggested to the Director of Kew Gardens, William Hooker, that rubber production should take place in both the East and the West.)

Despite their beneficial qualities, such as waterproofing, rubber goods were still not particularly popular as they had some major flaws, including dissolving malodorously and becoming pliant when warm and rigid when cold. Then in 1839 the American Charles Goodyear made the discovery that rubber could be stabilized by mixing it with sulphur while exposing it to heat – a process he called vulcanization – and the full versatility of this extraordinary substance become apparent.

Rubber goods could now be manufactured that had all the beneficial qualities of the material – such as durability, elasticity and variability – but which were not sticky, soluble or governed by the vagaries of the weather. (Unfortunately Goodyear did not apply for a patent until 1843, by which time Hancock had obtained a sample of the rubber – ironically from Goodyear – and discovered the secrets behind the process. He patented his own material called ebonite, which Goodyear challenged in court, but he lost the case.)

One of the most important rubber inventions was made in 1888, when an Irishman called John Boyd Dunlop revealed the first pneumatic tyre. Solid rubber tyres had been used for the previous 18 years, but Dunlop's new design, which he updated in 1890, immediately became popular. The first motor car to use a set of pneumatic tyres was driven in 1895, and with Henry Ford's mass-production Model T just over the horizon the rubber industry had never looked healthier. The import levels of rubber over the 19th century bear witness to its irrepressible rise. In 1830 Britain had imported just 465 lb (211 kg) of crude rubber; this had risen to 22,000 lb (10,000 kg) by 1857 and by 1874 levels were just under six times as much again.

RUBBER PLANT PROFILE

BOTANICAL DETAILS

More than 200 plant species from all around the world contain the rubber hydrocarbon that produces crude rubber. With such a wide variety of rubber genera it took scientists some time experimenting and observing the plant in the wild to conclude that *Hevea brasiliensis*, or the Para rubber tree, was the superior rubber producer. Other types such as *Castilla* (or Caucho rubber) and *Seringa* (or syringe rubber) have also been harvested, but proved less successful.

ORIGINS

Named after the port at the delta of the River Amazon in northern Brazil, the *Hevea* tree is now cultivated in many tropical countries and provides more than 99 per cent of the world's supply of natural rubber. Para rubber was initially collected as it grew wild in the rainforest. It is found in the milky sap called latex that flows through the vessels of the inner bark and seeps out when a careful incision is made (the Indians of South America called it the 'weeping tree'). When the rubber was collected in the wild, the tapper or *seringuiero* would have to follow a long jungle path that would lead to about 100 or 200 trees.

DESCRIPTION

The *Hevea* tree has smooth grey bark and produces small greenish-yellow flowers, palmate leaves and three-lobed seed capsules. In the depths of the jungle mature specimens can reach a height of between 100 and 160 ft (30 and 50 m) and are quite widely dispersed with perhaps only one or two trees per acre. The *Hevea* will start producing latex at age of 5 to 7 years and can be tapped for up to 30 years.

HABITAT

The *Hevea* grows primarily on the right bank of the Amazon up to an altitude of 2,500 ft (800 m). It is a tropical tree that requires constant heat and at least 70 in (180 cm) of rain per year. Harvesting rubber in the Amazon stops during the rainy season between January and June.

PROCESSING

Rubber is gathered by 'tapping' the tree, which involves cutting spiral-shaped grooves to the depth of about ¼ in (0.8 cm) into the bark half way round the tree (the tree dies if it is cut all around its girth). Its bark will recover in a few years if treated correctly, and in the meantime the other side of the tree can be tapped.

Tapping is done every 2 or 3 days, with the groove being reopened and the bark being cut in a downward direction. The latex flows down the groove, through a spout and is collected in a cup. The rubber content accounts for about 30 to 40 per cent of the latex's weight, and rubber now yields around a ton per acre on some of the larger plantations.

Originally the latex was turned into rubber by pouring it onto a ball of rubber attached to a stick and placing it over an oily, damp fire. The smoke ensured that mould and fermentation were prevented as the latex coagulated. Eventually the ball of rubber was large enough to be transported to the rubber merchants further downstream.

Rubber plantations only started producing significant amounts of rubber at the start of the 20th century. Each tree is planted about 16 ft (5 m) apart and is tapped every other day. The latex is sieved at the factory to remove large particles, and mixed with water and a small amount of formic acid to produce a uniform material as it coagulates. This is then left to stand for a period of up to 18 hours in aluminium vats. The resultant spongy substance is passed through rollers to remove the water content and is then dried in smoke houses for up to a week before it is ready for distribution as smoked sheets.

Finished rubber can be shaped in a number of different ways. A calendering machine, which resembles a mill with a number of rollers, produces thin sheets of rubber . The height of the rollers dictates the thickness of the rubber sheet. Extrusion shapes rubber by forcing it through a hole or die in a long, continuous line. Moulds are used for unusual or complex shapes and dipping an object into a rubber solution will produce a thin rubber image.

The economic potential of rubber was now clearly evident. It became an important component in the machinery of the nascent Industrial Revolution, employed in the gaskets of steam engines found in factories, mills, mines and railways. It made a triumphant entrance as a new and innovative material at the Great Exhibition of 1851, where shoes, airbeds, furniture and clothing made out of newly improved rubber were proudly displayed. Yet the success of rubber in Europe, which should have boded well for Brazil as its primary source, was to have a catastrophic effect on its country or origin, while becoming a golden plant transfer for the British empire.

Brazil's history in the 19th century shared in the general turbulence of the Napoleonic Wars. In 1807, the influence of its colonial master, Portugal, on the Amazon basin was strengthened when the king avoided capture by Napoleon in his own country by moving his court to Rio de Janeiro. The king was to depart again in 1820, however, and Brazil gained its independence two years later. Political structures in the new country were somewhat unwieldy, as the north was split into two regions: Belem was the capital of the eastern province of Para, while Manaus was its counterpart in the western province of Amazonas. The vital rubber industry, which at its peak represented 40 per cent of Brazil's export revenue and was second only to coffee in importance, was an ungainly behemoth, stretching 1,900 miles (3,000 km) from what was called Para City (Belem) at the mouth of the mighty Amazon into the dark and dense interior. The system of harvesting latex from rubber trees growing wild in the rainforest was facilitated by the multitude of tributaries and streams that provided excellent water transport access. As the demand for rubber increased, however, more labourers gave up agriculture to become tappers, and people had to push ever further into the forest to find trees.

The life of a tapper was a hard and lonely one spent collecting latex from dawn to midday and tending the smoking of the rubber balls during the afternoon. The rainy season must have seemed interminable, and many tappers succumbed to diseases while waiting for the downpours to cease — malaria was endemic and they were, of course, too poor to afford quinine.

DEVELOPMENT AND CHANGE

The first rubber boom came in the 1850s, following the discovery of the vulcanization process, when Brazil opened up the Amazon delta to foreign commerce. Ventures such as the Amazon Steam Navigation Company, which combined local Brazilian businessmen and foreign capital, were formed. The increase in rubber production resulted in goods having to be imported and tappers running up exorbitant debts to the merchants who bought their hard-earned rubber at low prices. This bondage was tacitly excepted by the large commercial companies who obtained their rubber from the merchants in the

RAINFOREST HERO: CHICO MENDES

Chico Mendes was born into a family of rubber tappers in Ecuador in 1944. He was raised in a remote area of the Brazilian Amazon and developed an intimate knowledge of the surrounding forest. By the age of nine, Chico was working alongside his father as a rubber tapper, or *seringueiro*, exploiting the resources of the Amazon in a form of sustainable farming that does no harm to the ecosystem.

In 1962, Mendes met fellow tapper Euclides Fernandez Tavora, a communist who taught him to read and write and instructed him in the basics of Marxism and Brazilian history and economy. The young Mendes began his personal mission to raise standards and opportunities in education for the poor of Brazil, and to improve the working conditions and economic power of the tappers. In *Chico Mendes in His Own Words*, published posthumously in 1989, he describes the history of rubber-tapping labour in the region, pointing out that workers were obliged to sell their rubber at artificially low prices. He goes on to say: 'In many parts of the western Amazon this system remains unchanged, although in the area around Xapuri the *seringalista* has given way to the rancher. This means the rubber tapper, instead of being exploited by the estate owner, is simul-taneously exploited by local merchants and faces expulsion at the hands of the rancher.' Mendes became leader of the National Council of Rubber Tappers and president of the Xapuri Rural Workers Union and continued a grass roots campaign that was to cost him his life.

As the value of rubber and the world market for the product declined with the increased use of synthetic substitutes, landowners in the Amazon turned to more profitable ventures, such as cattle ranching. Cattle need pasture land to graze, and the burning and wholesale destruction of huge expanses of the forest began. The Government of Brazil encouraged this expansion, aiding the process by imposing land redistribution laws that confused the picture of who actually had rights to the rubber-tapping lands. Chico Mendes fought hard to preserve the livelihood of the *seringueiros*, achieving international recognition and support for his cause. In December 1988 he was murdered on the orders of a rancher. The power of his grass roots movement for the protection of the rainforest and those who lived and worked there only increased in response to his murder. More than 30 union, church, human rights, political and environmental organisations now form the pressure group, the Chico Mendes Committee.

small market towns. At the same time as the trading restrictions were loosened, scientists were being given permission to undertake their work in the country. In 1854 the plant hunter Richard Spruce arrived back at Kew Gardens with the first complete specimens of a rubber plant following his tour of South America. A strange mixture of part hypochondriac and part dedicated naturalist, Spruce provided the first accurate description of rubber harvesting. The man who brought attention to the most successful rubber tree, the *Hevea*, was of all coincidences a Brazilian called Joao Martins da Silva Coutinho. He had developed an interest in rubber plants and had tried to promote rubber cultivation, but to no avail. He was asked by the Brazilian Government to be one of his country's representatives in Paris at the Universal Exposition of 1867. Silva Countiho was the chairman of the evaluation of rubber board and was able to prove comprehensively the superiority of *Hevea brasiliensis*.

In the mid-19th century, the British Government was eager to develop its eastern colonies and was looking for an appropriate crop that could be utilized

ABOVE This painting of a rubber tapper is by the Mexican artist Diego Rivera. It forms part of a mural in the National Palace, Mexico City.

in the regions of India, Ceylon and the Straits Settlements of Singapore, Penang and Malacca. The boom in the rubber industry in South America did not go unnoticed and the curator of the museum of the British Pharmaceutical Society, James Collins, read with interest the report of Silva Coutinho's rubber findings. Collins had been in contact with a number of travellers from Brazil and had been impressed by the opportunities rubber offered. He revealed the information he had gathered on the subject in the *Journal of the Royal Society of Arts* in 1869 and asked the readers for further information.

One of the responses came from Clements R. Markham, who worked in the India Office. Markham was something of a maverick figure possessed of imagination and a keen sense of adventure (later on he became the head of the Royal Geographical Society). His involvement with the cinchona transfer in the previous decade (see page 150) inspired him to tackle the rubber conundrum. Although there were similarities between the cinchona transfer and that of rubber, there were also some major differences. Rubber was to be purely an export crop and would have no inherent benefits for the local population. Indeed, it would rule the working lives of many more people than quinine and have more significant demographic consequences. The decimation of the South American wild rubber industry and the recruitment of indentured labour in southeast Asia were not matters at the forefront of Markham's mind when he envisaged the rubber transfer. He believed that cultivated rubber could be produced more cheaply and with less harm than the present method practised in the Amazon. There were also concerns about the damage being done to the rubber trees by over-exploitation, induced by the buoyant market and the inability of South America to keep up with demand.

Markham seems rather to have evaded the issue that plantation production in South America could be a viable alternative to Asia (it was, after all, closer to home and therefore the rubber market). His enthusiasm to be involved and the India Office's search for a cash crop probably negated any temptations to view South America as a serious alternative. Whatever the case, Markham said he had the inspiration for the rubber transfer in 1870 and began to work on his colleagues in the India Office. Towards the end of the following year, the India Office brought in Collins to research and report on the most suitable species of rubber. Collins still concurred with Silva Coutinho that the best variety was the *Hevea*, and in 1873 the India Office arranged for him to buy seeds. Joseph Hooker, the Director at Kew Gardens, was notified that a request had been posted out to the consul at Belem to obtain the *Hevea* seeds, and he assured them that he was prepared for their arrival and redistribution. (Hancock, interestingly, had suggested to the then Director of Kew Gardens, Sir William Hooker, in 1855 that rubber production should take place in both the East and the West.) However, before any reply could be expected from the consul at Belem, news

ATTALEA funifera.

reached Collins that one of his Brazilian contacts, Charles Farris, had just returned to London with 2,000 seeds. Markham immediately authorized the purchase of the collection and delivered them into the capable hands of Sir Joseph Hooker. Unfortunately, the seeds proved to be in a poor condition and only 12 managed to germinate. Six of the survivors were sent off to the Calcutta Botanic Garden, but the climate was too harsh for their frail state and there are no records of any survivors. It was decided that future consignments should be sent to a hotter, more appropriate location.

Soon afterwards Hooker received a reply to the letter sent to Belem. It was written by one Henry Alexander Wickham, who had offered to collect plants for Kew Gardens the previous year. Although Hooker had not bothered to reply at the time, when the letter was sent to the consul it was remembered that Wickham lived in the locale and could possibly do the job. Now aged 27, he was already an experienced traveller, having visited Central and South America. He had worked briefly as a rubber collector in the Orinoco and written an account of his adventures (which was fortuitously published by his wife's father). But Wickham had been dogged by ill-health and poor judgement. His attempts to establish a plantation with his family near Belem had repeatedly gone wrong. His mother and sister had both died and Wickham had proved to be a bad farmer – his workforce left him and he was forced to move to more moderate dwellings on two occasions. When the letter from Kew arrived at his home at Santarem, it must have seemed like a final opportunity to make a going concern of his Brazilian idyll, although he might in fact have seemed less than ideal to the India Office – his reputation as a rubber expert had spread through his book, but a closer examination would have revealed that his knowledge was flawed. He describes and draws *H. Brasiliensis*, for example, but the tree does not occur where Wickham was working – it must have been a different variety.

What really mattered was being in the right place at the right time, however, and Wickham planned to take advantage of the first bit of good luck he had been blessed with for some considerable time. When requested to estimate the costs of collecting the *Hevea* seeds, Wickham replied that the seeds were of a delicate constitution and proposed a better plan – he could grow seedlings on his property and forward those instead. The consul at Belem, Thomas Green, was suitably unimpressed with the suggestion to note on the letter that he could get any amount of the seed for a cheap price. Markham informed Wickham that the India Office was prepared to buy 1,000 seed for £10, but the offer was rejected as not worth the effort.

THE HUNT FOR THE SEEDS

A certain amount of gamesmanship seemed to be going on, and Hooker rejected the idea of growing the seedlings *in situ*. Eventually Wickham was told that

OPPOSITE The reports of European explorers such as Richard Spruce and amateur botanists François Fresneau and Charles de la Condamine helped to bring the potential of rubber to Western attention. As improvements in communications and transport opened up new areas, the stories and drawings of returned travellers fostered interest in the Amazonian region.

10,000 seeds were required. Another player, Ricardo Chavez, entered the contest at this time, offering to collect seed for the India Office, who commissioned him to gather as much as he could. Chavez and his team of Native American helpers managed to obtain 485 lb (220 kg) of seed, which were shipped off to England in May 1875. Unfortunately striking incompetence in the India Office resulted in the four barrels of precious seeds standing around for 10 days as nobody knew what to do with them. By the time Hooker was eventually informed of their presence they had been sent on to India, where they arrived in a hopeless state. Finally, in April 1875, Wickham received a letter from Hooker saying that he would pay for as much seed as he could collect. As the season was already nearly over it was not until 1876 that Wickham was able to start gathering substantial quantities of rubber seed. In March 1876 Wickham was to be found at Seringal on the Tapajos River busy collecting when he chanced upon a British ship, the *Amazonas*, on a new Liverpool to Manaus run. Wickham later recalled that the cargo of the boat had been spirited away at Manaus and, as the captain had nothing to fill his ship with on the return, Wickham had chartered the vessel and hurriedly set about collecting as much seed as possible. The ship duly arrived on the correct day and after carefully lifting the baskets of seeds on board Wickham followed his cargo. Clearly the life of a poor plantation owner had paled; Wickham felt that there was little else left for him in Brazil and his future lay with his precious collection of seeds. However, as Wickham recalled in 1908:

We were bound to call in at the city of Para, the port of entry, in order to obtain clearance for the ship before we could go to sea. It was perfectly certain in my mind that if the authorities guessed the purpose of what I had on board we should be detained under pleas of instructions from the Central Government at Rio, if not interdicted altogether. I had heard of the difficulties encountered in the Clements Markham introduction of the Cinchonas in getting them out of the Montana of Peru. Any such delay would have rendered my precious freight quite valueless and useless. But again fortune favoured. I had 'a friend at court' in the person of Consul Green. He, quite entering into the spirit of the thing, went himself with me on a special call on the Baron do S___, chief of the *Alfandiga*, and backed me up as I represented to his Excellency my difficulty and anxiety, being in charge of, and having on board a ship anchored out in the stream, exceedingly delicate botanical specimens specially designated for delivery to Her Britannic Majesty's own Royal Garden of Kew. Even while doing myself the honour of thus calling on his Excellency, I had given orders to keep up steam, having ventured to trust that his Excellency would see his way to furnish me with immediate dispatch. An interview most polite, full of mutual compliment in the best Portuguese manner, enabled us to get under way as soon as Murray [the ship's captain, according to Wickham] had got the dingy hauled aboard...

I got Murray to put me ashore at Havre, and there posted over to Kew, saw Sir Joseph Hooker, so as to enable him to dispatch a night goods train to meet the *Amazonas* on arrival at the Liverpool docks...

June 1876 was a time of commotion at Kew, as they were compelled to turn out orchid and propagating houses for service, and to make room for the sudden and all-unexpected inroad of the *Hevea*; but Sir Joseph was not a little pleased. The *Hevea* did not fail to respond to the care I had bestowed on them. A fortnight afterwards the glass-houses at Kew afforded (to me) a pretty sight – tier upon tier – rows of young *Hevea* plants – seven thousand odd of them.

In later life Wickham would dine out very well on this story of brazen duplicity. However, there are a number of inconsistencies concerning his account of the transportation of the rubber seeds to England that question the authenticity of all Wickham's adventures. The *Amazonas* did exist, but her first run took place a year earlier in 1875. Wickham's account gave the impression that the arrival of the boat was an opportunity not to be missed, but there were a number of steamers at Santarem that could have transported him to Belem and from there a British steamer left about once a week. The name of the captain of the *Amazonas* was J.L. Beesley and there was no reason for him not to be able to find a return cargo – it is highly unlikely that he owned the stolen cargo and any financial technicalities could have been solved by the owners of the ship's contacts at Manaus. It is very dubious that Wickham would have chartered the ship from the captain and there is no Government record of his claim that he chartered it in the name of the Government of India (he had no funds at the time). Finally, the impression given by Wickham that the exportation of the rubber seeds was an illegal act is erroneous. There had, of course, been several such cargoes, one of which Wickham himself had been involved with. The Brazilian customs regulations allowed natural history collections to go unchecked and unopened with the authorities rather generously accepting the veracity of the owners' statements as to the contents. Although the quantity involved in the seed transfers indicated an economic rather than an educational purpose, they were destined for an educational establishment. It was all irrelevant anyway, as there simply was no law banning the export of seed at the time. The Brazilian authorities must have known there were seed collectors roaming the countryside, for they made no attempt to conceal their activities.

All this is to miss the point of Wickham's story, which was the aggrandisement of Henry Alexander Wickham. He set about this task with some relish and was eventually rewarded for all his hard work with a knighthood. Rather like the person with only one interesting anecdote, Wickham repeated and embellished his great smuggling saga to anybody who would listen. Shortly before his death a gunboat appeared next to the *Amazonas*, which he was sure would have blown them out of the water if it had realized what they were up to.

Of the 70,000 seeds that arrived at Kew on 15 June 1876 only a disappointing 2,700 germinated, indicating that the seeds were not of the highest calibre. Nevertheless, over 1,900 seedlings were sent out in Wardian cases to the Peradeniya Gardens in Ceylon under the guardianship of a Kew gardener. Wickham was paid the collector's fee of £740, but he was frustrated not to be offered employment in Ceylon with 'his' seeds. Markham tried to persuade Hooker to employ their collector, but Hooker had doubts about Wickham's horticultural capabilities and steadfastly refused to find any service for him. Eventually Wickham lost patience and set off for Australia to try his luck once again. Markham was now embroiled in his own battle for survival in employment. He had clashed with Louis Mallet, the Secretary of State for India, who believed that Markham did not focus on one particular aspect of his job, but rather

RIGHT Small balls of rubber are laid out to dry in the sun on a rubber plantation in Sri Lanka, *c*.1950. Despite an initial lack of confidence in the *Hevea* seedlings, the plantations now provide the country with a valuable export, although working conditions for the tappers remain poor.

WOMEN WORKERS ON RUBBER PLANTATIONS

In contemporary Sri Lanka, almost half the labour employed in rubber tapping is recruited from nearby villages, and very many of these workers are women, usually of Tamil or Sinhala origin.

Rubber tapping – considered the lowest rung on the ladder of a rubber plantation's hierarchy – is physically exhausting, and a typical day's work starts at 6.15 a.m. Many of the women will have risen at around 4.00 a.m. in order to fulfil domestic tasks, prepare breakfast and ensure their children are ready for school. They will then set out on a 2–3 mile (3–5 km) walk to the plantation, followed by a further trek to reach the designated areas of the plantation for their work. Each woman is required to tap around 250 trees a day, the work to be completed by noon, before making a second round of all the trees to harvest the latex that has collected in coconut shells attached to them. The latex is poured into an aluminium bucket, which the woman must then transport over rough terrain – another physically arduous task. Failure to tap the required number of trees results in a woman's meagre wages for the day being halved by her employer.

After walking back home, a woman might typically spend the late afternoon collecting firewood in preparation for cooking the evening meal. Some women rubber workers are sole supporters of their households, whilst others receive scant support, or even worse treatment, from their husbands.

juggled several projects at once. For all his faults and his unconventional manner, Markham had been responsible for achieving the planning and implementation of the cinchona and rubber transfers. In typical fashion, when he heard that the 1,900 seedlings had been impounded at Ceylon for non-payment of the freight bill, Markham took it upon himself to sort out the problem. He spent a frustrating few days attempting to authorize the payment of the bill. For all the work that had gone into ensuring that the seedlings reached their destination safely, it seems incredible that plants could be risked at this late stage of the operation. A contingency shipment of 100 unaccompanied plants were left to wither on a foreign dockside for the sake of the tardy payment of a freight bill.

EFFECTING THE TRANSFER

By the end of the momentous year of 1876 over 2,900 rubber plants had made the long trek from South America to Kew Gardens and had then been distributed onwards. Many of these did not survive for reasons such as incompetent handling, bureaucratic blunders and a high level of natural loss. Of the 50 plants sent to the Botanical Gardens at Singapore in 1876, the superintendent, Henry Murton, records that only five arrived alive and these, too, subsequently died.

The first 10 years of rubber cultivation in southeast Asia was a time of experimentation and slow progress. At Henerathgoda, the new garden at Ceylon specially designed for the crop, they seem to have been unable to propagate seedlings and were still questioning the superiority of *Hevea* trees. The merits of *Castilla* and *Ceara* rubber were examined and it was only when the effects of tapping on the trees could be seen that *Hevea* was confirmed the victor. The best growing conditions were still a matter of some contention and when, in June 1877, some 22 plants were shipped from Ceylon to Singapore about half were planted on the edge of swampy ground while the other half were placed in well-drained soil.

It soon became clear that the stories about *Hevea* thriving in damp conditions were erroneous. Ceylon had the first trees to bear seeds in 1882, but although the subsequent yields increased in number there was not a great demand for seeds. Indeed, in 1887 the director at Peradeniya, the old Ceylon Garden, sent Kew 2,000 seeds with a note saying that no-one wanted them. The *Hevea* at Singapore Gardens had been moved to a more salubrious setting and 1,000 or so trees were prospering. Seedlings were dispersed around Perak and one pioneer planter, Heslop Hill, placed trees along the roadside of coffee plantations so that their progress could be easily monitored. Initial results were promising and it appeared that *Hevea* was adaptable to different soils and locations, but there were still doubts among the plantocracy about the benefits of switching to rubber production. The *Hevea* trees took at least five years to grow before they could begin to recompense the farmer, had never been tapped in an organized way before and would produce an unknown amount of rubber. This hesitancy was compounded by rising coffee prices and the disappointing results of the first attempts to tap the trees. Although the rubber produced was satisfactory, a cautious approach was adopted by those in charge of the Gardens (only in 1894 did Henry Trimen, the director at Peradeniya, conclude that the trees could be tapped every year).

The arrival of Henry W. Ridley, the new superintendent of the Botanical Gardens of Singapore, in 1888 would provide a much needed fillip to the slow development of rubber plantations. Ridley was a man of great enthusiasm and drive and for the next 24 years he focused much of his energies on the inchoate rubber industry. He had witnessed the tapping techniques employed in Ceylon and a year after his arrival in Singapore, Ridley began conducting his own experiments on the trees. First of all he cleared the land for the cultivation of more rubber trees and then raised 8,000 new plants to add to the existing stock of about 1,000 rubber trees. Abandoning the hesitant approach of the other garden superintendents, Ridley set up a broad range of tests and experiments on a budget of just £100 in an attempt to unlock the secrets of the trees. His work included investigations into which methods of tapping were the most productive, how seed could be best stored during transport and the possibility of disease during the tapping process. Ridley's energy was boundless, and he promoted rubber zealously. There are stories of him pressing seed samples into the pockets of uncertain plantation owners, and in his later life Ridley recalled being admonished by the Governor of Singapore for spending too much time 'growing exotics'.

Nevertheless Ridley enjoyed the continued support of Sir Joseph Hooker, who had trained him at Kew. The hub and spokes of Kew Gardens' network of botanical gardens that Banks and the Hookers had sought to create across the empire (see page 147) was kept in pristine working order by the dedication of men such as Ridley. The results of all Ridley's hard work soon bore fruition and he was able to demonstrate the best tapping technique and how often the tree could be tapped. Ridley discovered that the yields were increased with more frequent but careful tapping and that the morning was the best time to carry out this work. His concerns about disease infecting the open cuts were found to be groundless, indeed he discovered that repeated incisions made on the same cut could help stimulate the flow of latex. Progress was also made in rubber processing with the discovery by John Parkin in Ceylon of the acid method of coagulation. This produced cleaner rubber and meant that the latex collectors did not have to be involved in the first part of rubber processing.

After the disappointing levels of seed survival during the early days and the eventual growth in demand for seed, attention was paid to the most effective way of packaging. It was found that as long as the seed was fresh there was a good survival rate over moderate distances. Packing seeds in soil and coconut fibre was relatively efficient, but it was found that placing them in a sealed container of slightly damp charcoal was the lightest and most successful method. A highly profitable trade in rubber seeds evolved, and in 1899 over 1,000,000 seedlings were planted on the Malay Peninsula. Although Ridley encouraged private experimentation on the plantations of the Malay Peninsula, and was happy to disseminate rubber seed to those who requested it (and those who did not), he did have a competitive streak in him and he enjoyed a long running feud with the Peradeniya Gardens. He could also be disparaging about the work and influence of other people who rivalled his input into the rubber industry. In his retiring years Ridley, who lived to be 101, could be found pouring scorn on the legacy of Henry Wickham, whom he had once reprimanded for earning a knighthood writing nonsense about carrying some seeds home.

THE EXPANSION OF EMPIRE

Ever since the Portuguese had followed their noses and sailed to the enticing Spice Islands in the 16th century, southeast Asia had attracted the attention of avaricious European empires. The Dutch replaced the Portuguese and dominated foreign trade in the region, to be challenged in turn by the British. The two powers vied with each other until after the Napoleonic Wars. In 1824 they signed the Anglo-Dutch Treaty, which divided southeast Asia into 'spheres of influence' that were later to become colonial possessions (although the British ruled informally for much of the time). Britain ceded the trading posts in Sumatra, recognized Dutch control over Java, and agreed not to establish posts or enter into

ABOVE The leafy entrance to the Royal Botanic Gardens at Peradeniya, photographed c.1900, lined with mature, well-rooted rubber trees. Although seedlings were sent to Ceylon at the same time as Malaya, the Gardens' management lacked the driving energy of Henry Ridley, director of the Botanic Gardens in Singapore, and so progress was slower.

trade relations with the islands south of the Straits of Singapore. In return the Dutch handed over all their claims on the Malay Peninsula as well as some Indian posts. The British established themselves on the northern coast of Borneo when the adventurer Sir James Brookes was approved as the Rajah of Sarawak. Sir Stamford Raffles acquired the strategically placed Singapore Island in 1819 and established the most important entrêpot of the region.

As the 19th century progressed, Britain's hold on the territory tightened as the Straits Settlements of Penang Island, Port Wellesley, Singapore and Malacca came under British jurisdiction. Informal empire in Malay depended upon the harmonious coexistence of the peninsula's sultanates, but internecine war in the 1870s forced Britain into exercising direct rule over Perak, Selangor, Negri Sembilan and Pahang.

From the 1850s Selangor and Perak had experienced a tin mining boom, which resulted in an influx of indentured Chinese workers (there were 40,000 in Perak by 1870). Chinese tin miners had long been operating in the Malay Peninsula, and the establishment of British control enabled them to expand their activities. Roads and railway networks were constructed to transport the tin. Plantations followed the mining boom and soon large tracts of the dense jungle that covered the Malay Peninsula were being cleared for crops of tea, coffee, sugar, tapioca, gambier and pepper. These plantations covered an expanse of approximately 500,000 acres (200,000 ha).

After 20 years of experimentation and delay, the rubber industry in southeast Asia was now ready to start producing rubber in earnest. The experimentation with the crop in the later 1880s and 1890s had resulted in 5,000 acres (2,000 ha) being planted by 1900; over the next decade 1,000,000 acres (400,000 ha) were to come under rubber cultivation. *Hevea brasiliensis* had offered up its secrets a little reluctantly, but by the turn of the 20th century there was good general knowledge of expected yields, optimum planting density, tapping techniques, disease control and latex processing. As production increased it became clear that the choice of southeast Asia as a nursery for rubber had been an inspired one. Not only was there was an abundance of land, but also the climatic conditions were perfect, it was a politically stable region situated in the centre one of the world's most important trade routes and there was a ready supply of cheap labour.

The first successful rubber plantation on the Malay Peninsula was established in 1896 by a Chinese emigrant called Tan Chay Yan. He planted 42 acres (17 ha) of *Hevea* and *Ficus* with seed donated by Ridley. In 1898 the first commercial sale of Malay rubber occurred when 320 lb (145 kg) were purchased for £61. It came at a propitious time for the price of coffee was falling as output rose in Brazil, while rubber was experiencing a sharp rise in cost. The buoyancy of the rubber market encouraged greater investment in the plantations of southeast Asia as the

THE EARLY YEARS OF MALAYAN RUBBER

During the 1880s, coffee was the preferred plantation crop in the peninsula, and the first rubber seedlings were regarded with a certain amount of scepticism. However, the decline of coffee in the 1890s left many plantations of cleared land seeking a new crop to produce, and a willingness among their owners to experiment with a range of possibilities including cinchona, tea and rubber. The enthusiasm – considered by some an obsession – of H.W. Ridley, Superintendent of the Singapore Botanical Gardens, for rubber served to raise its profile in the region, in the process gaining him the nickname of 'Mad' or 'Rubber' Ridley.

A decision to grow rubber was an act of faith for several planters at the turn of the century. The natural delay before rubber can be tapped was compounded with uncertainties about the commercial life of a rubber tree, the number of trees that could be supported per acre and

how the plant would adapt to the habitat long-term. Nevertheless, the knowledge that motor manufacturers were causing demand to increase encouraged young planters such as Douglas Money to settle themselves in the region. In Money's case, he found no suitable accommodation at his first rubber plantation at Kampong Kuanton – conditions were, in fact, to remain primitive on the plantations for several years. His response was to erect an extraordinary building in pagoda style, six storeys in height and built from a then unknown material, reinforced concrete (all his knowledge in architecture and practical construction having been gained from the pages of the *Encyclopaedia Britannica*). It was a gesture of youthful confidence in a new and unproven industry that, perhaps more surprisingly, was shared by sufficient early investors to make rubber a viable commodity on the London Stock Exchange.

first harvests of the *Hevea* trees began to be brought in. The total area under rubber cultivation rose from 6,000 acres (2,400 ha) in 1900 to 100,000 acres (39,000 ha) in 1906. By the outbreak of the First World War, the figure had risen to 1,170,000 acres (472,700 ha).

Such a massive increase in land cultivation required a large workforce. The indigenous population was too small and more accustomed to following a simple agrarian lifestyle. Since the 1870s the British had made excursions into the interior of the Malay Peninsula to help settle the feuds between the Chinese over tin mining. Eventually, Britain began receiving the tax revenue from tin rather than the local sultans. In 1879 a regulation was passed decreeing that no land should lie dormant if there was anybody willing to work it. Soon private concessions on mining were granted and plantations began appearing. There was a tradition of using Chinese labourers in tin mining and so it was a natural progression to use them to clear the land and plant the crops in the burgeoning plantations. Many of the Chinese workers were imported under the indenture system from the coastal cities of China. They paid for their $10 passage out of their daily wage of 2.5 cents, and many of them were destined never to see their homeland again (the Chinese are today the largest ethnic group in Malaya).

However, finances were still a problem. The typical cost of clearing an acre of land was $220 ($550 a hectare), which was beyond the means of many farmers. Banks were unwilling to lend money to individual planters because there was at least a five-year wait before the rubber trees began to produce latex. In 1897 the Federated Malay States Government granted land on a perpetual lease for rubber growing at a peppercorn rate of only 10 cents an acre (25 cents a hectare) for the first 10 years and 50 cents thereafter ($1.24 per hectare). A 'Loans to Planters' scheme was set up in 1904 by the Government, which lent money at a fixed interest rate of 6.5 per cent per year over a maximum of seven years. This was aimed primarily at the European planters, but an increasing number of foreign businesses were investing in the burgeoning rubber industry. The high initial outlay of money resulted in plantations being owned by partnerships and corporations, financed by money from Europe, Ceylon, India and China.

Once the capital had been raised and the land cleared and planted, much of the day-to-day work was then carried out by Tamils from southern India. Tamils were imported under an immigration system contract sponsored by the Government, which levied harsh punishments on those participants who reneged on the terms of the contract or incurred debts. Despite these stringent conditions there were many Tamils who were prepared to work abroad (it was much easier for them to return home than for the Chinese) and by 1915 there were 144,000 Indians working on estates. In 1927 a record 120,000 plantation workers were imported. Eventually, in 1938, the Congress Party of India managed to stop the exploitative employment of Indians.

ABOVE In the early 20th century, the Michelin Company was at the forefront of the rapidly expanding motor industry. Its pioneering tyres were successful in many of the newly fashionable car races throughout Europe. This painted tile, from the Michelin Tyre Company's glamorous London headquarters, depicts the 1908 Dieppe Grand Prix.

After the initial success of the large rubber plantations, a number of smallholdings appeared. At first their numbers were quite limited, but by 1910 they covered about 125,000 acres (50,000 ha) of land. The prime advantage the smallholders had was the ability to regulate the amount of land they gave over to rubber production. At times of low return they could switch to alternative crops. The land was worked by members of the family, so the only outlay was for the seeds and the rent of the land. This was eased in 1913 when the Malays were allowed to buy cheap land in reservations set aside for them. By the 1920s rubber from plantations and smallholdings had become the major single source of export for the Malay Peninsula, rising to 40 per cent of the total revenue.

CONSUMPTION AT HOME

The demand for rubber was fuelled primarily by the success of the pneumatic tyre and the birth of the motor car industry. The market for motor passenger cars in the USA was already buoyant, rising from just over 4,000 sold in 1900 to over 24,000 by 1905, and sales were to escalate swiftly in 1908 when Henry Ford's first Model T drove off the production line, heralding the birth of affordable motoring for everyone. Average annual prices for rubber in London jumped from $5 per lb ($2.3 per kg) in 1900 to $12 per lb ($.5.55 per kg) six years later.

The confidence in the new industry seemed without limit. In 1909 there were chaotic scenes at the London Stock Exchange, as described by a witness: 'brokers,

THE MICHELIN COMPANY

Today a world-famous multinational, the Michelin Company epitomizes the wealth that rubber, combined with new forms of transport, brought to skilful and imaginative industrialists. The Company was founded by two brothers, Edouard and André, in Clermont-Ferrand, France, in 1889, when they took over a family business in agricultural machinery. Although small, the factory this contained was well accustomed to the commercial uses of vulcanized rubber in parts such as seals, belts, valves and pipes. The factory became celebrated in the region for its rubber products. A further opportunity for the material was spotted by Edouard Michelin when he was asked to undertake repairs on a tyre for a visiting cyclist. After a total of nine hours' labour, he recognized the potential for a tyre that could easily be repaired by the cyclist or driver himself, rather than being glued to the wheel rim. The removable tyre was subsequently patented by Michelin in 1891, providing an important stepping-stone to increased usage.

The new Michelin tyre met with further success that year when racing cyclist Charles Terrant, the sole competitor to use the new tyre, won the Paris–Brest–Paris race. His victory provided valuable endorsement for the idea, and a year later up to 10,000 cyclists had adopted the Michelin version.

In 1895 the arrival of the first motor car revealed the limitations of conventional solid tyres; the wheels, alarmingly, tended to break at speeds in excess of 15 mph (25 km/h). To resolve this, the Michelin Company designed and built an innovative car, the Éclair (so-called because of steering habits so erratic that it resembled a fork of lightning) and equipped it with pneumatic tyres. The Éclair competed in 1895 in the Paris–Bordeaux–Paris race, one of the newly fashionable car races, where its tyres were to attract so much attention that disbelievers wanted to cut them open to discover the hidden supports within. The journey itself was dogged with problems – water was accidentally added to the fuel; second, then third, gears were lost and the driver could only change from first to fourth on a downhill stretch; the tank caught fire, and the tyres required changing every 95 miles (150 km). Although the authorities refused to place the car officially because

of its wheel changes, it finished well within the time limit and was to assure the future of the pneumatic, changeable tyre.

Subsequent victories in many national races, such as Paris–Marseilles–Paris (in 1896), Marseilles–Nice (1897) and Paris–Toulouse–Paris (1900) were accompanied by international success. Cars fitted with Michelin tyres won the Paris–Berlin race (1901), Paris–Vienna (1902), Paris–Madrid (1903) and, most prestigiously of all, the Gordon-Bennett cup in 1905. In the last, the tyre faces were reinforced with steel-studded leather to reduce wear, an early precedent of modern tread patterns. By 1917 this had been further improved to make the RU, a tread tyre made with black rubber (supplemented with carbon powder to increase its strength and roadholding power).

In 1919 the development of corded tyres, which contained parallel layers of thread rather than criss-crossing canvas sheets, significantly increased their durability. As cars became more and more popular, test tracks for forward and reverse car manouevres were created at the Estaing factory in Clermont-Ferrand, which by 1927 was employing 1,588 people.

As the Michelin Company began to expand internationally (the first factory outside of France, at Turin, and the 'Michelin Tyre Co Ltd' headquarters in London were followed by a factory at Milltown in the United States), it sought to acquire direct control of the sources of rubber, its prime raw material, in Indo-China. In 1925, Michelin bought 22,500 acres (9,000 ha) of land in Dautieng and 13,700 acres (5,500 ha) at Thuan Loi, intending to create its own rubber plantation. In focusing upon the French colonial territory in the region, the Michelin company hoped to emulate the success of Malayan plantations.

The Company expanded through work in all areas of transport, including aviation and railways. The famous 'Micheline' carriages of the 1930s were much lighter than traditional trains and enabled the rails to guide the carriages, assisted by wheels with solid rubber tyres. They were used widely throughout France and in her colonial territories, especially in Madagascar where two 'Michelines' still run.

clerks, commissionaires, messenger boys and street porters fought their way to the counters to throw in their applications [for rubber company shares]. In a very few minutes two of the companies were over-subscribed and the lists closed, to the great disgust of disappointed applicants. Later on in the day there were dealings in these much-coveted lottery tickets at 500 and 600 per cent premiums.' Even the humanitarian disaster of the First World War was sympathetic to rubber's cause, showing how essential the substance had become.

The story of rubber is remarkable for its impact and its legacy. One of the most startling aspects is that the vast majority of the rubber used today can be traced back to a few seedlings that survived the journey from Brazil to southeast Asia, transforming the development of the crop and the international economy. The other feat of the rubber industry is its ability to meet consumer demand, and this is due to the proliferation of plantations in southeast Asia. Within its natural limits of 40,000 tons of wild rubber per year, Brazil could never have produced enough. In 1934 over 1,090,000 tons of rubber came out of southeast Asia alone. Brazil's economy was decimated by the rubber transfer: once the source of 98 per cent of the world's rubber, it has now fallen to just 5 per cent, and much of the land is being cleared for use in cattle ranching. How would Richard Spruce react if he learnt of the effect the innocuous tree he examined in the depths of the Amazonian rain forest 150 years ago would have on the world?

BELOW The wars of the 20th century created a dramatic increase in rubber consumption, both for military vehicles and civilian products such as gas masks. Reconstituted tyres helped to alleviate shortages in supply, such as these huge examples causing logistical problems for two women of the ATS in 1943.

Epilogue

L IFE WITHOUT RUBBER GOODS OR COTTON, or indeed the luxury of putting sugar in our tea or coffee, would seem impossible to bear, yet in today's packaged world relatively few people are aware of where these products come from and fewer still know of their remarkable history. Plants have truly changed the world: their cultivation and processing have been responsible, often simultaneously, for the creation of colossal wealth and unimaginable human misery. Directly and indirectly, plants and plantations enabled Britain to extend her territory to the four corners of the globe, and to rule over millions of people who would never set eyes on their mother country's green hills.

The sun began to set on the British empire many years before it finally died away. At the turn of the 20th century Britain was still arguably the most powerful nation on earth, but this long period of dominance was being challenged. Following the destruction of the Civil War and a worldwide recession towards the end of the 19th century, the USA was enjoying a period of prosperity. In Europe the new German nation was fast catching up in many spheres (there was a protracted naval build up) and the country became the joint world leaders along with the United States in the new chemical, engineering and car industries. Britain could still rely on the resources of India, the jewel in the imperial crown (Queen Victoria was crowned Empress of India in 1876), and the earnings from banking, shipping and insurance that came from being a major naval and financial power. However, the United States, Germany and Russia had greater populations, more indigenous resources and faster moving economies. The world was changing in more fundamental ways, too: conflict in the 19th century, for example, had been limited to regional affairs between armies whose techniques and tactics had consequently not progressed. The 20th century was to witness the first truly global wars, dominated by modern technology, that were to leave an indelible mark on humankind.

The new world order did not have room for traditional empires. While the United States and Russia fought to be the supreme global power in the blinking game that was the Cold War, Britain quietly sought to divest herself of her colonial possessions. Initially the Colonial Development Acts of 1940 and 1945 were established to make the colonies self-supporting entities, but with the financial profits being channelled back to Britain. However, the rise of the Indian National Congress Party and the ravaged state of Britain's economy following the Second World War meant that full independence for the colonies was inevitable (although at the time it was thought that it would take at least 50 years to accomplish). In fact there were two major periods of decolonization: the first centred on the Indian subcontinent in 1947–48 and the second on Africa, the Caribbean and Malaya in the 1960s. To Britain's credit, the disbanding of the empire was undertaken with an optimistic attitude and with a view of creating new nations with freedom, democracy and a harmonious relationship with the former ruler. On the whole, independence was executed with a reasonable degree of success, and certainly the handovers went more smoothly than those achieved by other European countries, such as France and Portugal. One of the reasons for this was the strength and calibre of the administration that was left behind; in 1946, for example, Indians comprised over half of the 1,000 or so senior civil servants in the subcontinent, providing an invaluable continuity after independence. In contrast, many African countries were thrown into disarray when Europeans hurriedly retreated without ensuring that there were competent people to fill the voids in the fledgling governments.

Part of the general problem of dismantling the British empire was the partitioning of land; the legacy of boundaries that divided tribes, cultures and languages was often hard to resolve. The disastrous Partition that followed Indian Independence resulted in racial violence that left over 500,000 dead, although India has subsequently managed to sustain the world's largest democracy despite widespread poverty and intermittent ethnic tensions.

In Africa, the British authorities were overtaken by events in some countries and independence was forced at a far quicker pace than had been anticipated. The West and East African troops who fought in southeast Asia saw the success of the Nationalists in challenging British rule in India, and when they returned home they determined to follow suite. Key problems were the redistribution of land and the restructuring of a colonial economy. Plant crops were also a source of controversy in the British West African colony of the Gold Coast. This area produced one third of the world's cocoa beans, yet although Africans ran the farms British companies retained the power and the profit. (Such was their influence that the best quality beans were known as 'Cadbury quality'.) To keep the cost low for the home market, the British Government fixed the price of the beans (although they claimed that it enabled the farmer to receive a steady income that was immune from sharp fluctuations in world price). The African struggle for self-rule started in the Gold Coast, where only 5,000 Britons – mostly traders who did not settle in the country – lived in comparative luxury alongside

2 million Africans. African army veterans led protests, which turned into violent riots that left 29 people dead. These were followed by a mass strike and a boycott of British goods. Eventually the British were forced to organize a local assembly election which one Kwame Nkrumah won by a landslide, and in 1957 the Gold Coast was granted complete independence, taking the name Ghana. Other countries followed suit, with 25 former colonies achieving independence in less than three years.

In East Africa the problem was exacerbated by the reluctance of the European settlers to relinquish power and control of acquired territory. Between the two world wars several thousand Europeans had settled on farms in the most fertile regions of Kenya, attracted by the more clement climate and the higher standard of living. When the British refused to hand back their coffee farms, a group of Africans established a movement called the Land and Freedom Party, or Mau Mau, in the foothills of Mount Kenya. They terrorized isolated farmsteads and attacked police stations, but were eventually defeated in 1956 after 50,000 tons of bombs had been dropped on their camps and 80,000 suspects had been detained. However, the British realized that they could not continue to protect the relatively small white population in Kenya and would have to compromise.

With the demise of the British empire came a corresponding decline in revenue from the former colonies. However, production of tea, rubber, cotton, sugar, tobacco, coffee, cocoa and other plantation produce continued to increase (although sugar beet dealt a major blow to the sugar cane plantation economy of the West Indies). Many of the deleterious plants of the empire have become a contemporary social and medical nightmare. Mass drug consumption is no longer a preserve of the Chinese, as opium and its derivatives – heroin and morphine – have become an integral aspect of Western society. For many decades American tobacco companies claimed that medical studies linking cigarette smoking to diseases such as cancer and emphysema were inconclusive, but in a series of litigation cases in the 1990s the top five cigarette manufacturing companies finally admitted that smoking was addictive and lethal. In a $368-billion settlement, the companies hoped to stop the lawsuits of 40 states by agreeing to place health warnings on cigarette packs and reduce their advertising, and to pay for the health treatment of smokers, anti-smoking literature and aid for smokers attempting to quit. However, the 'tawny weed' is still being produced, and tobacco companies are now focusing upon the new and lucrative Far Eastern market.

Initially, natural rubber was used for tyre production (the largest usage of rubber in the world), but it has largely been replaced by synthetic rubber, popularized as a consequence of war. The Germans utilized the new discovery of synthetic rubber in the First World War when they were cut off from their supplies of natural rubber. The United States also dramatically increased its synthetic rubber production when the Japanese captured the rubber plantations of southeast Asia during the Second World War. Synthetic rubber is now a component of many different products, including car tyres, footwear, matting, waterproofing agents and sponge and foam materials. Natural rubber is still used extensively, however, and there is now a cultivated rubber tree for every two human beings on the planet.

As we enter the 21st century, where are the plants that will shape the future? As our knowledge of the plant world increases, it is tempting to believe that we can change nature to improve our lives. Currently, the most controversial aspect of this ideology is the future of genetically-modified foods. European politicians and large retailers were surprised by the vehemently negative response to foodstuffs containing GM ingredients, and there has been widespread concern over many aspects of GM produce. Key issues include the ethics of tampering with genetics, the security or otherwise of experiments, the dangers of genetic pollution following the release of pollen or the interbreeding of fish, and the long-term effects of consuming GM foods on humans. At the moment there is simply not enough evidence to draw any conclusions over the safety or otherwise of genetically-modified foods, and further trials are being conducted in an attempt to resolve the debate.

Attention is also directed at more natural sources of plant material that could be of an immediate benefit to humankind. Without a doubt the richest biological storehouse in the world is the Amazon rainforest where there are literally thousands of potentially beneficial medicines derived from plants waiting to be discovered. Rainforests currently provide 25 per cent of the sources for today's medicines, and 70 per cent of the 3,000 plants identified by the US National Cancer Institute as active against cancer cells are only found in rainforests. Such is the potential for plant-based drugs and cures for viruses, infections and medical conditions that a new international industry known as 'bio-prospecting' has emerged. Bio-prospecting embraces an unusual amalgam of plant hunters, ecologists, conservationists, native shamans, drug researchers, US Government departments and the largest pharmaceutical companies who work together to preserve and examine the efficacious nature of rainforest plants. It has become a highly profitable industry (sales of plant-based drugs were estimated at $40 billion in 1990), and huge rewards await the discoverer of a cure for a major disease, such as cancer or AIDS. However, the destruction of the rainforest continues at an alarming rate — estimated at approximately an acre every second — and potentially beneficial plant species are being lost daily. The Madagascar periwinkle, for example, from which were obtained two drugs that increased child survival of leukemia fourfold, has already disappeared from its native habitat due to deforestation. Conservation of the plant heritage that has done so much to shape our past is no longer a matter of choice but necessity if humankind is to continue to prosper in the future.

Bibliography

No one writing in this field can fail to acknowledge the contribution of Henry Hobhouse, whose classic book *Seeds of Change* has recently been published in a revised edition. His unique interpretation of the role of plants in shaping the history of peoples and countries has transformed our understanding of cause and effect since its first publication in 1985.

Barbee, W.J., *The Cotton Question*, New York, 1866.

Barlow, Colin, *The Natural Rubber Industry: Its Development, Technology and Economy in Malaya*, Oxford University Press, Oxford, 1978.

Barraclough, Geoffrey (ed.), *The Times Atlas of World History*, Guild Publishing, London, 1978.

Beckford, William, *A Descriptive Account of the Island of Jamaica*, 1790.

Beeching, Jack, *The Chinese Opium Wars*, Hutchinson & Co. Ltd, London, 1975.

Berridge, Virginia, & Griffith Edwards, *Opium and the People*, Yale University Press, New Haven, 1987.

Blow Williams, Judith, *British Commercial Policy and Trade Expansion, 1750–1850*, Oxford University Press, Oxford, 1972.

Boorstin, D.J., *The Discoverers*, Random House Inc, New York, 1983.

Briggs, Asa, *A Social History of England*, Weidenfeld and Nicolson, London, 1983.

Brockway, Lucile H., *Science and Colonial Expansion: The Role of the British Royal Botanic Gardens*, Academic Press, Inc, New York, 1979.

Campbell, Mavis, *The Maroons of Jamaica 1655–1796: A history of resistance, collaboration and betrayal*, Mass., 1988.

Canny, Nicholas (ed.), *The Oxford History of the British Empire: Volume I: The Origins of Empire*, Oxford University Press, Oxford, 1998.

Chesneaux, Jean, Marianne Bastid and Marie-Claire Bergere, *China from the Opium Wars to the Revolution*, The Harvester Press, Hassocks, Sussex, 1977.

Coates, Austin, *The Commerce in Rubber: The First 250 Years*, Oxford University Press, Oxford, 1987.

Cotterell, Arthur, *China – A Concise Cultural History*, John Murray (Publishers) Ltd, London, 1988.

Crawford, M.D.C., *The Heritage of Cotton*, Grosset and Dunlap, New York, 1924.

Dean, Warren, *Brazil and the Struggle for Rubber: A Study in Environmental History*, Cambridge University Press, Cambridge, 1987.

Deerr, Noel, *The History of Sugar, Volume II*, Chapman and Hall, London, 1950.

Deford, Susan, 'Tobacco: the Noxious Weed that Built a Nation', *Washington Post*, 14 May 1997, © The Washington Post Company, 1997.

Desmond, Ray, *Kew: The History of the Royal Botanic Gardens*, 1995.

Dickson, J. *Address to the Members of the House of Commons, on the Relationship between the Cotton Crisis and Public Works in India*, P.S. King, London, (1862).

Dodd, W.E., *The Cotton Kingdom*, Yale University Press, New Haven, 1919.

Dowell, S.S., *Great Houses of Maryland*, Tidewater Publishers, 1988.

Dunn, Richard S., *Sugar and Slaves: The rise of the planter class in the English West Indies, 1624–1713*, Jonathan Cape, London, 1973.

Duran-Reynals, M.L., *The Pageant of Quinine*, London, 1947.

Edlin, H.L., *Man and Plants*, Aldus Books, London, 1967.

Egon, Corti, translated by England, P., *A History of Smoking*, George G. Harrap & Co Ltd, London, 1931.

Emerson, Robin, *British Teapots and Tea Drinking 1700–1850*, HMSO, London, 1992.

Fortune, Robert, *A Journey to the Tea Countries*, Mildmay Books Ltd, London, 1987.

Fryxell, P.A., *The Natural History of the Cotton Tribe (Malvaceae, Tribe Gossypieae)*, Texas A&M University Press, College Station and London, 1979.

Gabb, S., *Smoking and its Enemies: A Short History of 500 Years of the Use and Prohibition of Tobacco*, Forest, London, 1990.

Gandhi, M.P., *How to Compete with Foreign Cloth*, Calcutta, 1931.

Garrett W., *American Colonial – Puritan Simplicity to Georgian Grace*, The Monacelli Press, 1995.

Gill, C., *Merchants and Mariners of the 18th Century*, Edward Arnold Ltd, London, 1961.

Graham, Gerald S., *The China Station: War and Diplomacy 1830–1860*, Clarendon Press, Oxford, 1978.

Green, Daniel, *A Plantation Family*, Ipswich, 1979.

Guest, R., *Compendious History of the Cotton Manufacture*, Manchester, 1823.

Hall, Douglas, *In Miserable Slavery: Thomas Thistlewood in Jamaica, 1750–86*, Warwick University Carribean Studies, 1989.

Harnetty, P., *Imperialism and Free Trade: Lancashire and India in the mid-nineteenth century*, Manchester University Press, Manchester, 1972.

Haydon, P., *The English Pub*, Robert Hayle, London, 1994.

Hobhouse, Henry, *Seeds of Change: six plants that transformed mankind*, revised edition published by Macmillan Publishers Ltd, London, 1999.

Hsin-pao Chang, *Commissioner Lin and the Opium War*, Harvard University Press, Cambridge, Mass., 1964.

Inglis, Brian, *The Forbidden Game: A Social History of Drugs*, Hodder and Stoughton Ltd, Great Britain, 1975.

James, Lawrence, *The Rise and Fall of the British Empire*, Little, Brown & Company, Boston, 1994.

Kay, J. Phillips, *The Moral and Physcial Conditions of the Working Classes Employed in the Cotton Manufacture in Manchester*, 1832.

King, J.C.H., *Smoking pipes of the North American Indians*, British Museum Press, London, 1977.

Koskowski, W., *The Habit of Tobacco Smoking*, Staples Press Ltd, London, 1955.

Kuntz K.M., *Smoke*, Todtri Productions, Inc, 1997.

Kusy, Frank, *Cadogan guides: India*, Cadogan Books plc, London, 1996.

Lee, C.H., *A Cotton Enterprise*, Manchester University Press, Manchester, 1972.

Lyte, Charles, *The Plant Hunters*, Orbis, London, 1983.

Lloyd, T.O., *The British Empire, 1558-1995*, Oxford University Press, Oxford, 1996.

Lubbock, Basil, *The China Clippers*, 1914.

Marshall, P.J. (ed.), *The Cambridge Illustrated History of the British Empire*, Cambridge University Press, Cambridge, 1996.

Marshall, P.J. (ed.), *The Oxford History of the British Empire: Volume II: The Eighteenth Century*, Oxford University Press, Oxford, 1998.

Monckton, H.A., *A History of the English Public House*, The Bodley Head, London, 1969.

Morris, Sallie, and Leslie Mackley, *Choosing and Using Spices*, Select Editions, London, 1997.

Nicholson, Louise, *Cox & Kings India Companion*, Random Century Group Ltd, London, 1991.

Owen, David Edward, *British Opium Policy in China and India*, Yale University Press, New Haven, 1934.

Perdue, Bardeu and Phillips (eds), *Weevils in the Wheat – interviews with Virginia ex-slaves*, 1976.

Pitman, Frank Wesley, *The Development of The British West Indies 1700–1763*, Frank Cass and Co. Ltd, London, 1967.

Rawson, Jessica (ed.), *The British Museum Book of Chinese Art*, British Museum Press, London, 1992.

Ray, Oakley, and Charles Ksiv, *Drugs, Society and Human Behaviour*, Mosby College Publishing, St Louis, Missouri, 1987.

Roberts, J.M., *The Penguin History of the World*, revised edition published by Penguin Books, London, 1995; first published as *The Hutchinson History of the World* by Hutchinson, London, 1976.

Robinson, Carey, *The Iron Thorn: The Defeat of the British by the Jamaican Maroons*, Jamaica, 1969.

Steeds, David and Ian Nish, *China, Japan and Nineteenth Century Britain*, Irish University Press, Dublin, 1977.

Strickland, C.F., *Quinine and Malaria in India*, Oxford, 1939.

Strong, L.A.G., *The Story of Sugar*, Weidenfeld and Nicolson, London, 1954.

Summerscales, J.H., *British Cotton Growing*, F. & G. Pollard, Odham, 1928.

Trevelyan, G.M., *History of England*, Longmans, London, 1951.

Ure, A., *The Cotton Manufacture of Great Britain*, 1861.

Uyangoda, Jayadeva, *Life Under Milk Wood: Women Workers in Rubber Plantations: an overview*, Colombo, Sri Lanka, 1995.

Walvin, James, *Fruits of Empire: Exotic Produce and British Taste 1660–1800*, Macmillan, London 1997.

Warrren, W. Kenneth, *Tea Tales of Assam*, 1975.

Waley, Arthur, *The Opium War Through Chinese Eyes*, George Allen and Unwin Ltd, London, 1958.

Ward Fay, Peter, *The Opium War 1840–1842*, University of North Carolina Press, Chapel Hill, 1975.

Watson, Jack, *Success in European History 1815–1941*, John Murray (Publishers) Ltd, London, 1981.

Index

Acknowledgements

The Publishers would like to thank the following photographers and organizations for permission to reproduce their material. Every care has been taken to trace copyright holders. However, we will be happy to rectify any omissions in future editions.

Front cover Christie's Images, London; back cover British Library/ BAL; half title page Annabel Barrett/ Bridgeman Art Library (BAL); title page The Lindley Library/ Royal Horticultural Society, London
6 Fitzwilliam Museum, Cambridge University/ BAL; 9 Art Archive, London; 10 Library of Congress, Washington D.C./ BAL; 12 Art Archive; 14 Museum of the City of New York/ BAL; 15 BAL; 16 Library of Congress/ BAL; 18 Gary W. Carter/ Corbis; 20 Art Archive; 21 Wallace Collection/ BAL; 22 BAL; 25 BAL; 30 Cambridge Folk Museum/ BAL; 32 Bonhams/ BAL; 33 Christie's Images, London; 35 Mary Evans Picture Library; 36 Underwood & Underwood/ Corbis; 37 Wilberforce House Museum/ BAL; 39 BAL; 40 Tony Arruza/ Corbis; 42 Art Archive; 43 British Library/ BAL; 44 British Library/ BAL; 47 BAL; 49 Corbis; 50 Bettmann/ Corbis; 53 BAL; 55 Wilberforce House Museum/ BAL; 58 BAL; 60 Christie's Images; 62 Art Archive; 63 V&A Museum/ BAL; 65 Richard Hamilton-Smith/ Corbis; 68 British Library/ BAL; 70 Art Archive; 71 Mary Evans Picture Library; 73 BAL; 76 BAL; 79 BAL; 81 BAL; 82 Mary Evans Picture Library; 87 The Design Library, New York/ BAL; 88 British Library/ BAL; 89 The Lord's Gallery/ Art Archive; 92 Hans Georg Roth/ Corbis; 94 Bonhams/ BAL; 98 BAL; 101 Royal Geographical Society, London; 104 Art Archive; 105 Illustrated London News/ BAL ; 106 Hulton Deutsch Collection/ Corbis; 108 Bettman/ Corbis; 109 Christie's Images; 113 Mary Evans Picture Library; 116 British Library/ BAL; 117 Art Archive; 119 Michael Yamashita/ Corbis; 120 British Library/ BAL; 123 Honeychurch Antiques/ Corbis; 124 Berry Hill Galleries, New York/ Art Archive; 126 British Library/ Art Archive; 127 Hulton Deutsch/ Corbis; 134 Mary Evans Picture Library; 137 Museu Calouste, Gulbenkian/ BAL; 138 Mary Evans Picture Library; 140 Gianni Dagli Orti/ Corbis; 141 British Museum; 143 Royal Geographical Society, London; 144 Eric Crichton/ Corbis; 147 Mary Evans Picture Library; 152 Hulton Deutsch/ Corbis; 155 Illustrated London News/ Mary Evans Picture Library; 156 Hulton Deutsch / Corbis; 159 Christie's Images; 162 Christie's Images; 163 BAL; 165 BAL; 166 Wolfgang Kaehler/ Corbis; 170 Christie's Images; 174 Horace Bristol/ Corbis; 178 Corbis; 181 Philippa Lewis, Edifice/ Corbis; 183 Hulton Deutsch / Corbis; Endpapers Royal Geographical Society/ BAL.

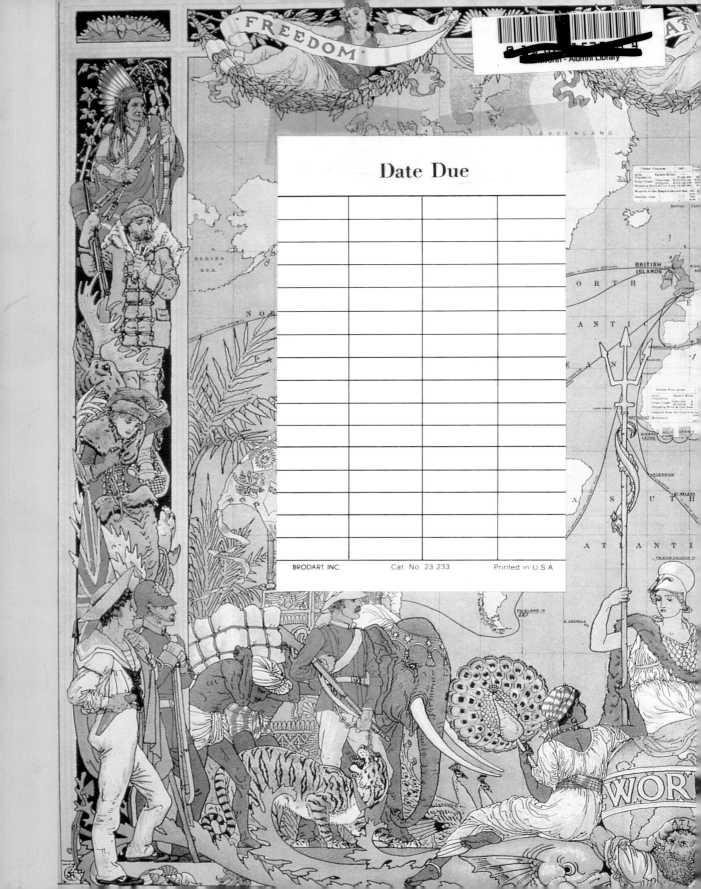